H45 777 406 1

D0514378

Try a Little Lowliness

Hertfordshire Libraries	
H45 777 406 1	
Askews	04-Aug-2009
	£9.99

Caldey Abbey – the cloister.

Try a Little Lowliness

Memoir of a
Cistercian novice

Paddy Lyons

GRACEWING

First published in 2009 by

Gracewing
2 Southern Avenue,
Leominster
Herefordshire HR6 0QF

All rights reserved. No part of this publication may be reproduced, stored in a retrieval system, or transmitted in any form, or by any means, electronic, mechanical, photocopying, recording or otherwise, without the written permission of the publisher.

© Paddy Lyons 2009

The right of Paddy Lyons to be identified as the author of this work has been asserted in accordance with the Copyright, Designs and Patents Act 1988.   −

ISBN 978 0 85244 694 2

The photographs on pp.ii, vi, 88 and 244 and the front cover are by Br Titus Keet, OCSO, to whom thanks are due. All other photographs are used by kind permission of Caldey Abbey.

Typeset by Action Publishing Technology Ltd, Gloucester GL1 5SR

Contents

'Domine illuminatio mea' (Psalm 27:1).

Foreword

Paddy Lyons joined me in the noviciate just as I was finishing my first year; a honeymoon period, though I didn't realise it at the time – it was soon to change. We were prepared for his arrival by the novice-master telling us that the Tiger had sent the Lions (!) which turned out to mean that Fr Clement Tigar, SJ of Osterley fame was recommending Paddy Lyons as a postulant. Who said novice-masters have no sense of humour?

Having read the typescript of Paddy's recollections I can vouch for the incredible accuracy some forty years after their happening. Reading them conjured up many memories and verified some of my own that I was beginning to doubt. He might have hyped up some of the details but only to keep his touch light and easy. I was also impressed as I read of how well Paddy is able to convey the very real spiritual lessons he learnt.

It was a great joy to meet Paddy when he returned after forty years' absence with his wife Elsie. We spent a wonderful afternoon in the guesthouse sitting room talking about everything at once. Elsie was a model of patience and I did manage to pause from my recollections long enough to hear a little about their happy years together. I can guarantee that Elsie has done much to round out and soften off the work done under Fr 'Lawrence'.

When Paddy told me he had written up a number of memories I was keen to share them. When he told me that Gracewing's publisher, Tom Longford, had expressed an interest I encouraged Paddy to get on with it. He sent me some of the chapters and I was all the more in favour. I even offered to write this Foreword.

Do read and enjoy the different happenings. Don't miss the wise comments under the humorous presentation. Paddy asked my opinion about using pseudonyms. My opinion was that it went better with the lightheartedness. I had no difficulty putting the real names to the characters.

And what characters those older monks were. Over half were the original founders who came over from Belgium in 1929 or who were sent to boost the Community in the aftermath of the Second World War. Caldey still has close and friendly contact with our mother house, Notre Dame de Scourmont in Chimay, Belgium. Indeed the last of Scourmont's monks died as recently as October 2004 at the grand old age of ninety-two!

Robert O'Brien, OCSO

Prologue

St Benedict lived in central Italy in the sixth century and wrote a Rule of Life for monks. Various rules had been written in the previous two centuries but Benedict's achieved a wonderful mix of ascetic purity and humane moderation. Although some of its directives will sound strange to the liberal ears of today, it has guided the lives of countless holy men who, in their turn, have played a large part in the civilising of the Western world.

But consider: a vegetarian brotherhood which takes away your liberty; your right to own anything; to marry or even to mix with members of the opposite sex; to have a choice in anything, to go anywhere or even to speak! And which then subjects you to unremitting hard labour, weird clothes and isolation for the rest of your life! Modern society hardly prepares a young man for that sort of life.

I've always thought mountaineers to be pretty mad people, but at least the mountains they climb are there. A monk has to find an empty space, then build his mountain and then climb it. And if he's good at his job and wants to break a few records, he has to go on climbing long after he has reached the summit and run out of rock and ice. A sort of Mount Neverest in thin air.

Yet a visit to such a place, made during my military service in Berlin, persuaded me to give it a go. The gentle, smiling monks, imparting a quiet wisdom when persuaded to talk, made such an impression on me, in stark contrast to the brutalising effect of army life, that, some years and several career moves later, I could resist the impulse no longer.

Saint Benedict says in his Rule,

> Let no easy entrance be granted him who newly arrives to
> change his way of life. If, after four or five days, he perse-
> veres in knocking at the door, and seems to be enduring
> patiently all the snubs he receives and all the obstacles put
> in his way, then let him in to stay at the Guesthouse for a
> few days. Afterwards let him come into the Noviciate where
> he will meditate and study, take his meals and sleep.

So one can only assume that things were different in
Benedict's day and that monasteries were sought-after
venues. Nowadays you can still find people, young and
old, waiting sometimes for days on end, showing all the
patience of the aspirant monk, to get into a special
concert, a sporting event, or even purchase a particular
item in a sale. They certainly don't line up outside
monasteries any more. But the prospect of gate-
knocking, insults and a long wait did not appeal. No. I
resorted to the convenience of the local library, the
appropriate directory, a nervous prayer, phoning the
abbey, speaking to the big man himself, who said,
'Come on down and see for yourself?' So I did.

Was I mad? No; though my girlfriend was pretty mad
but, I hope, forgave me. My mother was pretty sad but
saw it as an influence she couldn't match. She might
even have seen it as the likely outcome of a childhood
nurtured in the faith, a schooling which held out the religious life as a worthy aim, and that chance encounter
which offered nobility of spirit as an alternative to the
pursuit of material goals.

Chapter One

Arrival

'You goin' over to stay with the brothers, then?'

I turned to the boathand who had paused by me at the rail.

'Yes, I'm thinking of joining the Order.'

'Are you now!' he exclaimed. 'I dare say you'll be welcome. They say they're a bit short of young'uns at the moment.'

'Do you see much of them, then?' I asked.

'Oh no,' he breathed in sharply and pointed into the sky above the island we were now approaching. 'They keep 'em well out of sight up there. We mostly see Brother Thomas who runs the shop above the jetty, or maybe Father Stephen, sometimes the Abbot. No, reckon you'll get swallowed up like the rest of 'em.' He grinned at me as he moved away to prepare for landing.

Swallowed up, indeed! The whole idea, which had progressively become less appealing throughout the long, empty, jittery journey from Paddington to the Welsh coast, now gathered the hint of menace as we neared the beach. I observed the details of the land-scape with the sort of clarity you take in the decorations of a dentist's waiting room, beyond which lies uncertainty with the possibility of pain. It sat there like a picture postcard – a long strip of golden sand topped by wood-land and fields of ripened corn. The beach was flanked on both sides by rising cliffs, and a cluster of white cottages gathered round an unmade road leading from the jetty completed the foreground. And there, centre stage, towering above everything with its round towers,

The monastery boat on its morning crossing.

steep terracotta roofs, and punctuated by rows of windows glinting in the late afternoon sun, rose the high white walls of the monastery. The message was overwhelming: 'I'm going to swallow you up!'

We chugged alongside the jetty wall which was crowded with trippers waiting for the boat to return them home after a hot August Saturday on the sands. Hundreds, it seemed, of happy, endearing, carefree folk – golden girls and bronzed boys. The noise of their chatter, the drifting music of their radios, swamped me with its innocence – a rolling wave of fellowship and community to which I rightly belonged – all going one way; and one irresolute loner going the other. It was all so ordinary yet so unreal, a crowd scene on a desert island, a last sensuous play by the temptor to undermine my purpose. It contained an illusory delight, I knew, which, were I to turn to join it, would dissolve, and each sun-soaked element of it would go its own tawdry way.

Caldey Island, Pembrokshire – the abbey.

I threaded a confused path through the crowd and, leaving them suddenly behind, walked with a certain numbness on up the near deserted road towards the abbey, meeting only the occasional tardy tripper hurrying to catch the last boat home. The high ground to my right cast me in its shadow, and the hum of life which had surrounded me at the jetty only a moment ago seemed like a strange remembered dream. At that moment a bell started to toll up there among those roofs, slowly and steadily. Had somebody died? I felt small and insignificant, reduced by the high cliffs, the towering abbey, and that bell, enclosing the very air, capping all my scattered thoughts with the clanging of innumerable iron doors.

At last I was walking under the high walls themselves, regular windows spaced high above. The word 'cell' came to mind, and St Anthony's saying, 'A monk out of his cell is like a fish out of water.' What was I doing? I came upon a door marked with the sign, Guesthouse. It

was open and, as far as I could see, there was no queue
of aspiring or even perspiring young men being repulsed
or ignored as The Rule counselled. Here goes – I rang
the bell and walked in. It seemed like every other religious house I had ever been in – immaculately clean,
wood panelled walls and heavy Victorian furniture, the
sort everyday people had cleared out of their smaller
houses years ago. The faint smell of an oncoming meal
chased the clinging odour of an outgoing one.

Suddenly and silently a small man dressed in an
ankle-length tunic was by my side, his beaming face one
facet of a perfect sphere, head completely shaved
saving a neat circle of black hair balancing, it seemed,
on the crown. This unusual but by no means unpleasant
head rested on a severe black hooded tabard which
hung down over an all-embracing long-sleeved white
robe. Your Cistercian monk, I presumed.

'I know, don't tell me, you're Paddy,' he pumped my
hand enthusiastically, 'It's great to see you. I'm Father
Aelred, the guest-master. Well, I can't say 'Come in'
seeing as you're already in, but welcome to our community and, please,' he was still pumping my arm, 'make
yourself at home.' It was just the greeting my drained
spirit needed, full of warmth and white teeth. But such
was my unease by this stage that even into this artless
welcome I was capable of reading sinister designs – did
I want this to be my home? And why should it be so
great to see me? He must have sensed my unrest and
paused, looking down at my case, 'Look, let me show
you to your room and we'll make you a cup of tea
straight away.' Well, that seemed normal enough. He
seized the case and scurried ahead of me up some wide
wooden stairs and down a long dark corridor, stopping
at a door near the end. 'This one will be yours,' he
beamed, his bright eyes and teeth catching the available
light. 'Just shake yourself down and come back to the
parlour. I want to hear all about you.' He disappeared
down the corridor.

His very brightness emphasised the drabness of
everything in the tiny room, including a solid iron-
framed bed which took up most of it. There was a large

bowl on a bedside table with a ewer full of water. God, when was the last time I used one of these? Didn't they have running water here? Or any supply of water on this tiny island? I tried the electric light in the room – it worked – all was not stone age, at least. I splashed some of the freezing water over my face and it felt good, cooling my fevered misgivings – a shade.

Well, I was here now for the rest of my life, but to what purpose? How was I going to spend my time? I couldn't pray – there was nothing inside to come out. Even the pain of my torment was barren – just a growing emptiness, a draining away of the impetus which had brought me so far despite all the misgivings of parents and friends. I looked down at the confused reflection of my face in the water. I could see Mum crying at the bedroom window as I walked away from the house and, earlier, girlfriend Marian, deeply silent as I explained my grand purpose, the sunlight playing on the sheen of her hair. Well it looked like I was about to reap the harvest of the distress I had sown around me so cavalierly.

The linen towel was hard as I dried my face. Yes, the soft days were over and the quicker I put them out of my mind the better. Let's get out of this horrid little room. I met Father Aelred carrying my pot of tea into the parlour. 'Ah, good,' his face splitting into that grin again, 'let's sit down and chat a moment. The others will be coming back soon. The bell may signal the end of work for the community but it tells my guests it's time for a cup of tea.' My heart lifted at those domestic words. I was not alone. Maybe there was a whole group of us 'young'uns' waiting to enter.

'I bet you're feeling 'what have I let myself in for?' right now,' said Aelred as we sat down. 'We should have the 'Abandon hope . . .' notice above the door because virtually every postulant has that feeling when they get here.' He giggled. 'That's what you're called here, by the way. Means that you're claiming or demanding entry to the Order – about the last attitude you feel like adopting at this moment, I guess. Just as well you came on the last boat of the day.' He chortled. 'It will wear off, I assure you.'

'Now, to business; you'll be staying with me for a couple of days before moving on into the noviciate, which is that slightly separated part of the community in which apprentice monks like you live and learn our way of life over the first two years. So enjoy yourself here in the guesthouse while you can, eh! Luxuriate in the freedom of coming and going as you please with the novelty of the cloistered life all around you.

'There's a library next door, and over there,' he pointed to a notice board on the wall, 'is a list of the times of meals, Mass and the Divine Office – that's the series of church services which punctuate the daily, and nightly, life of the community,' he explained, though I did at least know that much.

I sat there, thinking of the old-time candidates at the gate. Insults indeed! This man was smothering me in kindness and I just wanted to run. I also wanted to pour out my story to him – the worthy, home-loving life I had sacrificed to come here; to tumble out the confusion of feelings writhing within me as I neared the moment of my commitment. But I couldn't utter a word of it. And anyway, he obviously didn't want to know about any of that. He wanted me to be looking forward, not back. I looked at him and smiled weakly.

'I'm afraid it's all weighing very heavily on me at the moment,' I heard myself saying – an understatement for the gathering scream of anguish I could feel inside.

'Like the impending execution, eh?' he smiled. 'We all have to go through it. What you're actually doing is catching up with yourself. The long cherished plan is about to become a reality. Right now, Paddy, you're entering a tunnel and everything is black, but look hard, go on, look hard. Think of God, heaven, Jesus, his mother – it doesn't matter particularly. There is a pinprick of light at the other end and over the next few days it will become larger and larger, and soon you will rush out into glorious sunlight and everything will suddenly be in technicolour, just like the Wizard of Oz.'

He looked up as footsteps approached and a middle-aged man entered the room. 'Ah, good, it's Tony. It'll be Vespers in a minute and Tony will take you to the church.' At that moment three young children burst in, followed by an adult couple, presumably their parents. 'Hi, there's Aelred,' said one; 'the unready,' said his older brother laughing, and the guest-master immediately went into an exaggerated martial arts pose. 'I'll cut off your head with one mighty blow,' he whispered fiercely, and then relaxed as they all rushed at him and tried to knock him over. 'That's enough, you kids,' grunted their father, pulling them off. Aelred turned to me. 'This is the lovely O'Connell family. Brother Kevin, the eldest of the tribe, is a member of the community in Simple Vows, and they're all enjoying a week down here with him.'

'Does Brother Kevin share the holiday with you all?' I asked, not sure I was hearing aright. How could such a thing happen once you'd renounced everything to come here?

'Oh yes,' one of the children piped up. 'We all went over to St Margaret's Island this afternoon and I got my feet wet when I slipped off this really slimy rock.'

'Yes, he can spend an hour or two with them if things are not too busy,' said Aelred. 'Soon we'll be bringing in the hay and then it'll be all hands to the pump – even yours,' he said, cuddling the smallest of the children. 'But you're going to be late for Vespers if you don't move, and so will I.' He gripped my shoulder and turned with me to the door. 'All will be well, Paddy me laddy,' he whispered in my ear.

Tony was waiting for me outside and together we walked towards the church which was set into the complex of buildings next to the guesthouse. 'You're the new postulant, I take it,' he said gravely. Yes, I suppose I am, I thought dully, and I nodded, still thinking furiously about Brother Kevin's afternoons off. A pinprick of light, he said.

We entered the church and climbed immediately into a small gallery which overlooked the interior facing the sanctuary at the other end. It was a simple building with no pretensions to style; the walls were plain white without decoration. The gallery was empty and I walked to the front and looked down on the body of the church, filled not with the benches of a normal parish church but with two long rows of dark wooden choir stalls ranged down each side. A tired sun bathed the walls in the faintest shade of pink and the shadows of the stalls stretched out in gentle coats of grey.

As I stood there a door at the far end opened below us and in streamed two lines of hooded men clothed in flowing robes of white. They made their way to the centre, bowed low and long to the Blessed Sacrament and then filed down each side of the choir stalls to their places. Near the rear of the procession came one figure dressed in civilian clothes and my heart pounded. This was going to be me in a day or so, enclosed, engulfed in this white impassive sea. Yes, swallowed up indeed! There was a loud clatter as they opened up some massive leather-bound books in front of them, and without a pause a single voice started to chant, followed by a line sung by the whole community – a tremendous but controlled sound coming from some thirty to forty throats.

I returned to sit by Tony numbed by the sudden power of the chant. Was I to be a part of this awesome heavenly choir? It was so different from anything musical I had experienced before that while part of me was elated by its other-worldliness, the rest of me was cowed by the largeness of it, just as I had been by the tolling of the monastery bell an hour before. I sat with my eyes shut, totally absorbed, no points of reference, like a raft adrift on the open sea. I opened them once to see Tony following the Office in a thick book flicking from end to end with great dexterity. Time enough for that later, I thought, and closed my eyes again. In no time it seemed the great books were banging shut and the figures filed out. I noticed with surprise that forty minutes had passed.

As we walked back to the guesthouse I wondered about my companion. 'Are you a postulant too?' I asked. 'Heavens, no,' he laughed. 'I'm happily married and an accountant in London. But I come down here once a year and try to recharge my batteries by reading and attending the Office – and enjoying the peace of this island.'

I found myself irritated by his casual if worthy acceptance of the place. Here, for me, the very jaws of purgatory were opening to consume me; where I would be waging bitter warfare with myself and the devil for the rest of my life; and all he could talk about was recharging his bloody batteries – tapping into the sacrificial torment of the likes of me for the sake of his good vibrations. At least the family down here on holiday was giving pleasure to a member of the community, not drawing power off it for selfish reasons.

Such turbulent feelings were a tonic for my morale, and a belligerent self-righteousness accompanied a wholesome meal obviously cooked somewhere in the monastery and served with much humour and horseplay by Father Aelred for the benefit of Brother Kevin's noisy family. Fortunately everyone left me to my own thoughts. Afterwards I browsed along the library shelves in a distracted way, and then strolled over on my own to hear Compline, the retiring Office for the day.

The church was in dark shadow with not a light turned on, and the absence of the noisy book openings told me that the monks were probably singing this Office by heart. It was a magical experience, so peaceful, and a beautiful anthem towards the end made my spine tingle. There was something in the childlike way this community of battle-hardened men swooped to the higher notes that brought to mind the times as a child I would sing for my mother. How, as my treble voice reached for the top notes, I would notice her eyes filling with tears. Now I knew how she felt, and I sat on after everyone had left, in the darkness, a mourner at the wake of my former life, and let the tears flow. I felt that I was bearing witness to a sense of ending and beginning, and a yearning deep inside me could only express itself that way.

Father Aelred made me a hot drink and disappeared with a promise to wake me in time for Prime, the first morning Office at six o'clock. I read a little and retired to bed at nine, the earliest for years, feeling more at peace than I had been all day.

I awoke in the dark to the sound of whispered voices

in the corridor and retreating footsteps. All my former anxieties rushed back and I was instantly awake and sitting up. I looked at my watch. It was not quite three o'clock. What was going on? Was somebody ill? It could hardly be the return of a late-night reveller. There was no way I could go back to sleep so I decided to make myself a cup of tea in the kitchen downstairs and see what was up. There was nobody around so I boiled the kettle and poured it on to a tea bag. While it was infusing I looked outside and wandered down the corridor to the left where I hadn't yet ventured. A door at the end was marked 'Monastic Enclosure' which presumably meant it was off limits to me. I was turning away when I heard that same thin voice starting a chant, just like yesterday evening. I opened the door a fraction and the full voice of the community echoed out. I shut the door quickly and leaned against it. At this time of the morning! I had heard that Cistercians sang the Night Office but I had imagined it to be on the other side of midnight before finally going to bed. This was ridiculous. Didn't they sleep at all, I wondered? How could I cope with such an inhuman regime?

A whole hour passed before I could get to sleep again. I dreamt I was on a boat and someone kept ringing the ship's bell which would toll oppressively, sending out waves of sound which made me feel quite sick. I awoke in a sweat to the knocking on my door. 'It's quarter to six, Paddy,' Father Aelred's voice was whispering. 'Prime will be starting in fifteen minutes time.' 'OK', I muttered, lying there feeling completely paralysed with a thumping heart. Could I possibly make it in time? Did I want to make it at all? I got to the gallery ten minutes late to find the Office in full swing but sung throughout on one note. Tony sat leafing through his book. At least he took the services seriously; a small contribution on his part, I thought.

'You didn't make the Night Office, then,' he grinned as we walked back together. 'Did you?' I asked in surprise. 'Yes,' he replied, 'not every night, but I'm leaving today and I wanted to go out on a high. It's very peaceful at that time of night. You realise that you're probably the only people in the whole world at prayer, apart from other Cistercian houses, that is, and it gives you a strange sense of responsibility, like a parent watching over sleeping children.'

I revised my early opinion of him – the man was obviously a tryer, but I was still worried about the three o'clock bit. 'Oh, they get enough sleep, I'm told,' he said in answer to my question. 'Many of them go to bed straight after Compline and that means about seven hours before they have to get up again. As a family and business man I'm lucky if I get six hours a night during the week. And Aelred tells me they eat well enough, too, though you know they're strict vegetarians.' I didn't, and my rosy vision of the life slipped back into black and white once more.

After breakfast, a good old-fashioned one of bacon and egg, I sought out Father Aelred in the kitchen. 'What further horrors are in store for me?' I said. 'First I find that the Night Office really means the middle of the night; now I hear I'm to be a complete vegetarian. I'm beginning to wonder what the next deprivation is going to be.'

He laughed, inordinately I thought, and disappeared next door to return with a small book. 'I'm surprised Father Abbot didn't tell you to read this, the Rule of St Benedict,' he said. 'It's all in here you know – a minute description of our life written down hundreds of years ago. We here are Cistercians of the Strict Observance which means that there have been times in the past when the observance of the Rule grew lax. You'll be studying it in great detail later on but do dip into it today sometime and get the feel of it. Horrors indeed!' he laughed again. 'Now if the Rule forbade any sleep or food at all, like some of those really enthusiastic monks in the deserts of Egypt in the early days, a raised eyebrow or two might be justified. But a slight rearrangement of your sleep pattern, and sparing the lives of a few cows and pigs is not going to deter a man of courage like you, I'm sure.' I took the book, reflecting that the Abbot had probably been wise not to have sent me this Rule, or I might never have come.

Terce was at nine o'clock, so-called because it was the Office of the third hour – following the ancient Roman practice of starting the day's clock at six a.m. This was immediately followed by the Community Mass, which provided another feast of plainsong. The sun was rising high and its rays cascaded through the upper windows of the church picking out the billowing clouds of incense, giving the whiteness of walls, cowls and smoke a hundred different shades. At the Peace the monks slipped back their hoods and embraced each other. There were many young men among them, I noticed, though their shaven heads (another 'horror' I had to come to terms with) made it difficult to classify them with any accuracy. At least the young chap in his own clothes still had his hair, I noticed with relief. I received Holy Communion at a hatchway downstairs, and the monk smiled as he put the host on my tongue, murmuring gently, 'The Body of Christ'. That Body, at least, I could cope with. It was this body of mine which was causing the problems.

There was nothing to do until the next Office, Sext at 12.30 p.m., so I wandered down a side road towards the cliffs with the Rule book in my pocket. It was a beautifully warm day and the smell of the yellow gorse in bloom was already heavy in the air. I sat down overlooking a calm blue sea and opened the book. The Prologue ran:

> Hearken, my son, to the commands of your master, and listen with the ear of your heart. Receive willingly and fulfil faithfully the warning of your loving father, that you may return through the labour of obedience to him from whom you had departed through the sloth of disobedience. To you my words are now addressed, whoever you are, that renouncing your own will, you take up the strong and shining weapons of obedience in order to fight for Christ the Lord, our true king.

Oh, if only it was a simple as picking up a weapon and slashing away. What a relief that would be to the state of tension I was suffering.

In the first place, whatever good work you begin to perform, beg him with earnest prayer to complete it, so that he who has deigned to include us among his children may not at any time be grieved by our evil doings. For we must always serve him by means of the gifts he has given us, so that he might never as an angry father disinherit his children, nor as an angry Lord incensed by our sins give us over to everlasting punishment as the most wicked of servants who would not follow him to glory.

Follow him to glory – me, in my state of mind! It was all so unreal here in this autumn paradise. One warning shot after another was telling me to make myself scarce and return from whence I came, but I just couldn't. Having come this far I knew I had to give the whole thing a try. And this was the strange turn around. It was now not the prospect of entering that was the torture but of sitting out here in this no-man's-land. Better to sit outside the gate with the insults – at least it would be nicer inside when I got in. All these prospects of discomfort and threats of disinheritance held like a sword over a chap's head were hardly conducive to the sense of leisure this serene environment demanded.

I felt so irritated and anxious that I was no longer able to sit still or read anything; I got up and strode around the perimeter of the island, hot and sweaty, up and down the cliffs, throwing pebbles into the sea, sprinting across the beaches, desperately filling in the hours until the bell rang out for Sext and I could sit and apply the healing prayer like a poultice to my shattered nerves.

I could hardly wait till lunch was over to corner Father Aelred. 'Look, Father,' I said almost fiercely, 'this waiting is beginning to get me down – Can't I go in any sooner? What's the point of keeping me in this never-never land?'

He grinned and led me outside where we strolled along the road. I could imagine him treading this path so regularly, reassuring the faint-hearted. 'So the suspense is killing you, is it? Not a bad sign. I've known guys drag it out as long as possible in the guesthouse until I virtually had to pitchfork them into the community. They rarely stayed long, and I remember one chap who actually went and got his bag and left when I told him it was time to go in. So in a way it's good that you want to leap in at the deep end, so to speak. There isn't a lot of point in prolonging the agony now that you've weathered the first shocks of encountering the awful reality of it all. Look, I'll have a word with the Father Lawrence, the novice-master, this afternoon and see what he thinks about taking you in tomorrow morning. Perhaps you would enjoy the afternoon more knowing that the process has begun.'

Suddenly a great weight seemed to be lifted from me and I put my arm round his shoulder and gave him a hug. 'You're my friend for life,' I said, and he laughed. 'Now there's a smile. I've been praying for that knotted brow of yours to clear ever since you came. Go on, run along and I'll have an answer for you at teatime.'

I walked down towards the jetty with a soaring heart and found myself wending my way through the trippers just as I had less than twenty-four hours before, but this time I felt totally different. I could give them back their golden skins and their pop idols and their vacuous chatter and all the busy life they clung to, where they found their security and fulfilment. That was fine by me. I now had somewhere else of my own to go, which looked daunting enough and had to be gone through, but was better than all this waiting. When the bell rang the sound was no longer ominous; it was like the bell telling me it was time to wend my way home, so I hurried back. Father Aelred confirmed that I could enter the community the next morning after Mass, and I spent the evening leafing through the Rule wondering how I could ever cope with eating a pound of bread a day, or what size a hemina of wine was, and why baths should only be allowed infrequently? Maybe the devil was in the detail but I felt I couldn't worry about that now. I just had to trust that all would be well, as Aelred had promised. I wanted to go out for a late evening stroll after Compline but again that great exhausting tiredness came over me. The night vanished in a great dreamless sleep.

Chapter Two

Swallowed Up

The end of Mass found me waiting restlessly in the guesthouse, bag in hand.

'Whoa, steady on, young man!' teased Aelred. 'Father Lawrence will still be sorting out the morning tasks for his novices. Give him a chance to brace himself for a new member of the flock.'

But I didn't have long to wait. Soon the door opened and a tall man about forty strode purposefully into the room. Aelred introduced us and added mischievously, 'A virgin postulant for you, Father Lawrence; mostly ignorant of St Benedict and his Rule; an empty vessel waiting to be filled.'

The novice-master grinned suddenly. 'That's the way I like 'em. No horror stories to be straightened out. OK, Paddy, come on through and I'll show you where to dump your things.' I whispered au revoir to Aelred and followed my new master through the doorway marked 'Monastic Enclosure' and into a world which, if not bathed in Oz-style technicolour, had a generous share of sunlight streaming in through the windows. Everything about Lawrence seemed swift and purposeful. I knew enough about monasteries to see that we were striding through one wing of the cloister, the central quadrangle which enclosed a small garden some thirty metres square and from which all the other rooms and staircases led off. 'Is this the . . .', I began to say, trying to catch him up. He turned round and put his finger to his lips, drawing me into the well of a nearby stairway. 'The first rule is that we must observe silence within the monastic buildings at all times, especially in the cloister, otherwise it would become a market place overnight. Don't worry,' he smiled as my face reddened, 'you'll soon get used to it.'

We now mounted a winding stairway and walked down a narrow corridor between rows of small curtained cubicles some four feet wide. 'Bedrooms,' he whispered, and pausing at one near the end he yanked the curtain back revealing a narrow bed and an upright cane chair. 'Here's yours,' he said. 'You sleep here and that's all, so you don't need any more than this – my cubicle's just the same, except the bed's a bit older' he grinned almost gleefully. 'The Rule takes community very seriously, and because we don't talk it's very necessary to be in touch with each other all the time – no dens, no hideaways, no private life at all in fact. That's the Benedictine way. Other orders manufacture other rules. We just live the contemplative community life to the full, and prove that the term is not a contradiction – though it can be a mixed blessing for light sleepers. Leave your things here but bring any pens, books and writing material you may have down to the noviciate.'

I followed him down the wooden stairway into the bare white-walled cloister. I was beginning to realise what the word austerity meant. You take every unnecessary or decorative thing away, including your possessions and your privacy, and what you're left with is austerity – simple but sublime! He ducked through a door in the cloister, down a passage with white cloaks hanging on pegs at either side, and into a room laid out as a classroom with some twenty desks and chairs in rows, a teaching desk at one end with a blackboard beside it, a large map of the Holy Land and long book-filled shelves against the walls. The noviciate.

'Here, put your things on this desk and come with me.' He led the way into a small room off the classroom which contained a desk, chair, bookshelf, crucifix, filing cabinet and nothing else. I sat down, muted, feeling excessive. Even the light conversational openings I could have made would have seemed untidy space fillers in a place like this.

'Well then, Paddy,' he said pleasantly, 'Welcome to this

little community of God. There are ten of us in the noviciate including you. There's another postulant, Terry,
and eight novices at various stages of their two-year
stay. Father Abbot gave me your formal application and
I can't see anything that would create a problem. Do
you think there might be?'

'No,' I answered, feeling reasonably at ease. 'Apart
from the whirlwind of anxiety that I'm doing something
incredibly stupid in coming here at all.'

'Well said!' he snorted with amusement and leaned
back in his chair. A long lean man, Father Lawrence had
a pleasant mobile face, a smile that flashed out and just
as swiftly retracted lest one might be led to think it
meant something, and eyes that never dwelt long on
any object but darted around picking up data like a frog
picking up flies.

'Of course you're doing something incredibly stupid.
The trouble is that you've been doing something incredibly sensible for twenty-five or so years, and look where
it's got you. You must have dropped your guard for a
moment and heard God saying deep within you, 'Listen,
I'm here. Come and find me.' You took him at his word
and you've ended up here. But you're no nearer to him
now than you were at the beginning of your journey. It's
just that this place and all this paraphernalia, or the lack
of it, depending on your viewpoint, is designed to keep
him visible, to stop other things from getting in the way.
That's the grim logic about the monastic life and that's
why it will always remain an authentic Christian vocation. It's not for heroes but for those of us who are not
really strong enough to resist all the distractions of the
world. We call it "Fuga mundi", flight from the world.'

'I know,' I burst in, everything suddenly falling into
place, 'I'd worked it out just like that. I hated the path
here I was being driven down because it all seemed so
single-minded, so oblivious of other more expansive
options, and seemingly rejecting of those I love and who
love me. But there seemed a snare in everything else I
looked at, and a voice saying, "No, not here, I'm not
here for you. Go on further." I knew that was not quite
true because God is in our loved ones and all his works,

but for me, well, I knew I just had to follow where he was leading me.'

'Spoken like a true ascetic,' Lawrence chimed in. 'You must read the sayings of the Desert Fathers. That teasing quest for God in solitude led them to some extraordinary places. If you think this is weird you should try living on top of a pillar in the desert as Saint Simeon did. Even I think that was a bit over the top.'

We both laughed. 'But how can I know that I'm not following a selfish and arrogant whim in coming to lead an extreme life like this and abandoning all those who love me.'

He sat back and looked at me steadily. 'Whims don't last too long in a place like this. And we don't abandon those we love any more than anyone who moves away to do God's work in a different place. Wherever we are, God always gives us people to love. After a few weeks of trying to love this crowd, you might not think it at all selfish or arrogant to stay. There's not one of us who doesn't need a great deal of love and support. Being a monk is a humbling thing I can assure you. You'll soon learn that both in the Rule and in the life we try to lead here in this place.'

He stopped as if he were about to add '. . . if I have anything to do with it,' but thought better of it. Here was a man who spoke his mind, amazingly vibrant for such a quiet and reflective way of life. Were they all like him and Aelred, I wondered? He seemed so sure about things, so positive. I instantly felt a rapport with him, someone I could really communicate with – however often that might be allowed.

'Anyway,' he continued, 'let me run through your day so that you know where you are. I've assigned Brother Samuel to be your guardian angel so he won't let you get lost in time or space. They're all out doing jobs at the moment, cleaning, laundry, that sort of thing. Normally we study the Rule at this time but today's a heavy day for duties and that takes precedence. They'll change and come back here before Sext – that's at a quarter to one, just before lunch. You'll stand next to Sam in choir and he'll tell you what to do. How's your Latin?'

'Rudimentary, I'm afraid. Remnants of Caesar's *Gallic Wars*, the Mass, a few ancient hymns.' Listening to the chant yesterday had been so sublime that the idea of understanding it, let alone praying it, hadn't occurred to me.

'Never mind, it'll come with practice and a few lessons. Anyway, after Sext comes lunch, then back here to read until None at about two. It's then time for afternoon work, so you'll change – I'll give you an overall and a pair of wellies, and then you'll go with the others to work with Brother Denis who'll be harvesting something or other or breaking new ground somewhere else. Then you wash and change and come back here until Vespers, the evening office. From Vespers we go into supper and then return here to read, something lighter, a biography, perhaps. Then we all come together, the whole community, to be read to. It's really a time filler to allow anyone who's wrapping up a job – at the farm or in one of the workshops – the chance to tidy up and join the last community activity of the day – Compline. We don't have a proper meeting room or Chapter House, as they're called, so all our assemblies happen in a wing of the cloister. And so to bed. I'm going to let you off the Night Office for a while, so I'll wake you in time for Lauds, that's at about half past four, and after that we read, gently and prayerfully, maybe grab a bowl of coffee . . . look, that's enough for you to remember for now – Sam will be on your shoulder to direct you; you'll soon pick it up.'

My heart sank. 'The Night Office,' I said, 'if Lauds is at half past four, what part of the rest of the night does this Night Office take up – all of it?'

Father Lawrence sighed – was I taxing his patience already?

'Of course not; we still get over seven hours sleep; at least I make sure my novices do. No, it starts at three o'clock and we sing, or rather monotone, a fair number of psalms with hymns and prayers, a bit like Vespers only longer. I'll explain the format later. At about four we have half an hour's silent prayer which you can either spend in your stall or walk a little if you're finding it difficult to keep your eyes open. OK?'

He picked two books from the shelf above him and passed them to me. One I recognised as the Rule; the other, a thick black book, *The Customs and Ordinances of the Cistercian Order,* made me nervous just to hold it. 'Look over these for a while. I have to do something but the others will be back soon and Sam will make himself known to you. No talking, mind; it would embarrass him dreadfully.' He showed me back to my desk with a flourish and was gone.

I picked up the Customs book and flicked through it. I paused at what seemed to be a set of rather strange drawings but which turned out to be the graphics of a sign language, presumably for monks to use when they needed to communicate something but keep the silence. To ask for bread you joined the tips of both index fingers and thumbs to make a sort of squarish circle. The additional 'please' was to kiss the tips of the fingers. God was the same sign as bread but vertical and made into a triangle. Salt was the tip of the index finger on the tongue. Wine, more to the point, was the same index finger applied to the tip of the nose. To be sick was to move the forearm from the vertical to the horizontal. This could be fun, I thought. God, I'm sick of this bread – pass the wine. Dead was signified by the rather grisly action of pressing the upturned thumb under the chin. Pass the wine or you're dead!

So engrossed was I that I didn't notice the novice standing at my side until he tapped me on the shoulder. He immediately shook me warmly by the hand, and from a cloudless face with large sky-blue eyes shone out a broad welcoming smile. He made some rapid movements with his hands which I realised with a jolt was the actual sign language I had just been reading about. I wrote down Brother Samuel on a scrap of paper and drew a pair of wings beside it and showed him, pointing at myself. He looked flummoxed but then twigged the angel bit and rubbed his chest vigorously, a sign I later learnt meant 'good'.

Other novices in their all-white tunics joined Sam and greeted me with silent lips and noisy eyes. One gave me the thumbs-up sign. They all moved to their desks and sat down. How strange, I thought, all these young men, teeming with life, sitting, walking, working, side by side, day in week out, yet never knowing what was going on in the minds and hearts of their companions. How could I ever care for or be supported by somebody I couldn't address except to ask for the salt or a lump of bread – with my fingers. But then, maybe, I would read the feelings in their eyes or gestures as time went by – reading between the signs.

I noticed several novices expertly 'signing' to each other, carrying on a sort of conversation, which seemed to make the whole thing slightly ludicrous, unless they were doing it illicitly. This turned out to be the case when Father Lawrence bounded into the room and all signs ceased and hands slid stealthily under their tabards or scapulas, as they were called. He pointed me out and waved his arms in the form of an embrace which I took to be the official welcome. I touched my lips, remembering the sign, which brought an instant round of silent applause. My heart leapt and I involuntarily made the embrace gesture in response.

Then Lawrence jabbed at his watch and they immediately formed into two lines and passed through the passage, picking up their cloaks en route and swinging them round their shoulders, hood up and metal clasp snapping in expert fashion. Sam brought up the rear in his line and slipped me into the place above him, following Terry the other postulant. We walked down the cloister and joined the end of two lines of hooded monks coming from somewhere else, and we all proceeded into the church and took our places facing the big black books.

Another new experience. Having been introduced to the noviciate I was now suddenly transported into the bosom of the whole community at prayer. Sam immediately opened the book in front of him along with the others in a chorus of creaks and bangs, and a single voice intoned the first line. Sam indicated the next line and with a thrill I added my voice to the thunder of the voices singing in unison, *'Domine, ad adjuvandum me festina,'* which I translated as 'Lord, help me quickly.'

You're going to have to help me, Lord, and pretty sharpish too, I reflected with an onset of panic. Otherwise I'm not sure I can cope with this cataclysmic change. Father Aelred and the guesthouse already seemed light years away.

Being part of the rolling flow was even more impressive than hearing it from the gallery. The pauses had obviously been honed to perfection over many years, and the hymn and psalms seemed so familiar that nobody paused or stumbled over a single word. The monastic style of singing – surging through a verse in brisk, evenly-spaced monosyllables, and then letting it die off in a soft cadence at the end – I knew in my bones it was going to be easy to follow.

After the psalms were over and the final prayer was being sung I allowed my eyes to stray to the back of the choir. There standing at the end of one of the lines, distinguished from the others by a cross hanging from a thick purple cord on his chest, was clearly the Abbot who had set all this in motion by inviting me down. I had imagined a rounded paternal figure but this one was tall and lean with a no-nonsense face, whose half-lenses added an austere, academic look. Opposite him on the other side of the choir, was a small, red-faced man with round, steel-rimmed glasses who seemed by comparison positively Pickwickian. He must be the Prior, or deputy Abbot, whom Father Aelred had referred to. Aelred I noticed halfway down the other side of the choir, and next to him stood Father Lawrence at whose raking glance I quickly jerked my eyes back to the text.

After about ten minutes or so the books clanged shut and the community stood impassively, faces expressionless, retracted into their hoods. Then another chant was intoned which I learnt later was a long grace or thanksgiving before lunch, and the lines moved out, singing, into the cloister, around two of its four corners, then turning into a large hall with long wooden trestle tables spaced around its walls. The regular places laid, each with their particular nameplate, to which each monk filed; the suddenly overpowering smell of cooked

The abbey refectory.

vegetables; the bustle of steaming trolleys being wheeled in: all shouted Food.

I suddenly realised how hungry I was and, ushered to a place next to Sam, I awaited the food with eager curiosity.

The lengthy grace completed, we all sat down. In front of me was a large white table napkin, a two-handled pint-sized earthenware bowl, a metal knife, wooden spoon and fork, and a nameplate bearing Postulant in Gothic lettering. I looked over to Sam but, like the others, he had his hood up and only the tip of his nose was visible. A tureen of soup was placed on the table by a serving monk with a large white apron over his tunic. Sam turned and grinned and placed the soup in front of me together with a large homemade loaf. I filled my bowl, cut a thick slice with the rather blunt knife (did I have to eat a pound of this a day?), and waded in. It was delicious and, conscious of the tension built up over the morning just slipping away, I pondered the scene before me.

Thirty-odd men, dressed and hooded like the Ku Klux Klan; reclusive, vegetarian, tonsured, purposeful ... what was all this really about? In this life of silent withdrawal, was there some moment in the day, week, year even, when, in community, the wraps would be put aside and the grand purpose of the charade proclaimed? Because just at this moment I could see no purpose strong enough to justify this extraordinary scene, like something off a medieval scroll. Was the Rule of St Benedict so inflexible that it was having to be visually reconstructed by these Cistercians in perpetuity?

I looked at the hunk of bread in front of me. Bread and circuses, I thought. I suddenly imagined the whole set-up as a latter-day miracle play which had, in the passage of time, lost its audience, and was now playing a continuous dress rehearsal to itself. Bread and surplices! As I paddled in these dangerous waters someone started to read aloud from a balcony set quite high up into the opposite wall. It was a passage from the Scriptures and my concentration wandered as the next stage of the communal meal began. Further bowls were placed on each table containing steaming potatoes and vegetables. I looked instinctively for the meat tray and remembered with a jolt that meat was now officially just a memory in my life. How would I cope? I looked around – nobody seemed to be wasting away. On the contrary, there were some ready-made Friar Tucks to be seen, their girth amplified by the flowing robes. Mind you, on a diet of bread and stodge, was that to be wondered at?

I looked around for a clean plate, but saw Sam wiping his soup up with his bread and guessed there would be none. The main course was soon gone and I took a pear from a bowl of fruit on the table and some water in my bowl. The reading had now changed to a biography of some modern-day saint, and as it droned on I followed Sam in washing my utensils over my dinner plate and wiping them and my bowl with the large napkin. Everything was then folded neatly and arranged just like the altar vessels after Mass, and the table was left as we had found it. At a pause in the reading a knock on the table from the Abbot signalled the end of lunch, and the community rose and sung another lengthy grace. Did it mean anything to them now, I wondered, singing the same old Latin verses year after year with never a simple, 'Gosh! Thanks Lord. That was a pretty indifferent meal but it keeps me alive to praise and serve you.' Maybe they said that inside while the tongue prattled away. We all filed out in the order we had entered, with the novices at the rear diverting back to the noviciate.

Now this was really hard. At the moment when, the meal completed, one just likes to relax into idle chit-chat and comfortable indolence over a coffee, even a cigarette – no, the novices all returned to their desks and began to read or write in what seemed a totally oppressive silence. No pre-lunch sign conversations now. Itching to find some diversion, I wandered over to the bookshelves and scanned the sections for something that would tempt the jaded palate. Spiritual development – that could came later. Biblical theology – not immediately after lunch, thank you. Monastic tradition – who cared! Lives of the saints – for heaven's sake!

In desperation I picked up a book on St Benedict and walked back to my place. I flicked over the pages but could find none that I was drawn to start on. I didn't want to hear of his great virtue, his cruel temptations, his courageous perseverance, even about his holy sister Scholastica. The passage describing how he rolled naked in a thorn bush to overcome a lustful urge did not impress me one bit. These were, after all, the sixties, and although the permissive society, as people were calling it, had its dangers, there had to be better ways of sublimating an impure thought than this. I realised with a shock that I hadn't had an 'impure' thought for days. Obviously, out of sight out of mind. But if the reading material was going to be as unappetising as this ... the occasional day dream was a distinct possibility.

A bell sounded and, as everyone got up, it was apparent that the time for None had come. At last here was something familiar, and I swung into the line like a pro. No longer bombarded by shockwaves I found myself enjoying the onward surge of the singing, each side of the choir taking up alternate verses as the psalms proceeded. I'm here to pray, I reminded myself, and plucked out words I recognised from the Latin such as '*jubilatio*' or '*peccatum*' as they sped before me; but it became easier just to be caught up in the sound of my voice blending into the measured flow of the single community song. Are they praying, I wondered, sneaking a look at Sam, but his peaceful face had a blandness about it that spoke of things happening either at great depth or not at all.

Lawrence pulled me aside as we left the church and led me up to the dormitory.

'Do you want to work outside with the novices this afternoon or would you rather go on reading. There's plenty of stuff about the Order – history, customs, rules, and that sort of thing.'

The idea of staying in the noviciate on my own with nothing to do but read the books I had seen on the shelves appalled me, and my instant response betrayed my state of mind only too clearly. Lawrence grinned slyly. 'I thought you'd prefer to get a breath of fresh air. Here, try these overalls for size.' He indicated a pair lying on the bed. 'When you've got them on come down to the boot room next to the noviciate and we'll find you some wellies.'

The boot room was already full of blue-denimed men pulling on boots and stamping them on the ground. Their breezy bonhomie was in such contrast to the silent gliders of five minutes ago that I wondered if indeed these were one and the same – but there couldn't be another crowd with haircuts like these, and their cheery silent greetings to me with the 'embrace' sign confirmed them as 'family'.

The novices were all wearing a sort of knee-length smock in blue denim which revealed a curious form of underwear. I could see the bottom of blue knee breeches fastened under the knee with string, with a sort of leg stocking stretching down into the shoe made of a stiffish buckram material. As one of them took off his shoe I saw that they ended underneath the heel with a separate soft felt slipper covering the foot. Obviously nothing had changed for centuries, with only the wellington boot making a gesture towards the twentieth century. I could picture some swain in the cornfield complete with smock and gaiters, pitch fork and pasty in a kerchief. I wanted to slap my thigh, point and guffaw loudly but Lawrence came in looking busy and I guessed that frivolous questions would be inopportune.

Having found a pair of boots that fitted I lumbered outside into a vegetable garden and, with Lawrence in the fore and Sam and I bringing up the rear, this happy band of novices walked off, again in the single file, again with blue denim hoods raised – each one of us estranged from each other in our own little world. The crocodile paused at the entrance to a large wooden shed from which emerged a sturdy monk dressed in a sensible boiler suit, driving a light tractor with some sort of plough attached. Driving slowly he led our file over many intersecting paths between a huge variety of vegetable plots, then across a close cropped meadow and into a large field, covered with neat lines of potato plants. The afternoon sun was pleasantly warm but the brisk pace made me wonder if I had not overdressed for the occasion. We were high up on the island and the blue sea shimmered all around us, distancing the mainland in a heat haze with nothing else beyond us but the ocean. Again I was suddenly caught thanking God for being here and then wondering what on earth for.

The reflective mood was swept aside as the tractor started without delay to turn the earth and throw out the potatoes. The novices followed the lanes it made with wide wicker baskets which we emptied into sacks placed at intervals. It's good to be here, I thought initially, but as the afternoon wore on and the tractor ploughed on at a relentless pace, my back first ached then blazed with pain. The others seemed impervious to the hardship and progressed behind the tractor in a permanently stooping posture, whereas I had constantly to stand erect, wriggle my hips to get some feeling back into the numbed area and then reach down again and try to catch the others up. The notion of praying to a provident God or communing with his creation was abandoned early on when I decided to fix my mind on the pain and dwell on the benefits of martyrdom and a swift and glorious death. The potato lanes shimmered in the heat and once or twice appeared to come and go like a mirage to my fuddled senses.

Lawrence had long since gone and eventually the tractor driver raised his plough and vanished from sight. The remaining potatoes were bagged and while I performed a series of stretching exercises to ease the agony which pulsated with every movement, the others stood in a group passing an occasional sign but mainly just looking out to sea. Sam came over to me and smiled banging his two fists together which I took to mean something disagreeable like hard work. I picked up two potatoes and banged them together and he laughed. Others now joined us and signed their approval of my efforts. My back began to ease and life once more held out possibilities.

The tractor returned, this time with Lawrence at the wheel driving wildly over the bumpy field, and we loaded the sacks on to a trailer and sat along the edges laughing and jostling during the painful and mercifully swift ride back to the shed. Hooded once more and in line we returned to the boot room just as that afternoon bell – was it really only forty-eight hours since I arrived! – began to toll, signalling, as I recalled, the end of work.

From the boot room Sam led me round the cloister, now quite a busy thoroughfare with monks in many forms of dress walking in all directions, and through a swing door into a large wash room. Here, several men, stripped to their undershirts, were washing vigorously, ducking their shaven heads under the taps. I longed to do the same as I was feeling hot and sticky all over but, with my long hair an obvious disadvantage, contented myself this time with washing just my face and hands. What you need is a shower, I thought. God knows what you do if you really want to get clean – jump into an icy pool, perhaps, so you can mortify the flesh at the same time. The very idea of bathing seemed somehow frivolous – a wanton exposure to feelings like pleasure or exhilaration! I mean, Jesus only entered the water for the serious matter of baptism; otherwise he simply sailed – or walked – on top of it!

We returned to the noviciate where the other novices were already seated in silence reading. The intensity of it was beginning to unnerve me. I couldn't imagine that they might possibly be enjoying their studies. I must get a grip on myself. Just maximise on the things you're actually enjoying, like the meals, the singing, this beautiful island, the new alliance with Sam (I couldn't feel brotherhood though, God knows, I was desperate enough), and maybe the boring bits would gradually be assimilated.

It was a convenient philosophy and it served me well during the next church service, the slightly longer Office of Vespers, with some interesting tunes to the psalms which, as they were repeated in every verse, I soon picked up. In the hymn, still in plainsong, I even detected a rhythm which evoked a corresponding movement within me, a balancing on the ball of one foot or the other. This immediately had me thinking of my rugby-playing days and the joy I would feel as, perfectly balanced, I could instantly decide which direction I took to deceive the opposition. Hey, this music was really up my street.

Supper, which followed Vespers, was another happy experience. The afternoon's labours had left a great hole in my stomach, and the bubble and squeak fried up from dinner's leftovers, along with some sublime homemade bread, butter and honey, gave me the overwhelming feeling that I was a survivor. Take one day at a time, I told myself, and who knows . . .

'Take every day as it comes,' said Lawrence, as if reading my mind, when he called me into his room after supper. 'God doesn't give us the strength to fight tomorrow's battles as well. As time goes on . . .' he broke off and looked at me closely as if he suddenly realised he was talking to that most fragile of creatures, the one-day-old novice. 'You are staying, I take it.'

'Where else would I go,' I said, with a lump suddenly in

my throat. I couldn't say anything and the novice-master, reading my misty eyes, looked rather uncomfortable as if mothering was a role he found hard to play. The stiff upper lip was his line, I was sure.

'Look,' he said, 'I've seen many novices come, and more go than stay, but if I were a betting man I'd put my money on you being a stayer.'

'Do you think that helps!' I retorted. 'I know I've got what it takes. I've been here a hundred times in my mind during the last months, but now that I'm here in the flesh, what scares me to hell is that it's going to take what I've got, all that I've got – it's going to swallow me up, and then . . . well, do I want to be what it eventually spits out?'

He got up and for a second I thought he was going to come over and give me a hug. God, I couldn't cope with that, I thought. But instead he walked over to the bookshelf and took down what I now knew to be the Rule of St Benedict, and stood by me thumbing through it.

'Well, if you see yourself being transformed into some sort of robotic monster, forget it. All sorts of people get fed into the system and what happens unfailingly among those who persevere is that they seem to become more themselves than they ever were before. The pursuit of a strict rule of life in a loving community will in the course of time ease away all that is not really you. You could say it removes the affectations to reveal the affections, the warm vulnerable person you really are underneath. The hard bit as you see it – the daily grind, the odd hours, the silence – they become habitual in a very short space of time, take my word for it. Just give yourself to them generously and you'll be amazed how snugly this life will fit you, even in the course of the next month.'

'I suppose it's all in the book,' I said lamely nodding at the volume he was holding, not really wanting to be consoled, resisting being given the good news.

'It is time for us to rise from sleep,' Lawrence picked out a passage and read it. '"Today, if you will hear his voice, harden not your hearts. Seek peace and pursue it. And when you have done these things my eyes will be upon you and my ears will be open to your prayers, and before you call upon me I will say to you, 'Behold I am here.' What can be sweeter, my dearest brother, than the voice of the Lord inviting us? In his loving kindness the Lord is showing us the way of life." That's St Benedict for you,' said Lawrence shutting the book with a sudden grin, 'He's all heart, really.'

But he could have been reading the Rite of the Dead over me, such was the gloom that descended on me as he rolled out the quaint wording. St Benedict's were not the comforting sentiments I wanted to hear just now. Oh for the familiar! The football results would have been more welcome. Couldn't he see that?

'After you've rolled in his bed of nettles,' I managed to blurt out.

'Oh, that was written to impress the hard men. Not for us softies. Putting up with each other is about the hardest thing we have to manage here. Starting to become what you really are deep down is a great adventure, so don't get too frightened by the size of the waves. You're on a safe ship. Look,' he said, 'you've weathered the first day. Congratulations! Just the communal reading and Compline to go and then a good night's sleep. I'll wake you for Lauds, the morning Office, so don't get up when the bell rings. And', he said softly as he showed me the door, '... one day at a time.'

The community sat on either side of the cloister as one of them read aloud from some spiritual book. My eyes were beginning to close and it was only seven o'clock – ridiculous. We filed into Compline which was sung, as I had guessed, without books, remaining always the same. The three psalms had a haunting tune with every verse seeming to end on a musical question mark, as if it never wanted to end. Eventually the beautiful *Salve Regina* anthem to Our Lady was sung and the monastic day was over.

Sam directed me upstairs to my cubicle, waved goodnight, and I sat on the bed almost too tired to undress. I didn't want to think about anything; to assess the impact of this 'adventure'; to contemplate what tomorrow might bring. I just wanted to escape into sleep and wake up to . . . another day? As I nuzzled into the pillow all the tears held over from the many attacks of self-pity I had suffered during the day flowed out, and a warm darkness enfolded my soul.

Chapter Three

New Clothes for Old

Whatever else it was – uncomfortable, self-abasing, not to say downright humiliating – it was certainly dramatic. Lying face downwards on those dirty terracotta tiles of the cloister floor after Prime, waiting to be received as a novice while the community sang what could have been the Lamentations of Jeremiah over my prostrate body. The horror film industry would have grabbed at the chance to use the set for one of their spooky spine-chillers.

It was all a little funereal for my liking but I suppose the symbolism was appropriate: Paddy, dying to the world, then rising as Brother Daniel (my new community name – there was already a Patrick here) to new life as a member of the Order of Cistercians of the Strict Observance. Not a lover of ceremonial I felt somewhat ridiculous as I looked out at floor level at the none too clean row of boots topped by the even dirtier hems of greasy off-white tunics. What on earth was I doing (an oft-repeated mantra during my weeks as a postulant) joining this crowd of misfits, stuck out on an island, yoked to an ascetic rule of life and denying themselves every known comfort?

Stop! The argument was now worn out. There was no justification for my lying here other than to accept these poor souls as my brothers of whom I was the least. And this way, this life was the only environment which was likely to force an acknowledgement out of me that God was my creator and his Son my redeemer. And that was that.

Monasteries, it suddenly dawned on me as I lay there

submerged under the ebb and flow of the chant, were
for the Don't Knows of this world. They had to be
because anyone who did know what they wanted to do
surely wouldn't be doing it in a place like this. I squint-
ed up at the craggy faces of the older monks. Had their
don't knows resolved themselves after decades of
monastic life? Or did a don't know gradually soften from
a wild perturbation of spirit into a gentle state of
unknowing, forging out of a life of self-sacrifice a
preparedness for whatever was to follow. A state of
being rather than of doing. Doing sublimated into being.
To be or not to be? That was the question a Don't Know
would probably never get round to answering.

But of course it was too late to ask myself a question
like that, nose down to the floor. A bit like a boxer on the
canvas wondering if he would have been wiser to have
covered his chin rather than chancing an uppercut.

It was Michaelmas, 29 September, a time-honoured
day for starting and ending. I had already suffered more
than enough, or so it seemed, in the six weeks since I
arrived. My body had been cruelly toughened by the
hard labour of bringing in the harvests. I had coped with
the rule of silence which forbade, for the sake of the
single-minded quest for God, verbal communication
with all save the Abbot and, in my case, the novice-
master. I had even survived the withdrawal, as real as
from any hard drug, of all the normal wordly distractions
– radio, TV, conversation, family and friends, reading
papers and books, girls even – all of which used to fill
my waking hours. There were days of unending pain
when the last thing I wanted to do was to pray or pick
up a Bible or spiritual book; moments when I just had to
grit my teeth not to rush in to Father Lawrence to say I
had had enough and that it was all so unfair. It was
supernature abhorring a vacuum.

And then, one strange afternoon, coming back from
collecting fresh butter from the farm, I had called into
the old island church of St Illtud, the hub of a former,
medieval community but now just a wayside chapel. I
had knelt on the ancient floor of rounded cobblestones
collected from the island's beaches. Amidst the pain

they inflicted on my knees, and the feeling of desolation as to the purpose and meaning of the life here – the utter ache of this whole futile exercise; amidst all this torment a sudden shaft of sweetness burst through within me, and brightness seemed to pour into the air around me, though I kept my eyes tightly closed not daring to see whatever, whoever, it might be.

This explosion of consolation must have been momentary, it was hard to tell – the merest tangential brush with God's inner life of blazing love – but the lightening effect it had on all that ache and desolation was both substantial and persistent. A vital conversion had taken place.

No, I had invested far too much for me to pull out now. And if I were to go, today, where would I go? What would I do? How stupid, I thought, ever to have started to climb the mountain from the bottom, the summit out of sight and probably out of reach. But what was the alternative?

I suddenly thought of my mother, not the one weeping as I left the family home, but the one in a recent letter, saying how proud she was of her monkish son and how impressed everyone in the parish was with my courageous decision. And even ex-girlfriend Marian, she reported, was looking great with the suspicion of a new boyfriend in tow. The letter shouted out a resumed normality with myself already a memory, albeit a favoured one. I was not the only one to have moved on.

The baptismal bit over, I was now summoned to be clothed in the basic white robe, a button-up tunic of unbleached wool, ankle-length and long sleeved. I knelt before the Abbot, a remote, burdened man, it seemed to me, whom I had met briefly when I had first entered. A man who rarely smiled and, I sometimes felt, regarded his flock as every bit as stupid and contrary as the sheep we were wearing. He asked me the ritual questions – did I wish to discard the life I had formerly led, embrace the Rule of St Benedict and clothe myself in the habit of humility? It went something like that for in truth I hardly heard a word he was saying. I remember thinking, do I have to sign anything, at which point the Abbot leaned forward and slipped the coat from my shoulders, took off my pullover, unbuttoned my shirt and carefully drew it over my head as if I were, in truth, a corpse.

Luckily, modern-day inhibitions sanctioned the retention of my trousers, so he simply eased the tunic over my head and did up the first few buttons. This was followed by the white scapula, a long strip of the same material eighteen inches wide and ankle-length back and front with a hood sitting on the shoulders. Finally he placed around me the all-enveloping white cloak, the formal choir garment which I would wear until it was replaced, by the cowl, the all-covering monastic robe, when I made my solemn vows in five years' time.

I'd asked Father Lawrence earlier if it was likely I would be trained to be a priest in due course since so many of the monks had been ordained.

'The answer is no for that very reason,' he replied. 'Up until a few years ago you were either a choir monk or a lay brother; the choir monks went on automatically to the priesthood, and the lay brothers, most of whom weren't educated and worked on the farm, didn't. It was then realised that, for most of the ordained choir monks, no priestly function was performed apart from saying Mass and hearing a few confessions. So now only enough priests to serve the needs of the community are trained. Which rules you out unless three-quarters of the community happen to be wiped out by some strange priestly virus. Anyway, let's not confuse the issue – a monk is a monk is a monk, and the least of these is a novice.'

So I was now dressed as a novice, though I would have to discard my trousers in favour of those quaint denim knee breeches which would serve as my underpants and be changed at bathtime every week (whether they needed to be or not). Father Abbot leaned forward once more and to signal that I was now formally a member of the community, kissed me on both cheeks. The light played on the silver stubble on his chin as our faces came together. Did I feel a sceptical tolerance in his embrace – how long will this one last? I gritted my jaw and took up the challenge. I was a monk now and

The author

the terms were uncompromising. We might dress like sheep; we might even be treated like sheep; but inside I felt like a battering ram.

The next stage of the initiation, however, developed the sheep theme even further. After the clothing I had to run an informal gauntlet of cheerful embraces from whoever I met on my way to the noviciate, my home for the next two years outside the main cloisters. Father Lawrence was there to embrace me and, ever a man to get on with the business, he took one look at my wild, unredeemed head of hair, incongruous above the chaste monastic clothing, and muttered like your genial sergeant major, 'I think we'll relieve you of that little lot right away.'

Yes, it was sheep-shearing time. I'm not sure why it is characteristic of monks to have shorn heads or why the various tonsures are so, but monks, both Bhuddist and Christian, and a diversity of other holy men all distinguish themselves by it. That original arch monk and prophet, Elisha, must have had it as well, for there's a lovely passage in the Old Testament where some mischievous village boys call him 'Baldy!' and, ever a man for a laugh, he summons bears from an adjacent wood to savage them. His tonsure must have meant a lot to him. Anyway, monks and close haircuts have always gone together. Certainly for ease of washing a dusty head after haymaking or to avoid your hair being pushed forward every time you raised your hood, the shaven head was a boon. And it must have kept down the nits.

I was led to the central washroom, an odd bare room lined with bowls but no mirrors, and one thankful concession to soft modernity, hot water. Father Edmond, a bowed but genial older monk, one of the original founding community from Belgium, stood by a chair with an ancient looking pair of electric clippers in his hand. Edmond was the choirmaster, razor-sharp when leading the community in song, but anywhere else he seemed transported to another world, so I was a little disconcerted to have to entrust my cranium to his other-worldliness. Would he remember that I have ears, I asked myself? And in so public a place, I fretted, as he ushered me to the chair right in the centre of the concourse where monks passed to and fro on their way to the loo or to have a late shave or wash. He waved a large blue cloth around my neck and with a grin drew his right forefinger across his throat. I didn't know whether to laugh or scream. The clippers buzzed into action and away he went.

I sat frozen as great locks of dark hair tumbled around me. In a way this unimportant ritual sealed my commitment to the new life. I could hardly walk out of the place now with a head like a grey egg. This was the sixties! Someone opened a door and a cold blast of air ran its icy fingers over my scalp. I shivered and Edmond, who had just expertly removed the last strands of hair around my ears, kindly drew my new hood over my head and patted my check. 'You are now a lamb of God, Brother Daniel,' he whispered and started to sweep up.

I stood looking at the great heap of dark hair, my pride

and joy, disappearing into a plastic sack. I reached up and felt my head over, naked with a range of ridges and bumps I had been totally unaware of before. 'More like a lamb led to the slaughter,' was the only sentiment which seemed to fit my predicament as another draught blew across from the door. A new, forbidding perspective on this romance, this quest, sent prickles of apprehension running through me. I remembered Lawrence's words, 'The reasons which make you stay here are never the ones which brought you here.' Dressed like a ballerina with boots on, with a head like a bit part in a Frankenstein film, I felt I had survived a drama only to be enrolled in a pantomime.

The bell rang for Terce and the community Mass, and I took my place at the end of the procession into the church alongside Brother Leo, who had been clothed just two weeks before me. Whatever my misgivings, it felt good to be part of that seamless flotilla of white gliding along like so many swans. I was still a mass of contradictions but at least I no longer stuck out like a sore thumb. As we made our way to our stalls it dawned on me that this uniform, this collective uniformity, served to conceal the mess and poverty of my life, possibly of all our lives. We stood accused of creating the impression of grace and order when, under the surface, disgrace and disorder was the more likely condition.

'Right, work,' said Lawrence as we returned to the noviciate after Mass. 'Denis is anxious to start reclaiming land for arable over towards West Point, so we're going to make a day of it, all of us, getting rid of the undergrowth to see what we've got for soil. Fr Maurice will prepare some sandwiches and tea, God preserve us, and we'll work through till Vespers.'

There followed a silent riot of jubilation and waving of arms – a day on the cliff tops with panoramic ocean views – which Lawrence cut short with a clap of his hands.

'You won't be waving your arms by four o'clock, I can promise you. And in case you think this is a party to celebrate Brother Daniel's clothing, forget it. We'll certainly rejoice with you, Daniel, when you've made your solemn profession in five years' time, and you'll receive the best funeral a man can have when you die, but in between we pick up our cross every day and stumble a few steps on the *Via Dolorosa*. That's our privilege.'

'Like a lamb led to the slaughter?' I expressed my earlier thought with a rueful grin.

'You said it, brother,' he replied without one.

Chapter Four

Making Hay

God knows why I loved haymaking. On our frugal diet the work was shattering, especially after wet weather when the bales weighed a ton. Furthermore, the tiny straw stalks would slide down your neck and snag into the weave of your shirt, making it worse than any hair shirt our forefathers ever wore. And as the weekly bath and change of underwear never varied for novices, winter or summer, a week of this constant torment would make my body look and feel like an overused pin cushion. Now a mature monk would have diligently sat and picked the stalks out even if it took half an hour a day, but not us would-be heroes, fed on Cassian's *Collections*.

This was a source book of anecdotes about the early Christian desert-dwelling monks, who seem to have made an Olympic sport of the virtue of bodily mortification, and who would no doubt have sewn needles into their shirts had this gained them an advancement in the race for the pearly gates. We novices, therefore, saw in it an invitation for self-flagellation and accepted any opportunity to suffer it even if it drove us to distraction. For the immature it was a constant flirtation with pride, for long after the harvest was home the conquest sang emptily in our heads.

Every part of the island was in the process of cultivation, some three hundred acres, and most of it was sown to barley. Some time previously Father Anthony, the farm manager, stout of girth and weather-beaten of face, who had, as a layman, been to agricultural college, decided that breeding large white pigs was a profitable livestock venture. So, as the larger part of their diet was barley, that's what we grew, on every last square yard. Such was his zeal to extend arable capacity that Anthony strayed far beyond safe angles in ploughing the acres sloping down to the cliffs.

One day the inevitable happened. 'Anthony's turned the tractor over!' 'Is he all right?' 'He had it coming.' The signs flashed around the noviciate. We were immediately summoned as a team (well, we were fitter than anyone else) and trotted to the spot in the traditional crocodile line, hoods up, with rope, first aid and novice-master in tow. We found Anthony, considerably paler than I had ever seen him before, sitting on the ground by the overturned tractor with a silly grin on his plump face; and how his rather pathetic-looking machine had not continued rolling over the cliff into the sea, such was the ridiculous gradient of the field, I will never know. It was quite easy to right it, but Anthony made us keep the rope taut (even breaking the silence in his concern that we knew precisely what we had to do) while he gingerly mounted and started up the tractor to gain the safer ground. That curbed his ardour for a while.

Yes, I loved the haymaking. The bright yellow of the corn and the deep blue of the sky, reflected in the sea, would create a backcloth of Van Gogh intensity for our short journeys across the fields which crested the island's humped terrain. The view across the corn-filled fields, past the old farm and the ancient monastic church, out over and beyond the endless silver-crested ocean into the blazing afternoon sun could be intoxicating. It could make life seem very simple, harmony a natural option and our community a blessing and reward. Strong liquor indeed!

The novices made up a cheerful team and the task, if exhausting, was finite. It had to be because the hay wagon had to be back at the barn and the hay stacked by the first bell for Vespers. And, country lad or townie, there was for all a deep satisfaction in finally gathering in a crop planted months before and watched anxiously through every high wind and cloudburst.

The pattern never varied. Father Lawrence would drive the tractor and we novices would sit with our pitch forks on the edge of the trailer kicking at pathside shrubs and grinning familiar messages to each other, 'Is it going to rain?' 'No, the clouds are too high.' 'Look at the size of this field! We won't get it finished in time.' 'Rubbish! Just you watch Lawrence move when he's up against it.' A shrug of the shoulder, a half-made sign with one hand, a raised eyebrow or pulled face was eloquent conversation among brothers who never spoke yet lived out their days in each other's company. Of course this signed chattiness contravened the spirit of silence but a good novice-master would not expect his fledglings to become perfect overnight.

Then the work would begin. One person would stay on the trailer to stack the bales and the rest of us would fan out from the slowly moving wagon bringing in the bales on the end of our forks. Crunch! I would plunge the sharp prongs deep into the centre and, with a jerk, lift and thrust made fluent over those hand-hardening weeks, raise the heavy bale over my head so that the weight of it was directed down through the pole, shoulders, back and legs. Only by doing so could I hope to keep going through the afternoon, and also keep my end up in the mortification stakes, this dangerous rivalry that went on in our minds – punishing the body to enliven the spirit.

Of course when the bales were damp or included some grass they were so much heavier, and then the simple decision (complicated, of course, by the stakes) had to be taken; do I bust a gut or call in the other guy? His attention attracted we would together fork the bale aloft and walk over to the trailer. As the afternoon wore on and the levels of bales rose on the trailer – six, seven, eight, even nine high, the effort required to pitch them up to the waiting brother up on top, fought cruelly with weakening legs and arms. Our pride discreetly sidelined, we worked more and more in pairs, grateful that no-one was going it alone, and now all working ever faster to beat the clock, or rather the bell.

The final part of the job was to transfer the bales from

the wagon to the hay barn. Two of the party would dismantle the load from the top and the rest of us would build up the permanent stack. The air became thick with dust and somehow the atmosphere would become slightly manic. Someone would inevitably be hit by a flying bale or a bale would fall from the stack and burst on landing. Suddenly we were all caught up in the spirit of the pillow fight which, with stiletto-sharp forks, held more than a hint of danger. Hay would fly, some of it intentionally down necks; bodies would roll and boys would be boys. For one hilarious moment the barn resounded with sneezes, snorts, and more than a suggestion of ill-concealed laughter. St Benedict might once have rolled in a bramble bush but that was to curb his lustful thoughts. This was nothing short of puerile delinquency.

Then the impatient stackers jabbed at their wrists to indicate that time was against us and, finally, the appearance of the novice-master would call a prompt halt to any such unruly behaviour. Shoulders were shrugged, 'It was an accident, yer honour.' Everyone minded his own business and, choking in the dust, would draw on dwindling reserves of strength to complete the job and regain the fresh air.

No one worked harder than Brother Rembert, a tall spare Scot in his last year of simple vows, the three probationary years in between the noviciate and solemn profession. Even at haymaking he would continue to wear his round rimless spectacles, looking ever the academic even as he sweated with the rest of us. This afternoon his job was stacker on the trailer. As the levels grew he worked like a master builder, keeping the rising platform square and even but criss-crossed so that the bales meshed together and could not be easily dislodged by a jerk of the tractor or sudden incline of the ground. There were occasions when a badly stacked wagon would not survive a sudden jolt, and the agony of restacking a fallen load halfway home wiped those dusty smiles clean off our faces.

But this afternoon level nine was achieved without accident, and up there Rembert had landed on board the last bale and wedged it into place. Lawrence attached a holding rope to the rear of the trailer and threw it up to him to tighten and pass down again at the tractor end to secure the load. Rembert, meticulous in all things pulled the rope taut as we stood idly by, thankful that our labours were nearly over. Then to our horror we heard a crack as the rope snapped, and saw Rembert, caught in the act of tugging hard, reel backwards and disappear over the edge down from a load as high as a house, down on top of the tractor.

In a silent order there are many silences, but the next moments seemed carved out of eternity. The wind twitched the odd straw. The incessant soft shriek of gulls became immediately apparent. We were all statues for an instant as a routine scene became dramatically etched with tragedy. He must be dead or maimed. Who could survive a fall like that without breaking his back or his neck? Even Lawrence was frozen in disbelief.

Suddenly all was mad activity. We rushed from where we each stood and converged on the tractor and then jerked to a halt, stunned by the impossible. Brother Rembert was rising to his feet unhurt, smiling in his boyish way and readjusting the glasses on his nose. Was this the same Brother Rembert who had plunged to certain death only a moment before. But no, or rather yes. Miraculously he had bounced off the expansive bonnet cover of the tractor, denting it quite severely, and simply rolled on to the grass. Silence was maintained, it was habitual, but we stood around him touching him in awe, flashing messages of concern and relief to him and to each other. 'Are you really all right?' 'Nothing broken?' 'Somebody up there's looking after you' 'God be praised!'

The first bell for Vespers boomed. God, we were going to be late. The rope was reknotted, hastily flung over and secured. We hurried home, flanking the wagon, subdued by God's majestic instancy. Rembert sat in the deepest of silences. Lawrence didn't have to say a word. There would be a scramble to change into choir dress, a quick wash (thank heaven for shaven heads) and bother the hair shirt. Then into the calm ebb and flow of Vespers where, like children, we could hide within a wisdom two thousand years old and let our tumultuous thoughts and feelings fall gently into place.

Chapter Five

Our Feathered Friends

As a child during the Second World War, I had a soft spot for hens. With government encouragement every house in our road sported a hen coop, usually a ramshackle board and wire affair, and placed at the bottom of the garden to keep rats and other interested wildlife away from the house. Only dimly aware of letters and postmen in those days, the daily arrival of eggs was of supreme importance to me; and to be allowed to rush down to the coop in the morning and collect the day's supply, ever so gently, especially if they were still warm, was a moment of unalloyed happiness. I loved our hens, cosy armfuls of clucking motherliness, and was mercifully spared sight of the necessary executions at the end of their useful lives. The wringing of necks meant no more to me than the feeble threat that accompanied my mother's warning to keep out of the vegetable patch or to come straight home from school and not play in the cemetery. The occasional bird on the table at Sunday lunch was never associated with my feathery friends down the garden. Such is the way we sanitise our memories of childhood – if we're lucky.

Luck was not on the side of our monastic fowl. No memories for them of a garden hen house and the joyful cries and cuddles of human chicks. The day I arrived on the island I noticed a large barn below the monastery with fowlish noises and smells emanating from it, and two days later, on my first tour of the monastic enclosure, I was led through another large shed of caged hens unrecognisable in their partially feathered skinny-ness from the plump plumed layers of former days.

'No such thing as free meal,' joked Father Lawrence, fingering the long food tray clipped to the cage we were passing. 'We've only got a few hundred acres here to support the community and pay the bills – fuel, machinery, repairs and maintenance. We're quite independent of the local diocese, you see. If we don't pay our way we go under like any business – not that that would happen with all the cheap labour we have at our disposal,' he punched me gently on the shoulder.

'No, the battery hens and broiler fowls are good earners and take up little space; and the compost their droppings make is out of this world,' he kissed his fingers.

I was confused and said nothing. Did these hens get a kick out of knowing they were good earners, I wondered, looking at the miserable specimens before me? But then, I knew nothing of farm economics, and the chicken industry must be really thriving judging by its use in the newly emerging fast food restaurants appearing alongside the traditional fish and chip shops. And who was I to judge the humanity of these gentle men?

During the following month I was introduced for several afternoons to the battery hen house. Father Oswald, though no doubt authorised to induct me into the arts of hen maintenance, chose to keep silent throughout our relationship, telling me with a few deft signs to watch and observe. All we did initially was to collect, wash and pack the eggs in boxes by size. Then we cleaned and refilled the automated meal and water flows. Oswald entered and left the shed like a phantom, careful never to make any more noise than absolutely necessary. I soon found out why.

On the second afternoon I accidentally dropped a water container which bounced on the wire cage with a clang and then thudded to the floor. Hardly had the look of horror appeared on Oswald's face than bedlam broke out in the cages. All 360 birds jumped six inches into the air, hitting their heads simultaneously on the cage tops, and barked out their consternation in a chaos of flailing legs and wings and wide-eyed crazy crowing. I froze, deafened and shocked until, having stopped attacking anything within pecking distance and being of a common mind that the world wasn't coming to an immediate end, the birds calmed down.

Not so Oswald. With constricted actions for fear of renewing the collective mayhem, his eyes and fingers told me that I had just committed the mortal sin of battery hen minders. Noise. With eyebrows that disappeared into his hood he despaired of their reaching their egg target for the day, and a complementary shrug of his shoulders indicated his doubt that some might be put off laying for the rest of their short lives. It was a bad news day for hens, and I couldn't wait for the session to end lest I compound my felony and further derange Oswald's equilibrium by disturbing my little sisters again.

I was, of course, forgiven by my next visit to the hen house, but a cruel penance awaited me. The shed stank of the ammonia in the hen's droppings which fell through the floor of the cage on to continuous band of toughened and waterproofed paper wound from a huge roll at one end of each row of cages and stretching to a disposal point at the other. With a sympathetic smile Oswald led me to a wheelbarrow which he placed at the end of a row. Signing that the paper roll was now full enough with droppings he took hold of a large handle attached to the floor of the row and started to wind the droppings out into the barrow. When it was full he cut the paper across and invited me to wheel the barrow, QUIETLY, to the door.

I followed him through the surrounding woodland for a hundred yards or so until, breaking through the tree line, we arrived at the biggest compost heap I had ever clapped eyes on. Except that it wasn't a heap but two ridges, head-high and six or seven feet across and both stretching some thirty yards to the border of a ploughed field. This, Oswald indicated, was the fertilizer source for the whole island and, by rubbing his chest vigorously presumably meant that we were fully organic. He than gave me a shovel which was leant against the heap and with a slightly gagging throat I dug into the droppings and added them to the accumulation of weeds, roots, old vegetables and leaves which made up the remainder of the compost. Still nauseous I followed Oswald back to the shed where, didn't I know it, he smiled again and waved his arm over the rows of cages, pressed his finger firmly against his lips, and disappeared.

It was penance indeed. There were six rows of cages and I had only emptied half a row with the prospect of eleven more journeys through bumpy woodland. I was tired already and – this was the worst thing – I would have to work on until the church bell rang a half an hour before Vespers and, with no watch, I had no idea of the time. However, things got a whole lot worse when, on the second row, I rolled the sheet in too quickly and upset the wheelbarrow, depositing the rolls of filth on to the floor, mercifully without too much noise. Righting the barrow I looked around for a shovel to reload the droppings from the floor, Father Oswald's spotless floor. But the shovel was back at the compost and the only shovelling implement I could see was a dust pan from a brush and pan set.

I was already in deep trouble, literally ankle-deep in it. The floor was filthy, the pan was too, and I was never going to finish this job before Vespers, not even before Compline at my rate of progress. The pan was not a good tool and before long my clothes were filthy as the sludge from the droppings oozed from the pan on to my person and, to add to my chagrin, I hadn't bothered to don an overall, thinking I would only be washing a few eggs. The scraping of the pan on the concrete floor was also beginning to agitate the more nervous of the birds and I could visualise an enraged Oswald bursting, silently, into the shed miming the reality of an apoplexy.

As I left the shed for the heap, breathing in the dreadful stench with every step, the bell rang and this was only my third journey of the twelve. What was I to do? A mature monk would have sighed, acknowledged his own unworthiness, perhaps added a verse from Scripture: 'It is when I am weak, Lord, that I am strong,' and pushed off, humbly, to Vespers without a care in the world. All I could see were six rolls of paper overloaded with excrement, all spilling over on to Oswald's precious floor, the whole thing grinding to a halt, with 360 frenetically expiring hens, overcome by slurping faeces and the sheer futility of going on living in such a disordered world.

I struggled manfully on, my mind indeed a disordered world. Fortunately there were no more overturned barrows but life stretched out wearily before me in hundred-yard journeys of increasing misery and muck. As I was rolling out the first half of the sixth row the shed door burst very noisily open to reveal a frowning Lawrence. At his thunderous approach the hens did their song and dance act with great fervour, eliciting from Lawrence merely a tetchy, 'Oh, put a sock in it, you stupid birds.'

He looked at me hard. 'Where did you get to, Daniel. I'm sure I told you that we stop working when the . . . Oh, phew-ee! Surely Ossie told you to take this stuff to the compost, not roll in it. Just look at you! I hope you've brought a spare set of clothes.'

He caught sight of my deeply and dirtily unhappy face and sniggered. 'Well, I suppose it's as good a lesson as any that the contemplative life doesn't always smell of roses. Come on, back for a bath and leave the rest for the next unlucky novice in the morning. Just walk behind me – well behind me, and sssh . . .' he pressed finger to lips convulsively in a perfect imitation of the absent hen-keeper.

I was relieved of hen duties for a few weeks and my next foray into the world of fowl came after my clothing as a novice.

'Time to induct you into the topsy-turvy world of broiler farming,' said Lawrence brightly, as he allocated jobs for the afternoon, or after None when our outdoor duties commenced. 'You'll be working with Sam. All I can say is that after a couple of work periods down there you'll be glad you're a vegetarian.'

Sam and I walked in file outside the enclosure and down to the barn I had walked past on my first day. Clad in our denim tunics, hoods up and wellies afoot, we entered into what I could only describe as a moonscape. A square perimeter some ten yards across was filled with a darkened sawdust material rising to the centre and hardened to a tarmac by thousands of claw steps and littered with a generation of droppings, the atmosphere pungent once more with ammonia. To complete the bizarre scene the mound was crowded with broiler fowl peacefully strutting around pecking at the ground and clucking softly. Unlike the hens these birds were amply feathered, and they only raised their voices, so to speak, when they felt their space was being invaded. But this was peace time, I was to discover.

Sam pointed to the bank of bright lights over the arena and signed that they came on for six hours and went off for six hours, simulating a twelve-hour day and thus encouraging a growth pattern twice the rate of the normal twenty-four hours. It was hard to know whether or not the birds thrived under this regime, but they certainly seemed happier than the hens, at least on that occasion. Our job was to tidy up, see that the water and meal feeds were working on the kiosks set around the arena, remove any dead birds and report any birds that were sick or demonstrating weird behaviour.

But to whom? My efforts to ask Sam that question failed miserably. The Cistercian sign language, designed for basic communication, only includes nouns which, attached to the finger tips-kissing 'please' cover all imperatives such as 'Go there', 'Give me', 'Do that' or maybe 'Do this with that' or even '. . . that with this'. It thus discourages information-seeking or anecdotal narrative, although I had noticed that the brighter novices, with gestures of the arms and rapid eye movements, could stray wilfully into that forbidden territory – conversation. I recalled the sign for head and made up a sign for chicken by raising my elbows, but 'head chicken' meant nothing to Sam and he smiled his winning smile and turned away.

So I followed him around, replenishing the food and water and tidying the place generally. We stopped by a chicken that seemed to be having some difficulty walking and Sam picked it up and turned it over for my

A supper for the guesthouse in the plucking.

inspection. The part where I assumed eggs came down was quite badly swollen and some part of its intestines were protruding from the orifice. Sam shook his head sadly implying that this poor bird's days were definitely numbered, and walked with it over to a cage by the wall and slipped it inside. As he did so the door by which we had entered open with a bang. 'Ah!' I thought, but it was Father Lawrence, striding across the litter, birds leaping, squawking, out of his path. Does he ever slow down for anyone, I wondered?

'Carry on, Sam,' he said, 'I'm just going to show this guy over the rest of the unit.'

He gripped me by the shoulder as we made our way over to another door. 'Disgusting, isn't it; like living in a midden in a time warp. Who'd be a chicken, eh?' What was this? Why was he trying to put me at my ease? Was it the preamble to yet another part of the process? I had somehow assumed that our broiler operation began and ended in this shed; that when the time was right cages would appear from within, packed with plump oven-ready birds, loaded on to the trailer and covered with a dark cloth to keep them quiet, and thence on to the boat, into the van, and delivered to the factory which converted them to food in whatever form. Lawrence opened the door and led me through – into the factory.

Well, it was more like a laboratory. White was the colour from floor to ceiling: white tiles and stainless steel tables and sinks.

'Voila l'abattoir,' Lawrence said with a wave of his arm. 'They may live in a midden but they go out in style. What did Shakespeare say: "Nothing became him in life more than the leaving of it."'

'But who does this?' I asked incredulously, 'Do people come from the mainland?'

'Not a bit of it,' he laughed, 'The answer is, whoever we've got available. Maurice, Dominic, Herman, Columba, even Father Abbot when we're stuck, and I'm no stranger to the murderous arts. On delivery day, I'm telling you, even the noviciate has its part to play.'

I had to know. 'How do you, er, kill them, then?'

'Ah, the dispatch, Madame la guillotine. Come.'

We walked over to a set of wire cages about eighteen inches in diameter and height narrowing to a round open-topped neck.

'This goes over the bird with its neck sticking out of the top. The executioner grabs the fateful weapon,' he opened a table drawer and took out an implement resembling secateurs except that the bottom blade was replaced by a spike about an inch long and the top was a curved muzzle-shaped container.

'You know our sign for dead, don't you? An upward thumb under the chin.' He performed the action and made a squelching noise. 'Long live the revolution.'

'You mean that dear old Herman and Dominic and Co stand here and . . .'

'To the manner born, though Herman may have to give it up soon if the arthritis in his wrist gets any worse.' He paused as if in tribute to the ascetic life. 'And then there's the blanching, the plucking, the gutting, the trimming and the dressing – all crafts picked up by repetition and honed

Preparing chickens for the market – the early days.

to a well-oiled operation – a bird ready for your table in a matter of minutes,' he paused again, suddenly serious. 'Never forget, for all their gentleness and their life of self-effacement, monks are a warrior breed.'

He can't be right. All evening I wrestled with the conviction formed on my first visit to the battery hens. Was it to do with the lack of quality in their short lives, the total lack of dignity; their exploitation by us for profit – a good return on our investment? Yet here we were, barely emerged from the era of human slavery, and I was worrying about chickens? And if these poor creatures, what about other barbarisms like your French pate de foie gras, or your Italian white veal? All conceived and processed by the Faithful – possibly even by monks!

Then suddenly I knew that the real issue here was obedience. The rest was a debate about relative moralities. Obedience was an absolute, the monastic determinant. Love your chickens, a voice within me whispered. Never give them cause to suffer on your account. Be an Oswald if you must, a fool for Christ. And if you do get the spike job, do it well and praise the Lord. Judge no man. The yoke of obedience.

A week or so later after the community Mass Lawrence arrived in the noviciate clad in his denims.

'Right,' he said, rubbing his hands, 'I need four novices: Sam, Luke, Leo and, yes, you, Daniel. I think it's your turn to be blooded – in a manner of speaking. It's Broiler Day, you'll be happy to know, so meet me, changed for work here in five minutes.'

My heart leapt to my throat. I wouldn't put it past Lawrence to slot me into the killing squad. My legs trembled as we filed to the shed. There a handful of chickens stalked the empty moonscape mound, pecking idly without a care in the world. Maybe it's all over, I prayed, and these ones are too small or too poorly.

Then the inner door opened and in strode Columba and beamed at us as he saw us huddled together. Suddenly he leant down and seized a bird by the neck, lifting it through his cupped arm to quieten its fluttering wings. He jovially thumbed under his chin, kissed the head of the silent terrified bird and disappeared back through the door.

'Looks like things are well under way already,' said Lawrence. 'We've lost a lot of birds through illness this time, and barely stand to break even on the operation. So come on, you lot, let's get in there and get it over with as quickly as possible.'

Through the door the scene was macabre indeed. Columba was in the act of securing the bird in its death chamber. Next to him, Dominic, in a blood-spattered rubber apron, spike in hand, looked up and smiled broadly as we filed before him. And here was Oswald, obviously more relaxed away from his nervous brood, with Kevin, plucking a couple of headless birds, steam billowing from the chamber through which the birds were passed. Next, by the sluice sink, stood a blood-flecked Abbot, behind a pile of necks and claws, testifying to his bloody part in the proceedings. All this, and here was the eerie bit, in complete silence. No light diverting radio music, no happy banter; just men listening to God, and converting life into death into food.

Before I could take in the rest of the operation I heard Lawrence mutter, 'Daniel, I think Father Abbot needs a hand cleaning out the birds. Here, take these.' He handed me a slim pair of latex gloves. 'Just watch what he does and do ye likewise.'

Oh mercy! Lawrence moved the others down the line and I was left with a tight-lipped focused Abbot. Cleaning was a euphemism for what he was doing; this was evisceration! He motioned me to watch as he picked up a very dead bird and plunged his gloved hand into the hole that had been its throat. Holding the bird down on the table he twisted his hand to and fro inside its meagre frame, pulled out a crimson mess and spread it on the table. From it he selected what I learnt later were its liver, kidneys and heart, washed them under the tap and then, oh horror, passed me the hollow torso and mouthed, 'Wash it out.'

I took the bird in my strange gloved hands and the next moment it had slipped through them and on to the filthy floor. I saw the Abbot's expression briefly pass through despair to resignation as I bent down to retrieve it; he watched as I washed it out under the tap, extracting little red bits from inside. He then picked up the tiny organs and popped them inside, finally ramming a portion of neck from a pile of necks into the hole to seal it. I could feel my throat gagging as I smelt the warm entrails – this had been pecking meal less than five minutes ago – but the Abbot was already passing me another evacuated fowl for 'cleaning'. So I just froze my senses, and any accompanying thoughts, and carried on as best I could.

After a while I stole a glance down the line and noticed the other three packing chickens which by this time had been miraculously dressed as table birds, bagged, and placed into cartons labelled, 'Abbot's Kitchen. Best Table Chickens. Organically Reared.' What on earth did that mean – organically reared? What part of the travesty of their lives had not been subjected to an artificial mass-produced hell? Except, perhaps, the meal they had eaten had been organically underpinned by the compost provided in part by their little sisters over in the hen house. So that was all right, then.

During the course of that memorable morning I was introduced to most aspects of the operation, a fierce rate of productivity being sustained by the presence of the Abbot and no distraction – not even a mid-morning cuppa. By lunchtime the job was finished, the cartons were bouncing their way down to the jetty on the tractor trailer to catch the high tide, and we were returning the shed to its former sanitised state. I stumbled over the crust of deep litter feeling drained and empty. Obedient, yes; but feelings? What was I supposed to do with them?

The next day we were dispatched with forks to break up the rock-hard crust, informed that the acid in the droppings would, amazingly, sterilize the litter, restoring it as a healthy environment for the next batch of cuddly day-old chicks, full of hope for a meaningful existence. I spent my anger forking the stinking mess like a demon, never knowing if my fellow novices felt as I did, or if they always worked this energetically. Soon the mound was transformed into a soft, somewhat neutralised floor to await its new tenants. A job well done, we reassured each other, rubbing our chests signifying our mutual pleasure.

During Vespers that afternoon a worried-looking Father Aelred entered the church and whispered something to Father Abbot who immediately left the choir taking the Prior and Lawrence with him. As the rest of us left after the Office the smell of smoke was in the cloister. Lawrence appeared and urged hurried the novices into the changing room. 'The broiler house is on fire. Get changed now and line up outside.'

We actually broke into a trot, unheard of for monks, as we hastened to the scene. The timber roof and walls were already well ablaze, and it was obvious that the island's precious water supply would be wasted on the building. Fortunately the shed stood apart but the Abbot organised us into a chain of buckets filled from the watercress pool to damp down the surrounding area. We all watched fascinated as the fire rose to its peak and finally brought the roof and walls crashing in. It then quickly became fiercely hot embers as everything of the broiler house was consumed. Supper was late; Compline was late, and from my bed space under the eaves the island was illuminated by a warm rosy glow which remained far into the night.

I was in turmoil. As far as I knew, we were the last ones in the shed, and it had crossed my mind at the time that the refreshed deep litter was fuel waiting for a match. Or a spark. All I could think of was the ferocity with which I had broken up the old litter, increasingly striking my steel fork against the concrete base as we worked our way in from the edge of the mound to its centre. It seemed clear to me that in the likelihood of having ignited a small fire from a wayward spark I was responsible, through my manic anger, for the destruction of part of our livelihood. When I confessed (in public because it was an act against the community) what would my punishment be – expulsion, excommunication? Additionally I would have to deal with my anger, the lack of acquiescence in a task enjoined under obedience. And self-imposed penances were always more painful! And what about the deep conviction that I was right all along about the injustice to the birds? It would need an excavator to sort that problem out.

I scarcely slept that night, and after the waking bell stumbled through the Night Office in a riot of conflicting emotions. At last the morning hour of Prime was over and I girded myself to confess to the Abbot and community after the daily recitation of a chapter of The Rule had been read. However, the Abbot had something to say and his measured monotone belied the seriousness of the issue.

'I should mention that the loss to the community due to yesterday's fire was limited by the decision we had already taken to terminate the broiler business. Broiler farming has increased exponentially and consequently market prices for table birds has fallen. We can't see how to expand our own productivity; therefore we can no longer compete in the field. Our only loss was the large shed ... which is regrettable.' He tailed off rather like the cadence in the chant at the end of a psalm verse, and raised his head to look at us – or was it at me?

Was this my moment of truth? I calmed my fluttering heart as I got ready to stand up. But he continued, 'We can't be sure of the cause of the fire, but it seems likely to have been due to a defective electricity cable in the processing area which, alas, had been reported some weeks ago. Clearing up will begin tomorrow when the embers have cooled.'

I wanted to shout out, 'No! You're wrong! It was me!' I even opened my mouth but nothing came. I was confounded. I wasn't ready for an acquittal before the trial; and what was I to do with all my feelings of guilt and disobedience? But I was aware of a new, stronger feeling: an upsurging of joy at the sudden, nay, miraculous conclusion of the broiler tyranny, that threatened to swallow all the other feelings in one gulp.

I was standing outside the noviciate when I became aware of Father Lawrence looming over me. Oh dear, had he rumbled me after all?

'Sorry for disturbing you in your moment of profound relief, Daniel. No more broiler fatigues, eh! Well, just so that you don't get let off too lightly, Father Oswald needs some urgent help in the hen house. Better get over there immediately after Mass, and Sshh!'

The joy in my heart deepened as I realised the symmetry of it all. I had received my absolution; now for the penance. Let the punishment fit the crime.

Chapter Six

Butter in a Lordly Dish

Once I had gained my second wind in the noviciate I determined to take seriously the *lectio divina*, the prayerful and reflective reading of the word of God, which St Benedict deemed so essential to the spiritual development of the monk. I suppose I had gained a better than average grasp of the New Testament through school and church-going, but my knowledge was still fragmentary, based on the regular gospel readings at Mass. The letters of St Paul and St John were largely untrodden territory as were the events of the early Church. The Old Testament was a closed book.

So I started at the beginning of the Book of Genesis and hoped to work my way through to the end of the Book of Revelations by the end of the two years. Of course, the trouble was that as I became more and more engrossed in the history of the people of God, so it acquired all the addictive characteristics of the best seller: the suspense of the whodunit; the intrigue of the historical; the sentiment of Mills and Boon.

One way of slowing it down was to supplement my reading with commentaries, explanatory maps and the generous range of biblical research on the bookshelves. This had the welcome effect of introducing a third dimension. I now knew exactly why the Assyrians came down like a wolf on the fold; though whether or not their cohorts were gleaming in purple and gold was left to the poet Byron's imagination and his need for a good rhyme. In fact the supporting literature was in danger of outshining the pages of scripture themselves.

'Of course you've got to know as much as possible

about the world they lived in,' said Father Lawrence. 'I mean it's a history of the people of God, so the better your background knowledge, the better your understanding of God's intervention in that history. But in terms of *lectio divina* you don't have to give it all the same weight. Most of the law-making in Numbers and Leviticus is hardly worth reading at all; much of the chronological history you'll probably never read more than the once; the Psalms, of course, you'll read every week and, hopefully, understand and use their prayerfulness. Then there's the prophets and some of the wisdom books which are almost on a par with the Gospel. In fact there are some passages, like the "suffering servant" in Isaiah, which are virtually pen pictures of the roles Jesus and the Father play in our salvation.'

So I devised the plan of studying a chapter in depth using all the aids, and then going back and reading it again, allowing all that came from it to nourish my fragile grasp on the mysterious activity of God within his creation and, for the most part, the devious, brutal and uncomprehending activity of his chosen race.

'The essential difference between the Old and New Testaments,' explained Lawrence about one rather savage episode in Joshua, 'is that the Israelites hated those who opposed or hated their God, whereas Jesus taught his disciples to love those whom God loves, that is, all his creation. Of course it all equals out rather when we consider how poorly we Christians have learnt that particular lesson.'

One afternoon we were being allocated our various tasks, and Brother Samuel was assigned to collect a couple of churns of buttermilk from Father Dominic's bakery where our baker had used his big electric mixer to separate the rich Jersey milk our herd produced.

'You've made butter before, haven't you, Sam,' said Lawrence, 'take a couple of trays and some cloths with you on the trolley, plus the salt and the bats of course. You know how to work the lordly dish.

'Lordly dish?' I mouthed. What was he talking about?

'Bringing forth butter in a lordly dish; part of

Deborah's description of a rather grisly murder in the book of Judges.'

'Oh, I haven't got there yet,' I replied, blushing.

Lawrence rolled his eyes skywards. 'Well, read it later on, chapter five if I'm not mistaken. Meanwhile you can join forces with Sam and learn how to make medieval butter in a very lordly dish, kept in the old monastery kitchen up on the farm. Come on now or we'll be reduced to eating curds and whey for supper tonight, like a certain Miss Muffet.'

Sam insisted on pushing the heavy trolley up the unmade road to the farm buildings which were part of the remains of a largely derelict monastery dating back to an earlier century, presumably before Henry the Eighth started closing them down. Here we entered an old kitchen complete with ancient oven set in the wall, a more modern sink with a tap, and a long wooden table. But set in the centre of the room was the strangest looking contraption consisting of a circular wooden table rising from a rim at the perimeter to a low cone at the centre. Straddled across the radius from a central spindle to a set of cog wheels meshed into a larger driving wheel at the edge was a cylindrical, fluted wooden beam. Set closely above the conical table it reminded me of the mangle my mother used to turn to press the water from the washing. A mangle on an angle. This, I presumed, was Lawrence's lordly dish.

Sam, who rarely used signs, busied himself moving the churns off the trolley, and putting the rest on the table. Then he ran some water over the conical circular surface to make sure it was clean, and washed two pairs of bats; the miniature cricket bats I remembered from my childhood, peeping over the high counter in Sainsbury's, watching the man in the huge white apron cut off and shape the little rectangles of butter from the yellow mountain in front of him.

Sam smiled at me and touched the corner of his eye, so I watched. He picked up a churn of buttermilk and emptied part of its sloppy contents evenly around the table and spread a little salt over it. Giving me a grimace he seized the wheel by its handle and leapt at it, heaving it into motion. The effect was amazing. The cog wheels, stiffened with years of salt, squealed as they grated together and the circular table slowly started to revolve. At the same time the fluted roller turned in conjunction with the table and the buttermilk squelched noisily through the flutings. Milky water immediately ran down from it to the edge and out through regular holes in the rim to fall into a circular tray attached to the table's legs.

Immediately I noticed the effort being wrenched from Sam's frail body, I leapt over to the wheel and took over the grinding of the rusty cogs. We both panted as we watched the butter having the whey squeezed out of it. Then, when he considered the butter firm enough, Sam signalled to me and I stopped. The butter now had to be gathered together but our clumsy attempts to move it about with the bats revealed it as the job of an expert. We exchanged glances, grinned at each other, and dived in with our none too clean hands, soon making a size-able block of it which I carried over to the long table. There the bats came in into their own and in no time at all a little row of rectangles brought respectability to our endeavours.

We improved our techniques with every repetition of the process, and after I'd smeared some butter over the cog wheels the whole action speeded up considerably. By the time the bell rang I felt we had made enough butter to satisfy the needs not only of the community but the provision of trippers' cream teas for the rest of the season.

I was disappointed when the fruit of our labour didn't appear at supper that night, and we had to make do with some unappetising grease from the mainland. But the reward was worth the waiting when it was served up the following night, cold and creamy, half of one of our batted slabs on a plate for each refectory table. As I spread it on a slice hewn from one of Father Dominic's loaves, tiny beads of water burst from the edge of my knife. The taste was delicious and a distant memory was tweaked as I recalled my Dad, in the midst of wartime rationing, unwrapping a parcel of Irish salt butter and

offering me some to accompany my boiled egg and
'soldiers'. I turned, trying to catch Sam's eye in celebration but, of course, his hooded face pointed tablewards,
sealed in reflective thought or prayer.

Butter on a lordly dish indeed. Immediately after
supper I took down the King James Bible from the noviciate shelf and opened it at the Book of Judges. What
had Lawrence said; Chapter 5? But in fact the story, I
quickly noticed, started in Chapter 4 where, yet again,
the children of Israel did evil in the sight of the Lord –
such short memories, these children – and they were
sold, this time into the hand of one Jabin, king of
Canaan, who reigned in Hazor, the commander of whose
army, Sisera, boasted 900 chariots of iron ready to roll
against the woebegone Israelites.

Now, Deborah the prophetess was the current judge in
Israel, and sat under a palm tree on Mount Ephraim to
mete out justice. She sent for Barak who ruled the roost
in Napthali, and ordered him, in the name of the Lord, to
raise ten thousand men from Naphthali and Zebulun,
promising to draw Sisera and his army to the river
Kishon where she would deliver them into Barak's hand.
After a bit of argy-bargy Deborah agreed to accompany
him but censured him, saying that he would lose some
of the glory as the Lord would sell Sisera into the hands
of a woman. Cue for the entry of Jael our heroine.

So, with the Lord at the head, Barak's army duly made
short work of Sisera's men. In the King James version
'the Lord discomfited Sisera, and all his chariots, and all
his host, with the edge of the sword . . .' (some discomfort!) with such immediacy that Sisera jumped from his
chariot and fled the field of battle. Unfortunately he
walked straight into the tent of Jael, wife of Heber the
Kenite, descendants of Hobab, the father-in-law of
Moses, thinking he was among friends. How wrong he
was!

Anyway, Jael, guessing who he was, invited him in,
gave him a drink of milk and covered him with a blanket,
whereupon he fell asleep pleading with her to tell no one
he was there. And thereupon Jael picked up a tent peg
and a hammer and skewered him to the ground through

his temple. 'And so . . .' the scripture blandly stated, '. . . he died.' Such an outcome undoubtedly discomforted the enemy completely, and the chapter ended with a prospering Israel destroying Jabin the King of Canaan.

Grisly murder indeed! I sat back horrified at yet another blood bath in the name of territorial possession. But there was more to come for I noticed that the next chapter repeated the whole savage episode, but as a song of vengeance and triumph by the prophetess Deborah and Barak. It was also laced with bitterness at the way they had not been supported by the other tribes of Israel: Reuben, who preferred to keep with their sheep; Gilead who stayed where they were beyond the Jordan; Dan who didn't bother to leave their ships; and Asher who remained in their coastal home. 'Curse Meroz, says the angel of the Lord, curse bitterly the inhabitants, because they came not to the help of the Lord.' Not that it mattered a great deal for, in the account of Deborah, a mini Red Sea type of massacre occurred, the river Kishon, the onrushing torrent of Kishon, sweeeping the army away and laying them open to that gory edge of the sword.

It was, however, the description of Sisera's death at the hand of Jael, '. . . blessed among women shall she be . . .' (some role model for the other 'blessed art thou among women' woman, I thought) that took my breath away with its gloating portrayal:

He asked water and she gave him milk;
she brought forth butter in a lordly dish.
She put her hand to the nail,
and her right hand to the workman's hammer;
and with the hammer she smote Sisera,
she smote off his head
when she had pierced and stricken through his temple.
At her feet he bowed, he fell;
Where he bowed, there he fell down dead.

But if that wasn't final enough what really took the biscuit was her mocking fantasy on the reaction of Sisera's household:

> The mother of Sisera looked out at a window
> and cried through the lattice;
> 'Why is his chariot so long in coming?
> Why tarry the wheels of his chariots?'
> Her wise ladies answered her, yea;
> she returned answer to herself:
> 'Have they not sped?
> Have they not divided the prey;
> to every man a damsel or two;
> to Sisera a prey of divers colours,
> a prey of divers colours of needlework;
> of divers colours of needlework on both sides;
> meet for the necks of them that take the spoil?'

And then the crunch line, the vindication of the servant of the Lord fully justified in her grim triumphalism:

> 'So let thine enemies perish, O Lord,
> but let them that love him be as the sun
> when he goeth forth in his might.'

And the result?

> The land had rest for forty years.

The bell rang for the evening reflection followed by Compline. It was right what Lawrence said; the difference between the two Testaments was that the Israelites hated those who hated or opposed the Lord (though whether or not Sisera and his mates had ever heard of the Lord is open to doubt). On the contrary Christians try to put on the mind of Christ and love all whom God loves – hate the sin but love the sinner. An exclusive love on the one hand and an inclusive love on the other. And wasn't Our Lady the very antithesis of Jael, the one immortalised for taking life and the other for giving life – bringing forth Jesus in a very unlordly manger. My mind buzzed as we ran through the Compline psalms (I hadn't heard a word of the reflection) and I looked for other evidence of this belligerent nation. But in the three Compline psalms all was peace and light, safety and protection, the wonderful imagery of Psalm 91:

> He rescues you from the snares
> Of fowlers hoping to destroy you;
> He covers you with his feathers
> And you find shelter underneath his wings.
> You need not fear the terrors of the night,
> The arrow that flies in the daytime,
> The plague that stalks in the dark,
> The scourge that wreaks havoc by day.

No, I didn't fear the terrors of the night but my dreams were turbulent none the less.

Father Lawrence was in ebullient mood the next morning and would have none of my protest at the behaviour of the Isrealites.

'I'm sure Jael didn't make a habit of driving tent pegs through people's skulls,' he said with a laugh, 'and there was a war on and her action probably saved a lot of Israelite lives, so in her own opportunistic way she was serving the Lord, I suppose. At least that's how our rather feisty Deborah sees it.'

He looked at me quizzically.

'Forget the detail – that's history and we can't change any of it. Just think of the *lectio divina* and what a splendid experience you've had; making butter just like Jael would have done, when she wasn't cracking heads open, that is. You've entered the arena of love and hate as it affects the people of God, both Old and New Testaments – and also today for that matter. You've thought about it, felt about it and, I hope, prayed about it. What more do you want for your money?

I went back to my desk with the 'Try harder' label on my conscience and picked up my Bible. I turned to the Book of Joshua but my heart wasn't in it any more – too much edge-of-the-sword stuff for my stomach. Judges too; their blood-soaked history suddenly palled on me. I couldn't face reading the whole lot through. What about a nice story for a change. The page fell open at the Book of Job. Hmm, don't know that one. Just the thing to cheer me up, perhaps.

Chapter Seven

As Good Cooks Go ...

Father Maurice was very French and very stout, short of stature and sometimes temper. A clown by temperament he could, with a gesture or look, convert an ordinary event into side-splitting farce, and then re-assume a dead-pan face which left you giggling, out of order and often in trouble.

Maurice was also the cook. He had not always been the cook. In fact, for the greater part of his monastic life he had been in charge of the vegetable gardens. One of the less attractive aspects of the Rule is the instruction that the duties of cook, being onerous, should be shared by all the monks turn and turn about. Maybe in the sixth century all men could cook a little, or maybe the nature of cuisine at that time demanded no higher standards than to throw a variety of vegetables into a pot, boil and season to taste. But twentieth-century man is a choosey creature although he rarely lifts a finger in the preparation of his food. Indulged and spoonfed by mothers and wives until his fairly restricted menu has been honed to perfect simplicity, he expresses a bovine response to all other preparations, 'It just doesn't taste like my mother's.'

Well, Father Maurice's fare certainly didn't taste like my mother's. Often it didn't even taste like food. The trouble was that, like all clowns, Maurice was a creative soul by nature, loving to experiment and innovate. But his genius lay more in the direction of mixing rare composts or cross-fertilizing hardy perennials. To toss an interesting salad or enliven the vegetables with a piquant sauce simply never occurred to him. What did occur to him all too frequently was to try and surprise us by serving old veg in new forms without reference to suggestion, advice or recipe. Perfectly good salad stuff like radishes or cucumber would appear boiled for the first time in their history, yet swedes would come grated raw. He would serve spaghetti with boiled potatoes or rice with lumps of cheese. He would boil fruit and neglect to add the sugar, or add so much bicarbonate of soda to the greens that they arrived with a head of foam like a glass of beer or else in the guise of iridescent algae.

It was obvious that he had the constitution of a mountain gorilla. For the rest of us, our lack of interest in food other than as a crude means of keeping body and soul together did us a credit as ascetics which would never have stood the test had a decent ratatouille or lemon sorbet been placed before us. One developed an inordinate love of the morning mug of coffee and slice of bread mainly because it had fortunately avoided any contact with Maurice's culinary zeal.

The Rule of St Benedict is quite generous in its provision of two meals a day, allowing a pound of bread per day per monk and all the veg he could manage. We ate in a large vaulted refectory as, on all formal occasions, solitary ruminants with our hoods raised. Knife, fork, spoon and a large two-handled bowl marked each place on long white-scrubbed tables, with a vast linen napkin to be tucked one corner under the chin and the opposite one under the dish to avoid staining our precious white garments. It was amusing at first to look across the refectory and see the constant stream of food disappearing into large black holes, all faces heavily shadowed within their deep hoods.

Silence pervaded the hall except for the distant voice of the week's reader sharing a worthy book with the community. Father Maurice would emerge from the kitchen after the soup was served, a perspiring aproned cumulus, hovering at the serving trolley thrusting steaming serving dishes towards reluctant diners. One day as he was bustling about, every inch the maitre d'hôtel, a sharp rap summoned him to the Abbot's table.

A solitary ruminant.

Every black-barrelled hood swung in his direction like guns lining up on a common target. The Abbot gesticulated with his spoon at his soup. Maurice bent over, peering into his superior's bowl. An offending object was removed and carried back to the kitchen on a side plate by the obviously unrepentant cook, who grinned broadly the instant his back was turned on the Abbot, eyebrows shooting up and down in mock disbelief accompanied by the Gallic shrug. We learnt later that the Abbot had come across a chunk of corned beef floating in his vegetarian broth, somehow transferred from the pot for guests and ailing brethren. Maurice traded on this misdemeanour for days, scandalising the zealous by making signs to all comers, 'He finds beef in his soup and complains? I should cry for him!'

Once I had worked in the kitchen my only reaction, apart from a certain chilling of the blood, was surprise that a whole variety of meat items, most of them alive, did not also find their way into the soup. The dirt around me was thickly spread and engrained. This summer's flies lay on the corpses of last summer's which lay on the skeletons of the year's before. Sticky fly papers hung in a row above the cooking range and one only hoped that insects made the common sense decision to choose the company of their peers on the paper rather than fall to their doom down into a bubbling pan below.

I took the earliest opportunity to convey my disgust to the novice-master. 'You know that cleanliness is said to be next to godliness,' I opened cautiously, not wanting to be thought a murmurer, a real baddie in the eyes of the Rule. But Father Lawrence rumbled me immediately. 'Of course, you're working in the kitchen this week, aren't you,' he smiled. 'Yes, it's a bit squalid. Just shows you the power of the love of God and my prayers, keeping you safe and well in the face of such dangers.'

'But surely God doesn't want us to live in filth,' I protested. 'No, he wants you to learn to live in obedience and docility,' countered Lawrence, 'don't let a little dirt get between you and the Lord – or Father Maurice for that matter. He may ask you to clean the place tomorrow, or he may not. Cleanliness next to godliness! – that's a very Protestant concept. I think it was Maurice told me what happened at our mother house in Belgium before he came here.' What was that? I asked, eager to learn of our folk history.

'Well, the Abbot General of the Order paid a visit there one year, and on his tour of inspection came upon an outhouse whose walls were filthy in the extreme, mould everywhere, dripping with damp. He was horrified when they told him it was the dairy where their celebrated cheese, a favourite in the locality, was made and matured. 'Well, it's got to be cleaned up, tiles washed, tables and tools scrubbed,' he commanded. The cheese monk bowed his head (there's heroism for you) and did as he was bidden. From that day the cheese lost the flavour its advocates would die for, and very soon they had to stop production because even the monks refused to eat it. No, leave well alone is probably Father Maurice's motto, and I'm sure it's that philosophy which gives the food here its

Preparing the midday meal.

unique flavour.' He added mischievously, 'Or else it's Maurice's little joke on the human race.'

The monastery's octagonal kitchen rose to an open windowless turret in the centre of the roof which acted as an efficient smoke and smell extractor. However, it also allowed the elements in, and one of life's compensations in this vale of tears was to see Father Maurice attending to a pot with his right hand while holding an umbrella over himself with his left, to the accompaniment of hissing raindrops bouncing off the glowing hotplates on either side. Once he espied an audience he would inevitably go into his 'Singing in the Rain' routine and jig along the range tapping the beat out on it with ladle or spoon. How he squared his bizarre behaviour with the dour demands of the Rule we all felt was his affair, but there was a wayward grace in those exotic rays of sunshine with which he infused our earnest lives.

On Christmas Day, in stark contrast to all the forces of

self-denial which measured every other day of the year, Maurice would provide, amazingly with abbatial approval, a table at the bottom of the refectory which groaned under the weight of a cornucopia of titbits both sweet and savoury, everything from cheese straws to rum truffles. The large, almost cavernous, hearth, usually clean and bare, would blaze out with a huge fire fed from a year's supply of fallen timber. As it was a rest day many members of the community would bring a book and sit toasting themselves like so many cats beside the fire, nibbling from time to time at the rich array of goodies spread before them. This was usually a short-lived self-indulgence, for stomachs, programmed to run on a year's vegetarian austerity, just couldn't cope with the richness of this Yuletide fare, and something approaching a queue would always form outside the infirmary door on the following day.

'I just don't know why they do it,' sighed Lawrence, 'I think our Continental brothers were brought up in a regime of alternating fasts and feasts for they do love a little indulgence when they get half a chance. Yet all you novices want to do is compete with each other to see who can eat the least – oh yes, don't think I don't notice all your surreptitious refusals. Either way, I can't see God giving out many brownie points around here.'

Another great indulgence at Christmas time, as well as at Easter, Pentecost, and on the feast day of our spiritual founder, St Bernard of Clairvaux, was a glass of wine, a gift from one of the Order's great vineyards in the valleys of Burgundy where the Cistercians were founded some 900 years ago. The Rule shows great humanity on the subject of wine, for while St Benedict doesn't see why monks should need to drink wine at all, he concedes that he was never able to convince his monks of this; and so he allowed each monk one hemina* of wine per day. The trouble was that no one seems to have remembered, or perhaps wanted to know, what a hemina measured, so that over the centuries it has fluctuated between parsimony and

*A unit of measure equal to about ten fluid ounces.

indulgence according to taste or craving of any particular abbot.

Anyway, our abbey must have ranked fairly low on the league table of drinkers, with a glass of Nuits St Georges on the four feasts and a bowl of homemade cider on the lesser ones. When those days came around the concession added a celebratory flavour to mealtimes, and it was noticeable that the old Belgian monks really cheered up, toasting each other as if some corporate memory of a norm rather than an exception flooded back briefly into their consciousness.

No one like his tipple more than Maurice, and on this Christmas Day who would have begrudged him of it? By chance, or as a result of corporate prayer, he had strayed into orthodoxy for once. We could scarcely believe our good fortune as roast potatoes were followed by sprouts and parsnips. He had even thrown in some chestnuts for good measure, followed by jelly and Jersey cream. Indeed, Maurice himself could hardly wait to get back to table to eat and to quaff the brimming glass set before his place. His grace was perfunctory but the energy he deployed in sitting down and grabbing at his napkin was disastrous. A resounding crash brought everything to a halt as all eyes focused on the shattered glass and a widening red stain upon the floor. There was an explosion of white as napkin flew heavenwards with all the savagery of a man who has lost everything on one throw.

Now it is the practice in Cistercian life that a monk causing a needless interruption in the process of a formal community activity, has to prostrate himself before the Abbot until he sees fit to signal him to get up and return to his place. Most perform this public display of humiliation with great dignity, but the utter torment of losing the craved for tonic propelled Maurice into a bravura performance. With face as burgundian as the wine he had just squandered he rushed from his place and literally threw himself down on the cold hard tiles. The jellies awaiting distribution on the serving trolley could not have quivered more than Maurice as he lay there caught in a cruel conflict between the rage which

engulfed him within and the sorrow which he was forced
to display without.

Normally the Abbot would rap the table immediately
to indicate the formal forgiveness for the formal contrition, but no such noise occurred. We wrenched our eyes
from the pulsating Maurice to observe that the Abbot's
head was bowed and his shoulders were heaving. He
was obviously choking but whether from mirth or from
the unaccustomed Christmas fare, or from a mixture of
both, no one knew. The dilemma was obvious, with an
Abbot temporarily *hors de combat* and a Maurice
becoming more distraught by the second, imagining
that his superior was taking the offence far more
gravely than the simple accident could ever have
deserved.

Both Prior and sub-Prior, who sat either side of the
Abbot, reacted with commendable speed. The sub-Prior
leapt up and smartly patted the Abbot between the
shoulders holding a glass of wine to his lips to help clear
the blockage. Father Jerome, the Prior, more alive to the
deeper needs of Maurice, went over and knelt beside the
prostrate figure, whispered something in his ear, and
raised the bewildered cook to his feet, though not
without a good heave. The Abbot, still coughing, rose
and left the refectory, whilst Maurice, realising that
somehow a later drama had overtaken his own, brushed
himself down, retrieved his napkin and returned, suit-
ably abashed, to his place. But matters were totally
restored when Father Prior came from the kitchen with
another glass of wine for his glowing friend. Mercurial to
the last, Maurice rose to his feet, toasted the community and took that first heavenly sip just as the Abbot
resumed his place at the table.

A skivvy, none other than myself on kitchen duty that
week, mopped up the wine and swept up the shards. As
I did so I glanced up at the beaming faces peering from
each hood-burrow around the hall. The reader, far above
in his little cockpit, droned on oblivious of the entertain-
ment which had so eclipsed his own. As we returned to
the meal and realised what a good, what an uncharac-
teristically good dinner Father Maurice had served up for

us, and reflected what a faithful, what an unfathomably faithful servant Father Maurice was beneath all those lovable eccentricities, we were all ready to forget the jaded appetites, forgive the rumbly tums of yore, and . . .

But then, a little unaccustomed wine does funny things to us all.

Chapter Eight

Try a Little Lowliness

It was Easter Monday and the euphoria of the great feast still sang in our hearts. It had been a hard Lent, very cold even though our little island was massaged by the Gulf Stream. It would have been hard to find something extra to do since, whatever it might have been, we were doing it already. It was also hard to give anything up since frugality was our second name and, anyway, Father Lawrence would have been upon us quicker than a frog on a fly if any of us had added the tiniest weight to the yoke which already spanned our tender shoulders. When I asked what I might do in the narrowed circumstances, a good book perhaps, Lawrence savaged me with a smile and said, 'What about The Three Bears?' Was he going dotty?

'That's my recommended subject this year, The Three Bears: Bear with the cold; Bear with each other and, most important; Bear with me. If you can do that you can forget about the rest.'

The Easter Triduum, or three-day-special, was an exciting time. In the never-changing humdrum of our penitential life, the liturgy was the vehicle through which our emotions peaked and troughed as we followed the annual path of salvation history. And Easter was more than a feast; it was a glut. It was an opportunity to penetrate more deeply the grace-gift of the Last Supper, the drama of the Good Friday sacrifice, and all the renewal contained in the Vigil liturgy for Easter Day. At the Easter Mass we really did feel like new men, drowned in the sorrow, raised in the joy. We basked in the glory of it all and it didn't matter that

Father Maurice's meal of new potatoes, broccoli and green peas lacked the traditional crown of roast lamb. It didn't bear thinking about what further indignity he might have heaped upon its innocent body.

Good Friday had been a strange, empty day, empty of work, empty of food, save for a little bread and tea at lunch. It was almost too much to open a book, and I wandered aimlessly around pondering on the futility of a world without a Redeemer. As if to express this communal sense of ennui we gathered at eleven o'clock and just sang the Psalms one after the other for two hours. Compared with all this tedium the afternoon liturgy was full of colour and pathos, and we emerged from it to find the sun, a rare visitor that spring, shining brightly. Nature was endorsing the sense of achievement embodied in Jesus' last words, 'It is accomplished.'

But now it was Monday morning and we sat in the noviciate, all bright and fluffy as if we had just been hatched. Would Father Lawrence, caught by the festive spirit, give us the day off to wander the fields, roam the beaches, listen to some music, read the book of our choice?

Would he . . . !

'Right.' Which normally meant right for him and wrong for us.

'Right, we're at the beginning again, a new creation, a fresh start. Which for novices means we start at the bottom, what I call the worm's eye view.'

This sounded very wrong for me, something rather unpleasant to underline the fact that while Eastertide might uplift the spirit, the body in the lumpen form of Brother Ass had not been asked to the wedding feast. Oh dear, what was it going to be this time?

It wasn't as bad as I feared.

'Humility, gentlemen, is the essence of the monastic life. In fact, although it is just one of the seventy-three chapters of St Benedict's Rule, it is actually a Rule within the Rule. Nearly all the other chapters are sets of instructions: what to do; when to do it; who's to do it, but Chapter Seven, 'Of Humility', is the Why and the How of monasticism. Why am I here, you will all have asked yourselves in your brief time with us. It's a question I often have to ask myself, so sorely am I sometimes tempted by the burden of my job to run off the nearest cliff.'

I had, of course, read the chapter on Humility, as I had read the other seventy-two, and had heard it read in passages during the morning chapter meeting. But it was not a chapter I had wanted to linger on in my tender state, wishing to salvage some self-esteem amidst the slings and arrows of this new, intense community life. I wasn't ready to grovel yet.

'In writing about the steps of humility, a sort of ladder between heaven and earth, like Jacob's Ladder in the Old Testament, Benedict begins by dispensing with the law of gravity. He says you have to ascend the ladder of humility to become more lowly. It doesn't seem to make sense until you realise that pride, its opposite, descends to this world and is bound to it and sustained by it, as our erstwhile friend, Satan, found to his cost. So, we'll be studying the twelve steps over the next few classes.'

Luke was always the first in with a question; dare I say in such a barren setting that he liked the sound of his own voice.

'Wouldn't it have been better starting this chapter at the beginning of Lent, Father. I mean that is the penitential season, isn't it?'

Lawrence paused to allow the paschal mood of joy to curb his acerbic wit.

'To say that, Luke, is not to understand what exactly you've come here for. Lent is the rest of the Church playing at being monks for a few weeks. We start where Lent leaves off, and there's no better time to start for people who take life seriously than Easter Monday. Any other si . . . any other questions?' He was trying hard.

'Right, tomorrow we will take the first step of Benedict's ladder which is about our mindfulness of God and his demands of us, sometimes referred to as the fear of God. Now this is a bit of an Old Testament view but that, gentlemen, is where we all start until we can move into the mind of Jesus Christ and start loving each other without reservation. And that's still twelve steps away. So today let's try being mindful of God, and consider the flip side, that he's always mindful of us. That should make some of us quake, eh, Brother Luke, being mindful of a God who has his eye on us three hundred and sixty five days of the year, multiplied by twenty-four, and then by sixty. And we're hardly off the ground. Lent!'

I was already well into my honeymoon period and mindfulness. I'd read Brother Lawrence's *The Practice of the Presence of God* and *The Jesus Prayer* by an unknown Russian monk, and was impatient to have that constant aspiration bubbling in my heart. Compared with these St Benedict's mindfulness seemed a bit negative, as if he were fearful of being caught out all the time – a sort of mind game. He quoted that verse of the psalm; 'God searcheth the heart and the reins.' I looked up the word and saw that the reins were the kidneys, once thought to be the seat of the affections and passions. So that's what he was getting at – those sorts of thoughts.

Anyway, surely I could choose what devotional ploy I used to acquire mindfulness of God. But no; I happened to peep at step number two, 'Seek not to carry out your own will.' Which was leading up to step number three, 'That a man submit himself, for the love of God and with all obedience, to his superior'. And who was that, the Abbot or Father Lawrence – probably both. And I knew what they'd say: 'Follow the Rule.' I was trapped.

I took it to my superior.

'Whoa, Daniel, whoa!' Father Lawrence exclaimed, 'You're up to step three in a few hours and it takes a good monk the whole of his life to get to the top.'

'Yes, but don't you think St Benedict's steps all seems so gloomy, so fearful.'

'I can see where you're coming from, Daniel, but that's a very modern concept, the idea that our sins are nothing compared to the infinity of God's love for us. St Benedict came from the tradition of the desert and the principle that you had to flee the world and its delights before they consumed you. Did you ever read *The Thirty-nine Steps* – yes, another set of steps. Well, what do you remember most about it?'

I thought for a moment. 'What comes back to me is that long drawn-out business of Richard Hannay getting up to Scotland, being chased all the way by the baddies.'

'Exactly,' Lawrence beamed, 'Flight, and along with it Hannay's preoccupation with his own danger and whoever he was trying to find. A perfect illustration of the early monks' double aim of fleeing the world and seeking God. Put yourself in their place: you've got this picture of the God of Mount Sinai, just up the road, watching you, counting off your sins; you're so aware, through bitter experience, of your weakness in the face of temptation. Where do you go when you can't really trust anything you do? Step three: submit yourself to a superior – in Benedict's case, the Abbot of a community of like-minded fugitives. That's the mind of Benedict, whether you like it or not.'

I was shocked. 'I'd never seen this place as a community of fugitives.'

'No, it isn't; it's a sanctuary, hence the enclosure, and for us the island as well; once we get here the fugitive bit is over – we've found our safe place. However, Daniel, the chase still goes on, inside, until we make that conversion. For Benedict that's when love casts out fear, to use his own words. And we won't reach that until the twelfth step.'

I felt I had to think this one through. It was serious because it challenged the motives I had for entering the monastery and the mind-set I now had to develop to continue under the Rule. Grovelling was not in my nature; self-effacement, yes, but in a happy-go-lucky way, not fearful nor breast-beating. But then, look at Lawrence; his didn't seem a cowed spirit. But then again, he might well have made it through by this time. I remembered the saying attributed to St Augustine, 'Love, and do what you like.' Was I already there, perhaps? Maybe I was exempted the twelve steps. Maybe not. It wasn't the first step or the third that bothered me, but the second, 'Seek not to fulfil your own desires' and that strange quotation which Benedict added, 'Self-indulgence carries its own penalty; necessity buys a crown.' That was going to be the problem.

And that wasn't the only problem. As if the scales had dropped from my eyes, the honeymoon was suddenly over. I no longer woke up in the early morning with joy singing in my heart. It was no longer child's play to spend a long afternoon in the fields or in the hen house, quietly mouthing sweet nothings to the Lord, oblivious of the drudgery or the boring, repetitive nature of the tasks. The well-being had dried up and what took its place was focus and discipline and dragging my mind back endlessly to stand in the presence of my creator and my saviour. It felt a losing battle, like a tired bare-knuckle fighter dragging himself back to the scratch mark for the umpteenth time.

So it was like meeting up with an old friend when we graduated to the fourth step and learnt, '. . . that if, in obedience, things that are hard, contrary, and even unjust, be done to him, he embrace them with a quiet conscience and, in suffering them, grow not weary, nor give over, since the Scripture says, "He alone who perseveres to the end shall be saved."'

Oh, what a relief to know where I was at last; not that I had left steps one and two behind as yet. I guessed that I might only know that I had climbed any of the steps when I had climbed them all, and reached that state of felicity, a bit, I supposed, like Father Basil or Father Jerome, who seemed to float through life in total serenity.

Lawrence seemed to have an affection for this step, as if this had been, or was still, a long-term parking lot for his humility.

'Get used to it,' he would say, 'and forget your rights. You might well receive kindness at the hands of your superiors, well, some of them,' he added with a bleak smile, 'but as Benedict says, you may not even get justice, let alone mercy, and there's no come back. Of course you can leave but this is a cross you're going to have to carry at some time of your life, if only at the end of it. So why not stay here and have your faith tested and strengthened with the rest of us on step number four.'

Step number five was, 'to open up to the Abbot, by

humble confession, all the evil thoughts of the heart, and the secret faults committed.'

'Remember this was written in the sixth century, long before private confession was practised generally in the Church, even though public penance was known since the earliest days,' Lawrence remarked. 'So as long as you trot along regularly to the confessor of your choice you can afford to skip that step, but ...' he glowered around the room, 'the spirit of this step is to be an open book to Father Abbot and me, whoever else might hear your confession. The Rule was written long before some namby-pamby came up with confessional secrecy.'

These were busy days in the gardens now that winter's iron grip had broken, and long days clearing, digging and planting put paid to further lessons on the Rule. But looking ahead, the sixth and seventh steps reduced even me, now a seasoned pessimist on humility, to a shocked disbelief. The sixth read, '... that a monk be content with all that is meanest and poorest, and in everything think himself an evil and worthless servant.' And the seventh, '... not only to pronounce with his tongue, but also in his very heart, believe himself to be the most abject of men and inferior to all, saying with the prophet, "I am a worm and no man, a disgrace among men and the outcast of the people."'

Now there are moments in all our lives (like the psalmist or the prophet) when, stung by contrition or devastated by the cruel turn of fate, we would feel that these sentiments reflected our condition. But this was to be my state of mind for life! This time I was wary of consulting Father Lawrence; I was in no rush to have my worst fears confirmed, so I pondered the implications over the long hours of work. Was it so bad to have no self-esteem at all; to consider myself evil, worthless, inferior to all? And, looking ahead at the eighth step: '... to do nothing but what the common rule of the monastery, or the example of his seniors, exhort him to do.' Could this be a monstrous confidence trick or, rather, no-confidence trick, to leave me no option but to submit to the Rule, which would then take the place of my emptied ego?

I looked around me at these, for the most part, soft-ened, gentle monks, my seniors. Yes, these were humble men leading blameless lives, I mean, you could tell that from the way they confessed to simple faults in Chapter or knelt before the community if they had broken some-thing, holding it in their hands, a 'disgrace among men'. But was that what they really felt: a disgrace (without grace!), worthless, evil – all the time? I was still disin-clined to talk to Lawrence who seemed, most of the time, as if he were following some alternative spirituality. No, I wanted someone who looked as if they'd been through the process, somebody like Father Jerome, the Prior, who was my confessor. Or, better still, though the prospect terrified me, Father Abbot, who certainly gave the impression that he held no high opinion of himself, but who acted as if he thought the worst about everybody else as well. And once I'd thought the thought, pride, or was it humility, gave me no rest.

I knocked on his door and received the answering knock. I'd rehearsed my questions but as I went to sit beside his desk (mercifully the days of kneeling at his feet having kissed his ring were long gone) and scanned his expressionless face while he kept his eyes on what-ever he had been reading, they vanished from my mind. His eyes flashed across to my face.

'Well, what can I do for you, Brother Daniel?'

I was a big boy, in my mid-twenties, once known for my fearless tackles on forwards twice my size, but my knees shook. For heaven's sake, here's Mr Big in my life, God's choice as my superior, for whom I had foregone all my rights. At that moment I heartily concurred with the psalmist, 'I am a worm and no man.'

'The chapter on humility – I have a ...' I paused stupidly, aware that what I did have was a great desire to run out of his room and not stop running until I was on a train headed for Paddington. But ...

'I'm having great difficulty with steps six and seven ...'

He stared into space for what seemed an age, and then seemed to sigh and said dryly, 'Most of us do, you know.'

'It's those bits about being 'evil and worthless', and then 'most abject and inferior to all'. Nothing in my life has prepared me to believe this of myself.'

There, I'd said it and, to my satisfaction, had put the thing in a nutshell.

'I don't suppose anything in your life prepared you for the Cistercian way of life. It certainly didn't for me.'

'Then how did you cope with seeing yourself as evil and a disgrace?'

'You know, Benedict wouldn't be alone in seeing himself as worthless and the biggest sinner of all time. St Francis, whom we all love for his wisdom and gentleness, both thought and said so of himself. And many other great heroes of the Church.'

'But I can't see myself as evil, however much I try.'

'Well, try another word, like rubbish or rotten apple, until you come to a word that seems to fit. Translations can be inexact.'

It was my turn to be silent.

'Every age has its own vocabulary, its own imagery. St Benedict was only reflecting and developing the spirituality of the desert, and most of his Rule undoubtedly existed in former community rules. What they were all trying to do was to provide a structure within which a monk could divest himself of self and put on Jesus Christ. Our Rule and the chapter on humility especially may seem rather crude tools to accomplish this but they haven't done a bad job over the last millennium and a half. Now you've reached the steps that mark the point of conversion, the actual surrender of everything you were so that what is now empty can start to be filled. Just look at the remaining steps: eight, do nothing outside the Rule; nine, be silent; ten, don't be frivolous; eleven, speak humbly when you have to; twelve, have your behaviour reflect the unworthiness you feel in your heart. These are doing no more than making a wholeness of the conversion made in six and seven.'

He had said all this quite quickly and almost wearisomely, looking into space, as if he had repeated it so many times to so many novices. Now he looked over to me quizzically.

'Why am I telling you all this? Haven't you asked Father Lawrence; he's your novice-master.'

'The fifth step told me to open myself up to the Abbot,' I replied with a fluttering heart. Would he have guessed why I couldn't speak to Lawrence? His face broke into a wry smile.

'Now that would be a novelty.'

And that was all he said; the interview was over and his eyes fluttered back to the papers on his desk. What did he mean – that he didn't understand why his brusqueness might put off those who sought confession or counselling or that he just didn't care?

I put off going to Lawrence as long as I could; about six hours.

'I went to see Father Abbot about the chapter on humility. I must say I found him quite inscrutable, but I think I've cracked it.'

'I'm beginning to think you're the one who's cracked. I must say I admire your courage, though having studied for the priesthood with him I know his other, more forthcoming side. But why on earth didn't you come to me?'

'I wanted another slant on it,' I lied.

'And what did he say?'

'He asked me why I wasn't asking you, and when I said that the chapter instructed me to open up to my abbot he just laughed.'

Lawrence sat back in his chair and giggled, complete-ly against the spirit of the tenth step, I thought.

'Well, ask a silly question, I suppose,' he giggled again.

'But he did convince me that, whatever vocabulary you use, to follow Christ the monastic way you have to . . .' I broke off; the conversation suddenly seemed futile.

'What?'

'Do what Chapter Seven tells you – to the letter, but gradually.'

'Oh, I was waiting for something more profound.'

I thank you, Lord, with all my heart;
I recite your marvels one by one (Psalm 9:1).

'That's deep enough for me,' I sighed with relief.
'Before, I was reading without understanding. Now ...'
There was nothing more to say.

'Well, I guess that's what abbots are for,' Lawrence
said, suddenly standing up so that I couldn't see his
face. 'See you at the pearly gates.'

Chapter Nine

Rest in Peace

As you would expect, death in a Christian community is not of itself a tragic event. Rather it is seen as a stage in the continuing process of life when the grandeur of God and our place in its mystery, though hidden from us now, become more fully revealed to us.

Because it is irreversible, however, death holds a dread for most of us, even mature Christians, because we know our own unreadiness and remember too many lost opportunities. It is that moment when everything catches up with us and we become overwhelmingly aware of the paltry nature of our response compared to the majestic love of God. We are wont to see our life as a balloon which, blown up and released, has darted around in a hapless, frantic way and now lies shrivelled and still upon the floor. Whereas God, fortunately, sees it as a vessel for air and light, ever capable of inflation (he's even given us a puncture repair kit, hasn't he) and rising, colourful and buoyant, giving joy to all.

Well, Father Basil didn't seem to have this problem. Already an old man when I entered, his daily life portrayed a state of felicity which never varied. When you live so close to each other, believe me, you become highly attuned to the variations of mood around you, and monks as a breed are as moody as anyone else.

But Father Basil was beyond moods. As the Rule says, 'Having ascended all these degrees of humility, the monk will arrive at that love of God which, being perfect, casts out fear; and he shall begin to keep without effort and naturally all those precepts which he had hitherto observed by fear.' This described Father

Basil to perfection. He was in overdrive, automatic pilot, coasting home, already living in the presence of the Father.

His skin was like a fine parchment drawn tightly over prominent cheekbones, with lively blue eyes and the quick mannerisms of the French – mobile shoulders for the Gallic shrug and all the expressiveness of a mime artist. His most endearing feature was that when he communicated in signs he softly uttered the sign at the same time, thus making it completely redundant. 'Father Abbot . . . seen . . . have you,?' he would mouth, or 'Look at your wet clothes . . . change them . . . you'll be ill . . . Daniel.' To hear my name from his lips gave me a glowing sense of being close to him, a member of his family. His saying 'Daniel' without a real need seemed to affirm me as my best self, and identify me as a luxury in his life and mine. Like all holy people he was a sort of two-way magnifying glass.

Too old for manual work, Basil assumed a natural responsibility for the humanities in our austere regime. The flowers in the cloister quadrangle owed their well-being to his loving care. Mornings in winter and spring would find him walking carefully with a brimming dish of finely shredded crumbs towards bird tables and appointed window sills. One saw him chatting softly to the birds as they received their daily bread at his hands. He was a softy in the company of hard men and rounded our rough edges with the motherhood of the Father.

One bright raw morning in April, just into Paschaltide, he died of a sudden heart attack – for him but a small step on his journey home. It had been some years since a death had occurred in the community and the experience threw our routine life into immediate turmoil. In our confusion and loss we novices turned towards the noviciate to seek solace and direction.

'The form', explained Father Lawrence dryly as we sat at our desks,' is very simple. As believers we celebrate his passage to the Father, and rejoice that one of our number has fulfilled his monastic vows. As a community we want to share this transitional time with Basil and so there will be someone praying with him and for him every moment until his burial. In a minute we'll be receiving his body into the church and sing the Office of the Dead over him. Then we'll all go to the guesthouse chapel where he will remain until his burial in a couple of days' time. We'll take turns at watching over him, in pairs, and reciting the Office continuously, so I'll be letting you know what time you're on when I have worked out a rota.'

As one unaccustomed to the business of death a gust of anxiety swept through me.

All work had stopped on the island. We waited in processional order in the cloisters, novices at the rear, at the foot of the stairs to the dormitories. Suddenly the creaking on the stairs signalled his arrival and, to my astonishment, four of the senior monks came into view carrying not a coffin as I had imagined (did we keep a spare always ready, I had wondered) but a wooden bier, a sort of stretcher, with Father Basil dressed in his white cowl, hood up, lying on his back, hands clasping a rosary on his chest. His mobile face was now still, grey and grave, and never was it more apparent that the life had passed from him and was its own sweet self somewhere else.

Everyone wore his hood up as was the rule for all formal occasions outside the church, so it was impossible to see how Father Basil's death was affecting anyone. It was not only a sober occasion as we made our silent way to the church. For me a primary colour had gone from the spectrum of my life. Everything had contracted and hardened a little and this larger body that we were collectively had diminished with his passing.

Who would soften our harsh austere lives in his old gentle way now? No, I couldn't share this celebration Lawrence had been going on about. What were all these impassive cowled figures, my only family now, thinking and feeling? I longed to know and be reassured that Basil's light and grace remained with them, enlarging their humanity. I desperately needed everything to stay the same.

As we took our place in the choir stalls, hoods were lowered, familiar faces reappeared around me and I was somewhat reassured. On the sanctuary floor lay the body and over it the antiphonal voices flowed back and forth like a gently undulating sea. There was comfort to be found in the psalms and prayers and, though he was temporarily lost to view, Basil was still with us in the universal body, reassuring us through the familiar words. I would have loved the Abbot to have said a few words of comfort and share with us his own feelings of love towards that still figure, but I knew that, apart from a few clipped sentences in Chapter tomorrow morning, there would be no comment, no exchange. Everything we felt and wanted to express would be channelled through the psalms and prayers of the liturgy. It was the penalty of our state and revealed monasticism at its purest and poorest.

The public gallery was full of the island's lay people and I guessed they would be celebrating Basil's death with many cups of tea and stronger liquor. But that was their way, not ours. For us life soon returned to normal after the reception of the body into church.

That evening my turn for watching over Basil came round and, together with Kevin, we entered the small chapel where he was resting. May he rest in peace. I looked up the word 'rest', in Latin *requies*, and learnt that it meant a deep quiet, and was used in the early Church to signify that period for the righteous between death and the second coming – a sort of well earned nap between the rigours of this world and the heavenly banquet. Ever in a hurry these days we seem to have cut out the sleep and promoted the active enjoyment of bliss right on the heels of worthy death. No peace for the blessed there either, it seems.

But Father Basil was definitely resting. The darkened chapel was illuminated only by the light of two large candles, one at his head and one at his feet. Beneath the lower candle the large antiphonary lay open at the Office for the Dead being recited by two fellow novices. As they came to the end of the passage they were reading they got up and, bowing to the Blessed

Sacrament, left the chapel consigning the care of the body to the two of us. The waxy smell of the candles gave the room an oppressive heavy feel, and in the flickering light the contours of Basil's face jumped this way and that, almost animating him. We recited the Office together out loud and started it again when we had finished. As I glanced intermittently at Basil I could almost see his lips moving, 'Beautiful . . . to rest . . . here . . . waiting . . . the Lord, eh, Daniel.'

By the end of the second day and my third turn in the stuffy chapel, the smell had gained an oppressive sweetness and now Father Basil's countenance had a tired air of resignation, not rest, about it. Our impatience for the burial to take place soon was matched, I felt, by his own.

The morning of his burial was grey and blustery and the liturgy was rich in hope and full of thanksgiving for the grace that God had showered on us all, including Father Basil. On that reassuring note we processed out to the community graveyard, opening for the first time in my experience the big door at the other end of the church. As we walked out with sharp snatches of the spring sun brilliant on our cowls and cloaks, we joined up with a cluster of island residents, well wishers from the mainland, perhaps some distant relatives from France, all dressed in black – a rather ragged bunch contrasting with our neat, parallel lines. They fell in behind us and the horizontal figure of Basil so that, as the two halves of Basil's human equation, we covered the short distance to the graveside. Here we arranged ourselves, black and white, on opposite sides of the hungry earth, like so many figures on a chess board. The final service was perfunctory; it had all been said in the Requiem Mass, but the ceremonial had a cheerful bustling air about it in the keen wind. Our grief was spent; our memories were enriched and secure. All we now had to do was dispose of the remains.

The Abbot duly completed this rite of passage by drawing Basil's hood down over his face and pinning it to the neck of his cowl. 'I am the resurrection and the life', he intoned the final prayer of divine union, and four monks lowered the stiff body on a sheet down into the grave and gently withdrew the sheet, leaving one poor frail old monk to contend with six feet of earth on top of him without the temporary sanctuary of a coffin. The earth was shovelled over him without further ado. Father Lawrence told us later that priests were traditionally buried with their heads towards the church and the laity feet forwards, respecting the quaint belief that at the last trump the priests would rise turned outwards from the church as the dispensers of sacramental grace to their facing lay flock. One of those remnants of a simpler credulous age – but then why change a winning formula!

As soon as Father Basil was dispatched the mood of the liturgy changed abruptly, and we walked back into the monastic enclosure leaving the world of temporal affairs behind us and reciting the seven penitential psalms. We were faced with the need for repentance as we looked now to ourselves and our daily preparedness for that last moment of our own.

And that was it. No more mention of Father Basil, and for those who joined the community after that date he might never have existed. A small wooden cross with his name appeared on his grave a week or so later and he now officially belonged to that other community in the cemetery, cleric and lay, toe to toe, awaiting the final call. I could see Father Basil winking at me as he watched over my slow ascent of the steps of humility; sign-speaking 'Not hard . . . Daniel . . . listen . . . to your heart.'

Or was his gaze turned permanently in another direction?

Anyway we swiftly got used to life without him. The only ones who really lost out were the birds.

Chapter Ten

Opus Dei

I've always been a tuneful singer and took to that part of our life like a duck to water. The Gregorian chant, or plainsong as the English call it, held a fascination for me ever since a memorable holiday, during my military service, by the Abbey of St Pierre de Solesmes on the River Sarthe near Le Mans. The research and study of the Benedictine monks there many years ago restored Gregorian chant to its original splendour, and it remains a centre of excellence for orthodoxy and performance. I luxuriated in it while I was there, alternating between bathing in the deep unhurried flow of both the river and the chant, and this probably influenced the decision that eventually brought me to this island community.

St Benedict says of the Opus Dei (giving the sung prayer life of the community the dignity of work): 'The presence of the Divine is everywhere, and the eyes of the Lord observe the good and the evil in every place. But especially should we remember this when we are assisting at the Work of God, and make sure that our mind and our voice are of one accord.'

The new-found popularity of this ancient song would have pleased St Benedict since he would certainly agree with General Booth that the devil should not have a monopoly on the best tunes. He might even have approved of the term 'stress-buster' applied to the chant by high-class DJs. For Benedict, however, it would be through dwelling on the words rather than absorbing the therapeutic tonality of the music, that stress, to which we are all prone in any age, would be busted.

I'm sure any comparison between the singing of

Solesmes and our motley choir would be odious, and there were fortunately many years between my delight in the one and my sufferance of the other. Our throaty efforts were good enough for me, however, and if a piece became too complicated for comfort then most of the community had the wisdom to keep quiet. Father Edmund, a ponderous but benign Belgian, was the choirmaster, and his knowledge of the chant and his ability on the organ were both profound. He also had the job of teaching novices the rudiments of plainsong, a task he performed with thoroughness and enthusiasm and for which the community should have been eternally grateful.

Of course the whole business of singing in Latin was absurd. English, Hebrew even, but never the imperial language, monotonous to sing and emotionally flattening. How else could we sing verses from an erotic love song like The Song of Songs and not even think of blushing. I had the benefit of a classical education and could make some sense of the psalms and prayers from the word go, but the effort of translating so often distracted me from the objectives of prayer and reflection that I raised the matter with Father Prior at confession one evening.

'Aha, Daniel, you worry too much. You must develop the attitude of the bumble bee,' said the diminutive Belgian with a twinkle in his eye. 'He does not take the pollen from every flower like a scavenger. Non, he hovers among the blooms and descends on the one he fancies. So don't wade through every verse you sing trying to extract the content of its meaning. You'll just end up with mental indigestion. Just alight on a word or phrase as the music bears you along and don't worry about the bits you miss. They'll still be there the next time you pass. Just nourish the moment.' It proved good advice and certainly stopped me worrying about lapses of concentration.

Father Edmund's language problems were of a different order. His English was poor and his inability to escape from dependence on his mother tongue was such that he would often prefer to use the French term to the

English, and on ears as untuned as your average novice the effect was bewildering and retention of the lesson minimal.

Once a week we novices crowded into a tiny practice room off the cloister containing a creaky harmonium and some battered psalters and hymnaries. Father Edmund was too other-worldly to see us as other than innocent babes, and far too gentle to reprove us when we overstepped the mark. Mayhem usually reigned for the duration of his lessons as he struggled in vain to find the right English words to pass on the knowledge he held so dear. Questions both serious and hoax were fired on him constantly while delinquent novices sign-chatted in the corner.

His actual task of teaching the theory of modes, the keys and scales upon which plainsong is based, was doomed to failure. He couldn't even explain the tonic-sol-fa without having to sing or play it, and the complex mix of binary and ternary (two-beat and three-beat) rhythms which animate plainsong and give it the nearest thing to sensual life never stood a chance. We keen ones picked it up as best we could, and would always end the lesson by singing a complicated Gradual or Alleluia together, all swaying and time-keeping with Edmund, stamping our feet in time with his gentle movements as we changed from one rhythm to the next.

One day Father Lawrence, passing the door while this tumult was in full swing, came in nearly to be trampled underfoot. He was about to read us the riot act when Edmund turned to him with eyes shining. 'Quel enthusiasm, mon Lawrence. We will all dance comme ça in heaven one day, non!' It was obvious that Lawrence's Anglo-Saxon concept of heaven did not include binaries and ternaries with the feet or on the harp, but it spiked his guns that day and our affection for Edmund deepened.

The whole community had a brief practice on Saturday mornings when Father Edmund went over anything complicated or out of the ordinary occurring during the coming week. In the larger theatre of the church he was no more successful in putting over the finer points of theory than he was in the music room, though his painful efforts to communicate were received with polite tolerance rather than our loutish pandemonium. However enthusiastic he waxed, when the necessities of English entwined him in an ever denser knot of unintelligible Franglais, it was difficult for the rest of us to sustain his vision, and the passion he constantly advocated was certainly never translated into performance from the choir.

Except for once. This Saturday we were rehearsing the Gradual for the following day which listed from the Book of Deuteronomy the type and number of beasts that were to be sacrificed as a burnt offering. The community with the single exception of Edmund gradually noticed that, through an open doorway on to the cloister, came wafting the rich smell of meat roasting for the guesthouse lunch. As the connection was made and spread around the choir the chant suddenly developed a new dimension (for we all remained carnivores at heart), and all Edmund's dreams and exhortations bore fruit as we, in a dreamland of our own, followed his swaying rhythms, surging magnificently on the alternating beats in time with his hand pumping the air. As we drew to a close he looked at the community with great affection. 'Merci, merci!' he said, 'that was a veritable feast.' The choir guffawed spontaneously and some even clapped their hands, which left our choirmaster a very happy, if slightly bewildered, man.

My enthusiasm for the chant soon earned me a place in the *Schola Cantorum*, the small group of singers who sang the more complicated parts of the Mass and special liturgies. There were six of us including the cantors from each side of the choir, Father Edmund and Father Columba, a barrel-chested Irishman with a rich melodious voice. It was with the *Schola* that Edmund was in his element. We at least knew and cared for his obsession with rhythms and, although we made mistakes, by and large we sustained a good tempo and finished at roughly the same time.

The community Mass which followed Terce at about

half past eight every morning was a time of great peace and consolation. I appreciated its leisured journey down the familiar lanes of our common faith and, as an attentive traveller, found new, deeper meanings in the words and prayers as we passed them by. It seemed to me a bit like heaven, this onward growth of knowledge and happiness in something lived repetitively day after day, year after year.

Of all the parts of the Mass the Allelulia plumbed the deepest joy in me, the nearest the Opus Dei got to a simple contemplation of the wonder of God. As we sang the protracted and rhythmic tunes on the final 'ah' syllable, we could have been watching a fabulous sunset or a breathtaking firework display, which strangely also evokes the same sound from the child in all of us. If ever the earth moved for me as a monk it was down there among the 'ahs' and the 'ohs', deep in the heart of God's Work.

But the more exacting pieces of chant could, of course, induce a stress that would be unimaginable to your modern DJ. Columba was a strange, unpredictable man who was prone to moods though his normal disposition was debonair. At one particular Mass I sensed something was funny right from the moment we come out to form the *Schola* in the middle of the choir. Columba was either not singing or he would increase his volume on the wrong beat and almost syncopate the chant. It seemed to be giving him a perverse pleasure and, as we started the Offertory, he threw any restraint aside and produced his own beat consistently. I glanced at Edmund and froze inside to see this mildest of men almost apoplectic with fury. He immediately started to heavily emphasise the beat, waving his hands to keep the rest of us in time. But Columba's response was to boom out his off-beat in a voice that would have shattered a tumbler.

The rest of us simply stopped singing, feeling sickened and unequal to the brawl that was taking place within the sacred liturgy; Edmund, shaking and perspiring, trying to control his precious rhythms, while a red-faced Columba effectively destroyed them. I glanced across at the Abbot who was as white as a sheet. The music blasted to a halt and Columba smiled and rocked back his heels as his face relaxed. Edmund bowed his head and seemed broken by the conflict. He stumbled forward, gained the Abbot's permission to leave the church and did not return.

The remainder of the Mass was a very subdued affair and, before going into the noviciate I had to walk a couple of times round the vegetable garden to collect my scattered wits. We gathered for our class time in total silence, each with his own thoughts. Lawrence muttered darkly, 'There's nothing I can say except don't any of you ever believe that a monk in vows has bought a one-way ticket to heaven. There's a lot of forgiving to do yet and there's only one place to do it,' he said thumbing at the crucifix behind his head.

'I think we'll take Chapter 7 today once again and have another look at humility.'

Chapter Eleven

Wandering Monk

Father Finbar was old, although his was not the ageing that fits the monastic picture of ultimate transcendence and other-worldliness. As Father Basil aged he seemed to withdraw materially from this life, becoming almost transparent as if his presence were strengthening somewhere else.

Not so Father Finbar. Senility had trapped him in the delightful if unbiddable world of the two-year-old, with its unquenchable zest for life and total lack of self-consciousness. It also dispensed him from the rigours and ordinances of the Rule under which we lived, so that when the rest of us were coming Father Finbar would inevitably be going. More disturbingly, when we were at rest Father Finbar would be at large. Sometimes at table, a period of quiet while we ate and listened to an edifying book, there, like some vengeful uninvited guest, would suddenly appear Father Finbar, smelling strongly of the farmyard and looking alarmed as if he had inadvertently stumbled across civilisation. He would pass along the tables peering closely at the name plates in the hope, we conjectured, of coming across his own, although he had not eaten in the main refectory for years. Muttering anxiously, as might anyone caught in such a time warp, he would eventually be led to the refectory for the sick where he had his place, and where he could eat a relaxed diet of meat, fish and eggs in addition to the vegetables that were the restricted fare for able monks.

One day at the community Mass we had just reached the Offertory and the cadences of the psalm were dying out when the main door flew open with a bang and there was Father Finbar. He had obviously been for a good trek through the fields because his rubber boots were twined about with long grass, caked with mud and dripping with water. The bottom foot or so of his habit was similarly soaked and burrs and twigs covered his cowl from the shoulders down. An inordinately long and large set of rosary beads that he always carried in one hand, trailed behind him like a centipede under vows, and his loose false teeth chattered away, programmed no doubt some time before on the joyful or sorrowful mysteries.

Father Finbar was a sorrowful mystery for Father Bede, our sacristan, who was responsible for the upkeep of the church. If ever a monk had modelled himself on the Rule it was Father Bede. Ascetic, self-abasing, silent as the grave, he kept the church like a new pin and the wooden boards of the floor gleamed under his loving care, the nearest thing to a mirror you would find in the whole place.

In stumbled Finbar, teeth chattering, rosary rattling, leaving a trail of water, chickweed and gobbets of mud as his wellies scuffed their way into the body of the church. All eyes turned at his appearance. The Abbot celebrating Mass – would he falter? He half-turned his head, took in the shambles, saw no obvious reason for instant excommunication, and carried on. Thirty pairs of eyes homed in on Bede – would he blow that Benedictine detachment he had spent a lifetime acquiring? Would he seize the nearest psalter and brain Finbar with it? Would he rush gibbering to the vestry or follow behind the plodding figure with pan and brush? But a slight sigh was all that Father Bede allowed to escape as he watched this walking disaster pass through his church and out through the side door. Good for you, Father B! We canonised him immediately for of such stoicism the monasteries of heaven were surely peopled.

Father Finbar, we were told (for we never heard him talk), had formerly been the novice-master and as such had been strict, hard and conservative. A small number of the community had been groomed by him, all hardy souls who had the inner resources to have survived his guidance. Of his mental decay we knew nothing nor of any special care he might receive. Yet some unseen hand raised him and bedded him, cleansed him and housled him.

On one occasion, being poorly, I ate with the sick and sat opposite Father Finbar. He ate noisily, oblivious of everything except the food which he devoured like a wolf. His chattering, loosely fitted teeth, driven by relentless gums, seemed in a state of active warfare at whose hands food was an innocent victim. The hand which held the fork also held the rosary, and at one point an extra quick movement flicked the beads between those machine-gun teeth. It said something of Father Maurice's cuisine that Finbar seemed not to notice the change of diet for some considerable time until he became suddenly aware that he was able to free neither fork nor hand. Contemplating this supply problem temporarily immobilised all his faculties as he froze with one elbow high in the air. Did the spectre of starvation stare him in the face? Was this the beginning of an unimaginable end? Then, in an explosion of movement presumably born of panic, he pulled his hand sharply and both sets of teeth (I swear they were still munching) and mangled beads all tumbled out on to the table. His amazement as he and his liberated teeth gazed at each other did not lesson in any way the now noiseless pounding of his gums. It was all too much too bear and I fled in silent hysterics from the refectory. The unseen hand must have swiftly redirected teeth and beads to their rightful places, for I saw him ten minutes later heading for the fields, the now battered rosary obediently trailing behind its shuffling master.

On another occasion we had assembled for Vespers when we were joined to our astonishment by Father Finbar who took his place gravely and silently (well, as silently as teeth and beads, momentarily set in a lower gear, would allow) among the priests at the top end of the choir. It was a novelty but no one could see any good reason why he should not attend, and the momentum of the evening prayer soon held the concentration

of us all. The show-stopping interruption that followed
had its origin in the refectory for the sick and one can
only surmise the sequence of events as follows: Father
Finbar, enjoying an early tea of pork chop and two veg,
emerged from some inner preoccupation to hear the bell
summoning the community to Vespers. Imagining
himself still subject to the Rule, but faced with the
tremendous need to protect his claim on the hardly
touched and deliciously fragrant chop, he obeyed a logic
that had completely escaped St Benedict, wrapped it up
in his large handkerchief and scurried, as he would have
done countless times before, to catch Vespers just
before it left the platform.

Perhaps he had seasoned the chop not wisely but too
well, for midway through the first psalm he felt a sneeze
coming, strong enough to threaten the stability of his
restless teeth. He was now a creature of instant reactions, and with the speed of a monk half his age he
yanked out his handkerchief to smother the sneeze.
There was a flash of white and then, like a magician's
trick that goes tragically wrong, a pink object flew over
the heads of the inner row and landed in the middle of
the choir. It was the pork chop, which should have had
the grace to shrivel up with embarrassment, for never
had this innocent porcine part been observed by such
incredulous eyes.

The psalm faltered as every nearside eye glanced
towards the spectacle of Father Finbar. He was in a state
of utter consternation as he suddenly twigged that the
chop was no longer lodged in the handkerchief, yet he
had failed to follow its flight through the air. He felt in
his pocket and then all over his person. He looked on the
floor beneath him and even behind the raised seat on
which he leant, then suspiciously at the monks on either
side of him as if they might have snatched it up and
concealed it, contemplating a later snack. At last a
confused quiet overcame him and he leant back, teeth
in neutral for once, to contemplate the terrible justice of
a mocked God.

His antics caused a ripple of snorts among the novices
but for the more mature the Opus Dei, the work of God's

servants, was above a mere chop. Good heavens, it had survived the dissolution of the monasteries. The offending and by now slightly offensive object lay prostrate in the middle of the community like the body of a deceased friend receiving its last blessing. Or so it may have seemed to Finbar who sat as at a wake, bereaved and without a comfort in the world.

One day Father Lawrence whispered to me in the cloister, 'Daniel, come and help me give Finbar communion of the sick.' Of course, that was what was odd about this week; there had been no invasions of our serenity, no sudden wild-eyed appearances, no muddy trails in the cloisters. A fragile peace had broken out in our world.

Together we proceeded to the infirmary, Lawrence stoled and serious, bearing the Blessed Sacrament; me walking ahead ringing the little bell. Into the infirmary, two cells joined together and granted a door, and there was . . . well, it was impossible to say what it was. A habit was reclining on bumped-up pillows, no face or hands visible. 'Is he . . . ?' I gestured my concern to Lawrence 'How do I know,' he growled. 'You'd better open him up and see.' I put the bell down and, kneeling by the bed, gingerly opened the front of the hood to reveal Father Finbar's white shrunken face, still of jaw, mute, inert. Had he snuffed it? Was he even now in his childhood heaven?

'Benedicite, Father!' Lawrence made me jump as he boomed the traditional monastic greeting. The effect was immediate. A noise like an approaching train rumbled from deep within the reclining monk and emerged, it seemed an age later, as a rasping cough which shook his entire frame, plus the bed. One eye opened, as bright as an eagle's. There was a face-splitting yawn revealing a mouth and throat as pink as a baby's palm and then, as if all this preparation had activated a mechanism only turned off when sleep intervened, those gums swung into gear and the 'Hail Mary . . . Holy Mary . . . Hail Mary . . . Holy Mary . . .' rolled out once more from Father Finbar's programmed prayer wheel.

Father Lawrence, at great personal risk, deftly slipped the communion wafer in between a 'womb' and a 'Jesus'. The noise changed slightly, as when a bin bag is fed into the dustman's van, and then reverted to normal. The other eye opened, a hand reached for the rosary and Father Finbar's day had begun.

'He never opens his eyes until you say "Benedicite",' whispered Lawrence as we tidied the room. 'I think he's afraid it's the grim reaper who's coming in ringing the bell. Though what he's scared of I can't imagine. He must hold the world record for rosaries by now.'

At that Finbar eased himself out of bed and indicated to his rubber boots standing by the door. The years of asceticism, which push a man out of bed as soon as he hears the rising bell, still worked for Finbar and he deftly slipped his stockinged feet into the boots. Lawrence, whom I now suspected was the unseen hand, held the cowl open to pop over Finbar's head like a pullover on an infant schoolboy.

As Father Finbar stood there, hands held up awaiting the cowl, it seemed to me that he could equally have been inviting an embrace, as naturally as a child who turns from fierce independence to its mother's arms. Father Lawrence, in the simple role of provider, was answering Finbar's tacit request to be loved and cared for. I suddenly felt clothed in the quiet dignity of God, who for all the unfathomable riches of knowledge and experience to which he gives us access, nevertheless prefers us to come to him as children. There was a fierce struggle as hands and head fought for air, and then Finbar emerged, more or less dressed, more or less unready, more or less alive.

'This is his big day,' whispered Lawrence, 'I said he could go out for a short walk and, look, he can't wait.' But there was something wrong. Father Finbar paused and looked wildly about the room. Then, in a glass beside the bed, he espied his teeth, and with what approximated to a joyful snarl he snatched them up, rammed them in place and made for the door. As we followed him the pattern was complete – shambling gait, rattling jaws, trailing beads, off down the corridor towards the stairs. Watch out, world. The Lone Ranger rides again.

Chapter Twelve

About Love

With Sam it had been love at first sight. How could I not be immediately attracted to that fresh open face, those enormous blue eyes and the soft smile which so often broadened into a grin of great beauty and depth. He had not long been received as a novice when I arrived, and on that first anxious day I was given into his care to follow all that he did and to take my first faltering steps under his watchful eye. His ingenuous friendship contrasted with the more reserved welcome of the others and, needing someone's affection in my insecurity, I clung to his ready acceptance of me as a drowning man clings to the first buoyant thing he encounters.

Yes, when I wanted a straw God sent me an oak tree. Not only was he decorous and welcoming; he was also the perfect model of a novice. Silent as the grave yet he attended to my every whim. He seemed to know intuitively when I was going to need him for as I turned towards him he would already be in the act of turning towards me.

And when didn't I need him in those early days when everything invading my senses was too demanding, too insistent, too other, too alien; when everything within me recoiled with distaste from the challenge of the singular life. He provided the warmth and the food that sustained me. In fact he was playing Jesus' role for me, and when every fresh turn of events bade me run for sanity's sake from this idiot life his smile said, 'Stay with me and share my life.' So I stayed, but initially, I think, only for Sam. Far from perfect, perhaps, but God, giving no other leads for me to follow, was obviously content to stick with that one. Yet how like God, and his Son for that matter, to base all his best enterprises on a dodgy relationship. Didn't he learn that lesson in the very beginning when he created Adam to manage his garden, found him totally useless on his own, and had to revise his grand eternal plan, kill Adam off (the Bible puts him into a 'deep sleep') and invent a married couple out of the pieces.

All the classic indications of an infatuation were established in a matter of days. If he wasn't at his desk in the noviciate when I walked in, it seemed empty. If he looked at me without his characteristic smile my heart missed a beat – had I done something to displease him? But when the smile returned my heart danced.

I remember being warned at school in those high, moral, post-war days, against having 'particular friendships'. A Jesuit school, they no doubt followed the rule for young Jesuits themselves, which was probably designed more to encourage the greater good of community life than to discourage the unthinkable inclination towards the unmentionable. Or was it? Anyway, St Benedict doesn't mention the danger of 'particular friendships'; but then, in the context of a life where the people never speak to each other, and are counselled to focus on their unworthiness and to be subject in all things to their abbot, it would have seemed superfluous if not downright paranoid if he had.

Of course, my dependency on him didn't remain total for very long. As those first desolate days passed and there I was still in place, little by little other aspects of the life came into an acceptable focus and were absorbed. Some books became less unapproachable than others. The Bible became palatable through archaeology, literary forms and other aids to understanding. The Rule became a marginal possibility just as long as I didn't apply it to myself and could keep it at arm's length like a dangerous virus in a test tube. The manual work became easier as my body toughened, and I could enjoy its physical challenge and the fleeting camaraderie it afforded with the others.

The novices around me became more real as I gradually accepted them into my active life. Their smiles, signalled comments, and their little gestures of support supplemented Sam's attentions but never supplanted them, just as welcome supplements to a diet never replace the staple food. If I asked a question of Father Lawrence in class concerning the construction of the Temple in Jerusalem or a detail in the Rule, before the day was out Sam would place a detailed plan of the Temple on my desk or the relevant page marked in the Order's Ordinances and Customs. His special guardianship was long over yet I still basked in the warm glow of his close attention. And of course I returned this favour, helping in whatever way I could during work, lifting the heavy bales of hay with him, for he was of a slight build, or helping him move the big sacks of vegetables.

The two of us were despatched one afternoon to clean out some cattle pens on the old monastery farm. I was thrilled and excited that the two of us could be on our own and, as soon as we were out of sight of the enclosure, moved up to walk abreast of him and elbowed him to point out Father Anthony driving a tractor towards a distant field. With a soft smile and a slight blush Sam put his finger to his lips, pulled his hood more firmly about his ears and resumed his place at the head of our file of two. I fell back in confusion, rebuffed, yet my admiration for him grew, seeing his single-minded devotion to our way of life.

We worked hard together cleaning out the cows (always easier than cleaning out the pigs who somehow knitted every hay stalk together with their constant burrowing). We shared many a silent joke together as one or another thing happened to amuse us but, at the bell, Sam simply straightened up, grabbed the tea cans, grinned at me and bowed, raising his hood, and moved off on the journey home. 'That's ma boy!' I sang quietly to myself as he trudged slightly bowed before me, his ridiculous denim smock catching the tops of his wellies. Everything about us smelled sweetly of sweat, hay and dung, and my inclusion in his aura made even my rough ways smooth.

I knew so little about him. When he spoke (which was seldom and only in class in response to a direct question from Lawrence) he betrayed a soft Irish accent which matched his dark hair – when it grew long enough to show – and ruddy complexion. But what became evident after only a short while in community was that all you needed to know of someone was revealed though their body language, their gestures, reactions.

In Sam's case, the words from the Gospel, 'I was hungry and you fed me', 'I was naked and you clothed me' came alive in a thousand and one small indicators. The spirit of the Gospel which filled him, as yet eluded me. His humility and correctness seemed only to high-light my arrogance and faintheartedness. Yet I never saw a glance of judgement by which I might accuse him of perfectionism.

Some time after I had been clothed as a novice a new postulant arrived, Tom by name, showing all the uncer-tainty and anxiety that had characterised my arrival. Sam was again given the task of guardianship and I moved over to the other side of the choir while Tom took my place alongside him. Well, for a start I was a little miffed at not being assigned the task myself as it would have given me a little status in the noviciate pecking order.

But what really reared its ugly head was jealousy, a passion to which I had not thought myself prone, perhaps because I am wary of the vulnerability of love. It took me completely by surprise that when Sam conferred on a grateful Tom all the caring he had lavished upon me in choir, on desk or at table, all I felt were the gusts of abandonment and mortification. Battle against it as I would, for reason told me that there was no lessening of his regard for me, every act of caring elsewhere on his part turned a knife deep in a part of me where logic and reason held no dominion.

It was as if all the pain involved in acclimatising myself to this harsh regime, which had been postponed by Sam's attentions, had now to be gone through, later rather than earlier. On reflection, however, the pain and anguish I now suffered had little to do with adapting to a new life, but came from the misplacement and mismanagement of my affections which were rooted largely in fantasy. That was what hurt when it was shown to be so, not the noble gift of love given without condition.

None of this was easy to acknowledge because the passion was still very much alive, but now I had to cope with the possibility of love turning sour and hatred taking its place. One dreadful dream I had brought this to a head. I was approaching Sam from a distance and, as we drew closer he opened his arms in the gesture of peace. We closed on each other and I became aware of the hugeness of his features, those enormous eyes, the roughened redness of his face, and those full rose lips which parted in his characteristic smile. And then we were kissing, not cheek to cheek, but mouth to mouth, and my head swam with his particular odour. This made me bite deeply into his lips and I could feel the skin part, taste the hot tang of his blood, sense him drawing away in panic. But I carried on until his whole face was a bloody mess, and when he eventually wrenched himself away he was not screaming with pain and rage but uttering pitiful inarticulate cries of grief and his arms were still cruciform in his embrace for me.

I awoke in a torment of disgust and loathing and a dreadful taste in my mouth stayed with me for the whole night. In this wakeful period I resolved to go to confession and share the whole shameful secret with Father Jerome, the Prior, who, behind the fierceness of his austerity, was soft and shy and would surprise you with a sudden gleeful smile. Had I had Sam's orthodoxy I should have gone to Father Lawrence or the Abbot, but my fear of the acute embarrassment of the former or the taut overtones of censure in the latter directed my faltering steps towards Father Prior's door that evening after Compline.

'Bless me, Father,' I started after he had welcomed me without surprise, having heard my confession several times before.

'Come and sit here,' he interrupted, 'come and sit here and pause for a moment after all the noise and bustle of a busy day. Let's put ourselves in the right disposition for repentance.' I recalled he had said once before that he had no business accepting my repentance unless he too acknowledged his own tendencies to fall short of the mark.

The room was not cold nor were the bare walls and surfaces unwelcoming. This was Father Prior's combined office and bedroom but he could have vacated it for good inside five minutes with time to change the sheets – if he had had any! No, the warmth in this room emanated from the little man himself. A man in his fifties, he was small and energetic with bird-like eyes which darted glances of reproof or affirmation through steel-rimmed circular spectacles. I guessed the Abbot must have appointed him his deputy to act as a link with the ten or so older monks who, like the Prior, were French and Belgian, and had come over with the founding party many years before. His response was usually predictable. First he would receive the confession, comment or whatever it was with great gravity, as if he were putting it through some monastic test to search out the weaknesses, the resonances of a choice made not wholly for Christ. Then over that sharp enquiry would roll a great wave of humanity and a warm smile, almost of relief would break out, dismissing reproof, accompanied by a light touch of your sleeve or shoulder.

Now he sat in silence, eyes closed, fingertips touching, waiting on God. I could wait no longer.

'Bless me, Father, for I have sinned . . .' It was the ritual address learnt as a seven-year-old but never had it seemed more appropriate. I wasn't scraping around for the peccadilloes of the past tonight. 'I've developed an unhealthy attachment to another brother . . .' As I hesitated he opened his eyes and looked at me evenly waiting for me to unfold – I couldn't fudge or hypothesise. 'It's for Brother Samuel . . .' At the mention of the name he turned his head fractionally and the light glancing off his glasses felt like an incision. What was he thinking? What judgements was he making? What penances was he preparing? Was excommunication or even expulsion on the cards? I had to know so I rushed on.

'This attachment, infatuation, call it what you like, is obsessing me so that I can't think straight any more. It's ruining my relationship not only with him but with everyone we share in common. I feel so ... twisted, so full of hate masquerading as love.' As I said the word 'love' the sham of it all caught at my throat preventing me from saying any more. I could feel a tear furrowing down my cheek ... God, what sort of a man let alone monk was I becoming?

Another thought – perhaps he would deny me absolution; was it an unforgivable sin – the sin against the Holy Spirit? Was I repentant or was I obdurate? I didn't know any longer. I saw his eyebrows draw together, saw him redden slightly, and then, without his smile but with an expression of great tenderness he reached forward and enclosed my hand between both of his and gently squeezed it. 'My poor Daniel,' he said, 'How long have you been suffering this? You should not have kept this to yourself and help the devil do his dirty work.'

The mixture of compunction, relief and common or garden self-pity now brought the tears coursing down in great profusion, nor could I attend to them as Father Prior was still holding my hand quite tightly. I stumbled out the sorry tale of my one-sided affair, ending with the jealousy which had precipitated the confession.

His eyes narrowed again. 'How do you feel about him? Do you have a sexual inclination – do you desire him?' His hands tightened slightly.

How could I tell, I was so confused. 'I'm not sure, Father. I want to be near him all the time but I have never contemplated anything intimate. I suppose I look forward to and enjoy the kiss of peace at Mass but not in a homosexual way.' I didn't, dared not mention the dream. Surely there was no truth, no hidden desire locked into that ghastly vision. I wanted absolution, not a Freudian analysis.

Father Jerome withdrew his hands and sat looking at me for an uncomfortably long time. I had never seen him so grave and a fluttering panic began to return. 'An infatuation is not uncommon among novices,' he said gently. 'The impulse to create fantasies at times of stress and loneliness does not disappear just because we opt to dedicate our lives to God. But it will go if you acknowledge your own weakness and put yourself completely in God's hands. It will not be easy because we cannot change the situation; Samuel must stay where he is and it would be wrong to burden him with the knowledge of your sentiments. But have you told Father Abbot or Father Lawrence of this?'

'Oh no,' I breathed anxiously in anticipation of his command. The eyebrows contracted again.

'You know, Daniel, that worries me almost more than the infatuation. It is hard to survive in a singular life like ours, but without trust in our superiors it is impossible. You have been slow to share this problem because you feared the judgement of those with greatest responsibility for you. There's pride there and I would rather you addressed that with your tears of repentance or else it will follow you biting at your heels for the rest of your time here.'

As if he sensed the piercing accuracy and gravity of his assessment, Jerome's face suddenly split into that boyish grin and he leant forward and took me lightly by the shoulder, 'That's enough correction for one night. Look, Daniel, come and see me after Compline every night for a while and tell me how you are getting on. And if you feel you can share this with Father Lawrence, then do so in your own time and strength. I can hardly tell him myself since we are still in the confessional.'

His decisiveness drew back a curtain in my heart and gave wings to my tongue. 'Father, I should confess to you all the occasions I have judged the other novices and professed monks, comparing them to Sam. All the times I have claimed his attention like a drug to ease the misery of the early days. How I have trusted in him rather than in the Lord.'

'I know, I know,' he said soothingly, 'it's all part of the same tune the devil plays on our weakness, once we let him in. Vigilance, Daniel, vigilance. Be sober and watch for you know not the hour. Come tomorrow night and tell me how you are going to keep him at bay.'

'But what about penance and absolution,' I blurted out, ready now for the sackcloth and ashes.

'There you go wanting to replace the wound of your transgressions with the pain of penitence. You are altogether too active about everything. This is a reflective life; go away and think. We don't give penances here.' He grinned again, ' but I did forget the absolution.' He reached out suddenly and placed his hands on my head, more a characteristic of healing than penance – perhaps that was what he felt I needed. I saw him muttering the words of absolution and I made my act of contrition, 'Oh my God, see how I have offended you and my brothers here. Help me through your steadfast love to root out the evil and make a new start in this place.' I said it very slowly, half aloud, and when I opened my eyes Father Prior was there grinning. 'Now you can sleep the sleep of the innocent, I hope,' he said. 'If you want a penance, say a Hail Mary and ask your Holy Mother to help you release your emotions in appropriate ways, eh.'

I was free, liberated. I practically scampered from the room and although it was well past my bedtime I had to get into the fresh air. In the dark I ran round and round the vegetable garden pumping both arms into the air more like some boxing champ than a repentant sinner. I felt that if I didn't celebrate my release the very Brussels sprouts would have jumped out of their beds.

The jealousy went straight away and I found myself wanting to make it up to Tom the postulant in whatever courtesies I could bestow. I tried to look on Sam just like the others but this was very hard. He was such a perfect model of a novice that I didn't seem to be able to get a grip on such a smooth surface. He seemed to command either hatred or idolatry in me. All I craved now was peace and looked forward to those nightly blessings from Father Prior.

'The devil plans like a general,' he said one evening. 'He knows all our weaknesses and has a special hatred for contemplative communities like ours: a strategy for every monk in this Abbey which involves every other monk. He seeks to sow jealously, envy, anger, covetousness, yes, even lust in all our hearts. And our only weapon is the very weakness he wants to exploit, for we have to learn not to trust in any strength we might think we have but in the strength of the Lord and, Daniel, in the good counsel of our superiors. Never forget that the devil, just as St Benedict says, prefers us to take him on single-handed. That is why we have chosen to live in community, not as a bunch of hermits, eh.'

A few weeks later Sam and I were once again assigned to mucking out duties at the farm, this time with the pigs. Walking behind his hooded figure I was aware I still had that lightness of heart in the knowledge that we were to be together for the next two hours. I reflected on Father Prior's final words as he dispensed me from my nightly visits: 'You have the tools now, Daniel, to fight the devil when he "trifles with your affections". Remember, self-knowledge is the beginning of wisdom.' I took a swing at a bed of nettles with my shovel. I'll knock him for six, I thought aggressively. The awful dream had not re-occurred, but I found myself not looking at Sam's face, not wanting to provoke the memory.

We worked hard in the sties, thankful that the base was made of smooth cement rather than the lumpy cobbles of the old pens, for this made child's play of the removal of the knotted straw. Having cleaned out four pens we now had to fork the debris on to barrows, wheel them over to the main dung heap and fork each barrowful up on to the top of the most recent stack, where it would mulch down gradually and be spread over the barley fields in the early spring prior to ploughing and planting.

As we wheeled the last barrow-loads over to the stack we grinned tiredly at each other. We were locked in our own worlds without distraction, worlds of constantly shifting thoughts about our studies, our relationships, our weaknesses and our strengths, the work of the moment, sometimes a memory of the old life, nothing forced. In this drift I would, every now and then, make a little acknowledgement of God, a word of thanks or praise – a device to keep everything centred on reality.

The last barrowful we forked up together and, as I

jerked playfully but too vigorously in setting it free, Sam's fork sprung from his grasp and followed the flying hay on to the top of the pile. I beat my breast in apology and he flushed slightly and clambered up the sloping side of the stack to retrieve his fork, helped in his ascent by my steadying hand. He smiled down at me and jumped over a little mound of hay and, with no more than a strangled yelp of surprise, sank out of view.

A chill of fear swept over me as I recalled the warning from Lawrence when he had once accompanied us to the farm. 'Don't play around on top of those stacks,' he had said harshly as one of us started to climb up. 'When they've been standing a few weeks in the rain, vertical channels of pure manure sludge form where the hay has not knitted together, and these could be as deep as the stack itself. It's not good standing and you should always carry your fork with you to use as a lever or bridge if you should slip into one of them.'

I flew to the stack and, fork in hand, leapt up the sloping side praying aloud, 'Please God, please ...' as I went. I reached the spot where Sam had disappeared and my worst fears were confirmed. All I could see were his hands gripping the firm hay, the top of his head covered in the browny green slime. What could I possibly do? In desperation I threw my fork across the churned up liquid and stood astride Sam with my feet on firmer hay. Reaching down I grabbed his sleeves near the wrist and pulled upwards. The suction of the swamp was tremendous and I could feel my feet sinking in the slime but it was now or never. I continued to gasp out prayer commands, 'Give me strength, Lord ... Give me strength!' and grabbed the sleeves and shoulders as they jerked slowly above the surface in response to my frenzied efforts. Finally I knelt down on the shaft of my fork which was across the black hole, and plunged my hands deep down and under Sam's arms, pulling with all the strength that remained in me. As his body came clear with his face towards me, completely covered in the slime, I slid backwards so that he slumped across the shaft. Then, with one final tremendous heave around his waist I straightened up, pulling his legs free, and together we fell to one side on the firm hay.

I felt totally drained and wanted just to lie with him where we had fallen, but the dark soggy heap that Sam was didn't move. He's swallowed the stuff and choked, I immediately thought. I had to overcome the desire to do nothing. I've done enough – surely he can do the rest. But it was the filth I couldn't stand. If he were clean and his face at peace it would have been easier . . . I turned him on his front, head to one side, and knelt astride him pressing his back hard and in an upwards direction as I imagined it must be done; but why should a load of theory work for me out here in this place? Nothing. 'Oh God, what do I do now,' I sobbed. Was his tongue free? I jerked his mouth open and felt inside with my finger and thumb. Yes, it was there but his mouth was full of slime. More pushes, irregular, panic stricken, but yet I noticed a stream of manure flowing out of his open mouth . . . and was that a gurgle I could hear in the stillness of that barren darkening afternoon.

Please, God, please . . . what now, what now? I couldn't cope with the dreadful sense of time and life slipping away. I reached into my tunic for a handkerchief and wiped his face feverishly but there was no sign of life. I knew then that I had to try mouth-to-mouth resuscitation, the kiss of life; a vain attempt, probably, but it had to be done. Even in the cold a sweat of terror swept over me. Could I possibly be doing this to Sam? But it's not Sam, I told myself savagely. It's a sad inert body waiting for breath, the spirit of life, the Adam in Genesis. I'm the holy spirit here, the giver of life.

All these thoughts tumbled through my head in a split second as I turned Sam on his back. I wiped around his mouth and bent low over it. The smell was appalling and I could feel my own gorge rising. I held his face between my hands and placed my mouth over his and breathed hard. Was this the right thing to do or should I be sucking to get the stuff out. I breathed again desperately trying not to be sick into his mouth, and again, harder. The detached part of my brain suddenly thought of my nightmare dream of the devouring kiss. Was this it? Worse than any nightmare . . . Then suddenly I was gasping into his mouth the familiar age-old prayer: 'Come, Holy Spirit, fill the heart of your faithful; kindle in him the fire of your love. Send forth your spirit and he shall be created; and you *shall* renew the face of the earth.' My head was spinning but I just went on saying the mantra, breathing it into his waiting body.

Suddenly there was a convulsive heave beneath me and a great wave of manure, vomit, and whatever else had gathered in his lungs and tubes, swept up and into my mouth before I had a chance to snatch it away. I rolled over pulling Sam on to his side, and as I lay there unable to control my own heaving stomach, so he continued to retch and writhe, moaning after every convulsion. And, thank God, his eyes were open at last, looking wildly about as he lay there in his terrible distress.

I knelt beside him, breathing deeply to keep down the rest of my nausea, shattered but elated beyond measure, thanking God in tune with the breathing. But the next crisis was already upon me as Sam now started to moan and shiver violently, obviously in deep shock. As I was trying to turn my numbed brain to cope once again, I caught a movement over by the piggeries and saw Brother Wilfrid, the farm assistant, just about to enter.

'Wilfrid!' I screamed, waving my arms weakly, 'Wilfrid, over here, quickly, quickly!' He looked up, surprised at the noise of my voice. 'Quickly! Quickly!' I repeated, and he began a loping run across the littered yard. Wilfrid I scarcely knew, as his onerous duties at the farm excluded him from all the choir duties other than the Sunday community Mass. The occasional encounter in the cloister or on the farm hardly laid bare anything I could have called knowledge.

'He just slipped down into the manure and I nearly lost him,' I croaked as his wide-eyed stare took in the scene and Sam's caked, trembling figure. 'We must get him back to the monastery . . . as soon as possible . . . he needs to be wrapped up . . . and warm . . . a blanket or something . . . can you get the tractor . . . and trailer.'

Brother Wilfrid's appearance had given me a new lease of life and I knew exactly what had to happen. And so, fortunately, did Wilfrid, for without a word he stretched down and picked Sam up in his muscular arms, leapt from the stack, and started to run across to the piggery. I ran behind him, confused and anxious. What was happening; was there something I had forgotten? Was Sam in even more danger?

I followed Wilfrid into the piggery, a different block from the one Sam and I had been cleaning, and was struck by a wave of warmth and light. A sow had obviously just farrowed and the heating and arc lamps were still on, God be praised. Snuffling and snorting came from a number of the pens around me, and it was hard to believe that all this life and domesticity had been going on just yards from our barren battlefield on the stack. Wilfrid made a cradling movement and pointed to a pile of straw. I sat down and he gently lowered Sam into my arms. He tapped me on the shoulder and as I looked up into his face he smiled calmly as if Sam were just another successful piglet delivered to its suckling mother. 'Cuddle him,' he mouthed, and made a steering sign indicating that he was going to get the tractor, and then disappeared through the door.

I looked down at Sam whose shivering was beginning to make my body vibrate. Beneath the heavy streaks and clots of slime which covered the whole of his head, his flesh had an ivory hue like a much neglected plaster bust. Every now and then he would retch on nothing and I thought, God, what must your inside feel like. I knew he must drink some water soon since he would certainly be very dehydrated by now, but I was fearful of disturbing him until Wilfrid returned.

As we waited our eyes met and he opened his mouth and the word 'Thanks!' crackled out. It was the first indication to me that he knew what was happening, and even though so much still had to be done – that he would have to recover slowly and painfully from this trauma, yet a great peace sang in my heart. I wanted to cry and pulled him closer to me to fill him with my warmth.

What an extraordinary realisation of all my fantasies, I mused as we waited. I had kissed my hero and was now holding him in the closest of embraces. I had been able to serve him in his direst need. And my perfect monastic model had even, just now, broken the rule of silence – for me. Yet I could truthfully say that I felt not the slightest ripple of desire nor controlling power. It was as if I had broken through a barrier, burst a bubble, which released him to be just himself in my eyes, like any other loved brother in need. Here was Sam, but it could as well have been Luke or Leo or any one of my fellow novices. It could even have been Father Lawrence, though that was perhaps stretching credulity a bit far.

Chapter Thirteen

Promise to Obey

Obedience is a very complex precept and one which strikes at the very stuff of our human condition. Battles and trophies are won on it; order and structure depend on it; yet children fly the nest to escape from it, and despots use it to underpin their power.

It is the anchor of the monastic life and features large in the sayings of the founding fathers of Christian monasticism. These were the characters who lived, for the most part, in the desert off the green fringes of the Nile in the fourth and fifth centuries, and whose larger-than-life practices of self-denial and mortification render them objects of curiosity rather than inspiration to the self-indulgent society of today.

To some the injunction of a novice-master to his novices to plant seedlings upside down in the earth as a test of their obedience and their faith is an outrage. It is not only an affront to dignity to have to perform such a futile task. For dignity can sometimes be dispensed with if a greater good is served. But what if the miracle happens and a healthy crop of vegetables appears? Isn't the growth of a plant bedded the right way up a miracle in its own right, though one of the natural order? And what of that nasty scheming novice-master – not only was he humiliating his poor novices; he was putting the Lord his God to the test to boot. No, unquestioning obedience is not favoured today. It is not even understood.

St Benedict drew heavily on the tradition of the Desert Fathers in laying out his way of life for monks, but such was his remarkable sense of discernment and

A rare photo of the community in 1963, commemorating the transfer of a Norwegian member (bottom row, fourth from right) to Oslo as bishop.

wisdom that he managed to eliminate all the excesses of practice and teaching of the earlier centuries, presenting a Rule full of reason and compassion. In Chapter 68 of his Rule he says, 'If on any brother there be laid commands that are hard or impossible, let him receive the orders with all mildness and obedience. But if he sees the weight of the burden altogether to exceed his strength, let him patiently and in due season lay before his superior the reasons for his incapacity to obey, without showing pride, resistance or contradiction. If, however, after this the superior still persists in his command, let the junior know that it is expedient for him, and let him obey out of love, trusting in the assistance of God.'

In other words, if you can't beat 'em, join 'em, for love will win in the end.

Well, this lover was so anxious to please on entering the life that I was deceived into thinking that I was already through the hoop of obedience and doing it all without effort. But this, I was informed by Father Lawrence with a wicked glint in his eye, when I was explaining with some embarrassment how easy this particular monastic virtue was proving, was my honey-moon.

'When you first embrace life under a Rule,' he said in a plummy sort of voice – he was obviously going to enjoy himself, 'it is like a love affair. You are only too eager to be given an order, the quicker to carry it out. Slay a giant, walk on water, and you scurry off to work miracles under obedience. But just you wait till, after a while, you go off the boil and are asked to perform, not the impossible but the grindingly ordinary. And then go on doing the grindingly ordinary, month after month, year upon year, not only with a smile on your face but also a smile in your heart.' He looked at me with a smile on his face – I wasn't so sure about the heart. Maybe he was recalling wistfully the fervour of his early days. 'But do enjoy yourself while it lasts,' he added with a hint of sarcasm. And I did.

I can't remember when things began to get hard and my scrupulous observance of the Rule changed from automatic to manual. But one morning in June (I had been here some nine months) I was walking through the vegetable gardens before Prime. It was one of those marvellous June mornings when the sky, even as we rose some three hours earlier, was the deepest of blues and had improved by the hour. By now it was comfortably warm and being alive was a thrill rather than a fact. Every growing thing was praising God with a bursting heart.

I was passing through the rows of young strawberry plants. Our main income during the summer came from the sale of Cream Teas to the tripper hordes who invaded the island. The strawberries were complemented by cream, milk and butter from our Jersey herd and Father Dominic's home-made bread rolls. Anyway, there at my feet one gorgeous strawberry had ripened before the others and shone like fire with a dewy sparkle. It seized my attention and I paused (fatally) and pondered on its beauty. 'It's a special day today,' I reasoned, for indeed it was the feast day of St Stephen Harding, one of the founders of the Cistercian Order and an Englishman to boot. 'I feel extra strong today,' my reasoning went, 'so strong that I can do anything I like because I am doing it in strength and not in weakness. I am going to celebrate this feast by picking this fruit and popping it into my mouth.' And no sooner pondered than popped even though the Rule said no eating outside the refectory.

As my throat was closing on all its fragrant splendour I felt slightly foolish – like Adam must have felt as he surveyed the apple in his hand with a big bite out of it. I had been conned by the devil and had lost my innocence. My bubble had burst. My mood turned into midwinter and self-deception dogged me like a bad smell for the rest of the day.

On Saturday mornings the community observed the Chapter of Faults. This was the occasion when one could confess, in the presence of the community, to breaking one or other of the observances of our life together. Such a fault was not considered sinful and demanding of absolution but rather an offence against community life, hence the need to raise it in community.

Consequently, the next Saturday morning after Prime and Chapter I took a deep breath, stood up and stumbled out my confession. One of the professed monks had just confessed to speaking in the cloister and the Abbot had not said a word, merely nodding his head. I half expected my whopper to raise a titter, or perhaps the Abbot would say he quite understood and often fancied one himself, etc, etc, but no, not a smile; just a closing of the eyes accompanied by a deep sigh.

'That's a rather stupid thing to do, Brother Daniel. I mean, we try to subdue our appetites in this place, not whet them. How on earth can you keep your mind on God and your own unworthiness, and stuff yourself with strawberries at the same time. Ultimately it's a question of obedience and conversion of life, and you must think seriously about these vows as you are coming to that moment when you have to chose whether to take them in earnest or not at all. Please go on thinking about that, brother.'

As one of the Desert Fathers remarked, 'If a monk wishes to be humble let him seek humiliation.' The

Chapter proceeded but the buzzing in my head blocked
out all further listening. I felt less a strawberry, more a
raspberry – a loud, rude noise, an embarrassment. One
or two fellow novices gave me a wry smile but the
others seemed to turn their hoods away. I dreaded to
contemplate Lawrence's dark thoughts. The honeymoon
was over. It may have been a simple strawberry but I
had picked it off the tree of good and evil.

All around me, I discovered, were people doing things
under obedience. In an ideal world monks would have
divided their time between prayer and study, but St
Benedict, and the Cistercian founders some five
centuries later, saw the value of manual work, not only
to provide food and pay the bills but also to put monks
in touch with their bodies and communicate their
mortality through the pain and labour of honest toil. It
was also an excellent vehicle for obedience.

Father Maurice, who had spent his long monastic life
working in the garden, now cooked under obedience,
obliging the rest of us often to eat under the same
virtue. Father Oswald, who had once been a parish
priest, looked after the chickens; not only the pleasant, clucking, laying type, but inhabitants of that
monstrous tribute to mechanisation, the windowless,
timeless deep-litter house. Here the lights clicked on
and off simulating fast breeder days and nights of a
few hours each, while 300 hapless fowls, desexed,
deprived of sunlight and scenery, would roam, when
not pecking at the ever present food and each other,
over an acrid landscape of crusted droppings and
sawdust. It would have required the sensitivity of a
depressed warthog to enjoy caring for this unhappy
breed, one or two of whom we would usually find trampled to death, hard and flat, when we went in to renew
the food and drink each day. Yet Ossie took up his task
with seeming willingness, nay, enthusiasm, and would
caringly pluck out of the milling herd birds he felt
looked under par and likely to fall and be flattened by
next daybreak. These he consigned to Maurice and the
pot but, in such a nightmarish life, this could only be
seen as act of kindness.

Father John, who had entered the monastic life straight from action in the war as a bomber pilot, made perfume under obedience. Perfume! Well yes. Many monasteries make beer or wine; great liqueurs like Chartreuse or Benedictine come from orders other than our own; but we seemed to be fairly unique in making perfumes based, in the beginning at least, on the abundant supply of lavender, gorse, thrift and other wild flowers on the island. But when, with a heart sickened by war's senseless attrition, John turned to the simple life, could he ever have imagined that he would be spending his days making up a high-quality lavender water and gorse essence and, far worse, negotiating deals with hard-nosed London perfume distributors.

One evening I had to take a note to his room (he had a room – with a door!) and, after locating it in an obscure corner of the dormitory, knocked and was summoned. I was amazed to see him seated at a table, smoking, yes reader, smoking, listening to some jazz on a portable radio and sticking labels on tiny perfume bottles. After a year of fume-free, God-filled silence I couldn't believe my eyes. Was this the ante-room to hell itself, or some devilish punishment for who knows what monastic crime?

'Oh, John,' laughed Lawrence tersely, when I put it to him as if it were something I shouldn't have found out but felt he ought to know. 'Poor chap. Nerves in tatters; needs a few props to get through life.' 'But wouldn't he be better working on the farm in the fresh air, close to nature?' I asked naively. 'Then who would we get to run the perfumery?' Obedience.

I wondered what my particular cross would be, since I wasn't that foolish to believe I had already entered that state of serenity to accept whatever task I was given with a cry of praise. I didn't have too long to wait.

I was with the Prior making my regular confession. 'Just accept the sacrament as part of your weekly routine like changing out of your soiled clothes,' he had said. 'Penance for a monk is all about vigilance – acknowledging slip-ups, general frailty, desires not sufficiently under control, falling short of the mark – that's what the Hebrew for sin actually means – and in return receiving new directions, a touch on the tiller.' In short, repentence and grace.

'Now, Daniel' he said with a sudden gleam in his eye, sitting up in his chair. 'Father Edmund isn't getting any younger. Last week while he was ill there was no one to play the organ, as you know.'

What was he driving at, I thought. No, surely not, not that . . . Oh my God . . .!

He went on. 'We need someone to deputise for him from now on and take over progressively as he gets older. Already he sometimes plays as if he's in a world of his own. I remember you telling me that you were able to play the piano, and Father Abbot agreed that it would be an ideal arrangement for you to help him out. And Father Lawrence thinks it's a good idea as well.'

So was this it? This was my cross, my chicken house, my perfumery? I felt a great weight crushing down on me at the same time as a wave of panic rising through my chest and lodging in my throat. Was this happening to me, who died every time I was ever asked to perform in public; who would leave the house and hide if ever I thought my mother might make me play some Mozart or Chopin for a visiting friend or relative. I could vaguely hear the Prior talking, '. . . and Father Abbot says he doesn't want anything complicated, just basic accompaniment.'

What was I to say? How could I reasonably protest? Well, I knew that the Rule allowed me to protest if the burden was impossible to bear, but how could he understand my reason for it being impossible.

'You know I've never actually played an organ, Father. Wouldn't it take me a very long time to learn the pedal movements?' Maybe that would deflect him. 'And I haven't done any sight-reading since I was a boy,' I added for good measure.

'Oh, never mind about the pedals. Just learn a few of the basic tunes and keep it simple, that's my advice, Daniel. I'm sure you'll soon get used to it.' The conversation was over, I could see that, and he smiled his blessing over me and waved his extended arms, the Cistercian non-contact embrace.

'I'll start practising immediately and tell you when I think I'm ready,' I said lamely, but he saw through my procrastination.

'A good idea, let's say a couple of weeks or so,' he said. 'We'll start with Compline, then the Little Hours, and so on.'

This was obedience with a vengeance; right from the top, even cutting out the middle man, in this case, Father Lawrence. When I mentioned it to him, some seconds later, pouring out my woes in a stream of pure funk, he smiled, not unkindly, rather with a dash of fraternal sympathy.

'Join the club, old fellow,' he said, adding desperation to my desolation. No help here, then. 'Do you think I wanted to be a novice-master; do you think anyone would honestly want to be a novice-master? The only thing you have to worry about is playing a few wrong notes. I'm playing with souls, remember, for whom I'm responsible to my Father Abbot in heaven, ... as well as my Father Abbot here,' he added as an afterthought. 'At least you've got a musical cross to bear; look at what I have to carry.'

As I practised on the old harmonium in the music room the dread of playing in front of the community lessened a little. The notion that I had been asked to perform the impossible, and had accepted the task, made me feel rather good in fact. It was all a question of mind over matter and, anyway, accompanying plain chant didn't seem too difficult. I had applied my playing-by-ear techniques to the recurring patterns of the music. The community could sing the ordinary daily stuff blindfolded so they didn't need a melody line. The three-chord method I'd learnt on the guitar seemed to work for nearly every tune, and the only difference between me and Elvis or Cliff was that I had to use the ancient modal scales where they used the diatonic. Also, I reflected smugly, my rewards one day would make their millions seem like a drop in a bucket.

Compline is the last Hour of the daily Office and never

changes, so I made it my first task to learn its accompaniment by heart. For much of the year it was sung in darkness; this added to its haunting quality as the repetitive tunes ebbed and flowed from one side of the choir to the other, and forty tired monks relaxed under its soothing influence as if it were a herbal bath. The day of my public initiation (and the community's as it turned out) was a dark, squally day and, with a comforting 'good luck' signal from Lawrence (the rest of the novices seemed to be as blissfully unaware of my imminent ordeal as the community).

I walked to the organ rather than to my usual choir stall.

Immediately I arrived the full import of what I was undertaking broke over me like a thunderclap. My eyes had in no way accustomed themselves to the gloom, and I couldn't make out the black keys from the white keys, let alone focus on the stops. I wasn't even sure if I had opened the lid, and where was that button for the power?

The community was quickly in place and there was no delaying. The first thing I had to do was place my finger on the A Natural so that the Invitator, Father Herman this week, could intone the opening prayer, *'Deus, in adjutorium meum intende!'* ('God, reach out in my help!'). How appropriate! In the gloom, however, my panicky finger brushed the G not the A. Now, most monks have indifferent voices; some are tone deaf, but when you have sung an A for thirty years you know that G is a bum note. Father Herman's brain and ears received different messages and the result was a sort of strangulated G sharp. I sensed my mistake immediately and struck the A with firmness. The tone deaf decided to follow Herman and the others corrected their tone so that the response, 'Lord, help me quickly!' was both discordant and apposite. One note in and we were already in chaos!

By this time even the sleepiest monk was aware of alien fingers on the keyboard. I noticed suddenly and with great interest that I had developed the propensity to sweat through my fingertips. I was now sliding through the first psalm and what should have been even time had become the skater's waltz. In my frenzy I didn't stop at the last verse of the psalm and played an extra verse while the community tried to sing an antiphon. There was no time to pause or correct my bloomers before the Office rolled remorselessly onwards.

I saved my tour de force for the *Salve Regina*, the beautiful anthem to Our Lady which closes the monastic prayer for the day. Stumbling from one wrong chord to another I so confused everybody that at the halfway stage some were a line behind the rest while others had stopped singing altogether. Then I too trailed to a dismal halt leaving the more dedicated singers to fight it out unaccompanied over the last two lines. I sat bowed down under a wave of complex emotions – relief, fear, despair, and a tremendous urge to giggle. Perhaps the Abbot would sack me there and then. But again, knowing him, he might use me as a stick to beat the community with. Could I be excommunicated for destroying the Divine Office?

What I did know deep down was that I had, indeed, joined the club – the toilers under obedience, though God knows when my task would, in Lawrence's term, become grindingly ordinary. I guessed there was that to look forward to.

Things were never that bad again, though with unfamiliar masses this organist was known to lose his way completely, leading the choir many a time to an untidy and uncomfortable silence. The sudden call on the Cantor, Father Edmund, to pick up the thread unaided often caught him completely unawares. He was the doormouse of the community, and it must be hard for anyone to know exactly what to do, what note to sing, when roused from a deep sleep. But it was quite remarkable how a quick nudge and a pointing finger on the text from his next-door neighbour would have him singing fluently in the right key in seconds from a standing start.

Father Edmund was a quiet man among quiet men, whose obvious love of music became evident when he sat at the keyboard. No dozing then as his bowed shoulders would weave and pitch with the complicated rhythms, and his use of the stops would make the instrument leap into another dimension and the church shake with the fortissimo or throb with the tremulo. But his irresistible use of the stops to bring different shades to the tedious process of liturgy, which obviously gave him such pleasure, was the very reason why the Abbot so urgently sought his replacement. To be removed from the position of resident organist must have been a big disappointment to him, but to be replaced by an incompetent clown like myself must have taxed his serenity to the limit. Yet he showed never a trace of animosity towards me and if I ever caught his eye in our travels, which with his propensity for sleeping on the move was rare, his soft old face would light up and his hand would rub his chest. 'Your playing . . . getting better', he would sign. Is he joking, I would ask myself? Is he taking the mickey? Is he deaf?

Several months of continuous playing on my part had taken its toll on the community. Now deeply suspicious of my continuing inconsistencies they became more watchful, less likely to accept a note at its face value. But either the Abbot was himself tone deaf or he accepted my travesties of accompaniment with the ascetic zeal of a fervent penitent. When after one particularly painful performance I bared my feelings of guilt at so regularly haemorrhaging the supply of our liturgical lifeblood he just shrugged his shoulders.

'Please carry on. No frills, no heavy pedals. A lean accompaniment. You're doing fine.' Such insensitivity made me despair. The years ahead grew bleaker at the thought. Obedience was beginning to grind me down.

One morning, on one of the feasts of Our Lady, Father Lawrence called me in.

'You don't have to play the Mass this morning. Father Edmund asked the Abbot if he could do this one. Apparently it's a very special feast day for him. So that lets us off the hook for one session at least, eh.' I didn't miss the barb in the 'us'. Lawrence did not share the Abbot's zeal for my efforts and had remarked, albeit with a smile, that crosses were in good supply these days – you only had to attend the Office to pick one up. Now that wasn't very nice.

It was sad to watch Father Edmund under such restraints as the Mass got under way. The Abbot had obviously got to him. A thin reedy accompaniment was all we got for the *Kyrie* and *Gloria*. It was as if he had modelled himself on my playing, and though it was hard to see his face it seemed as if he were playing in an emotional straitjacket. The Creed and the Offertory proceeded so quietly that we scarcely heard them and, just as I was beginning to doze off, as if a signal had been given him from on high (or had he negotiated a deal with the Abbot), he threw caution to the winds and broke loose.

At this transitional stage of the Mass he had formerly been wont on feast days to play a voluntary, a classical interlude, which had long since disappeared as it formed no part of my repertoire. But he obviously saw it as his special offering to Our Lady and, with all the stops out, the opening fanfare shook the church. It was as if the bowels of the organ had been given an enema. Everyone jumped a foot including the celebrant. As he launched into the work Edmund's shoulders could be seen rolling and pitching like the lunatic organist of the Victorian melodrama.

Then as the theme developed he trod majestically on the pedals. Now the large wooden pedal pipes were ranged along the walls sitting above the choir stalls. There was a slight pause and then a loud wheezing grunt as if some ancient asthmatic brontosaurus were clearing its throat. Then came a soft popping like a muted machine gun or the distant expulsion of champagne corks, and out from the lower orifices of each pedal pipe a little carpet of woollen fluff burst forth. Evidently all the dust and fibres from our habits which had accumulated in the pipes during their last inactive months were now being ceremoniously released.

As we watched transfixed in wonderment these little felt carpets descended like snowflakes and a number of them landed on the shorn heads of the monks beneath, the Abbot among them. For a moment they sat there like little mortar boards while their incumbents either stoically continued to look out over the choir or, unfortunately, looked upwards and received more of the debris full in the face. It was not for me to instruct Father Edmund, but he had obviously learnt my technique of stopping the holy liturgy in its tracks.

Father Abbot threw a glance across at Edmund which spoke eloquently of his short-lived reprieve. Any hopes I might have entertained of my release from the organ withered as I watched, and I resigned myself to bearing the grindingly ordinary burden Father Lawrence had predicted for the rest of my days. But for a few minutes more Father Edmund, blissfully ignorant (or was he?) of his imminent banishment, had the world at his fingertips, and blithely saluted the music and memory of Wolfgang Amadeus across the centuries.

Chapter Fourteen

The Coal Boat Cometh

Living on a small island had its drawbacks. God provided the soil and what we could we grew in it; the rest had
to be brought from abroad. Even the water had its problems. It flowed in through a natural seam dividing the
sandstone from the limestone which, at high summer,
mercifully brief in our climate, dried to a trickle. Thanks
to St Benedict ablutions didn't account for much of the
supply, but in a dry spell the market garden suffered
and the pigs missed their mud patches.

Everything else came in by boat: the people and the
goods. This included the day chicks, destined for a brief
life of service in community; and the monastic aspirants,
most of them also destined for a brief island life of confusion, pain, a settling for all that they had so carelessly
discarded back home, and a safe withdrawal – also by
boat. There were no known escapes by borrowing the
island boat, and the sea channel could be dangerous for
fugitive swimmers.

What also came in was coal, some 300 tons of it, to
feed the boilers and the ovens, and to provide a
modicum of heat for the sick in the calefactory, a
warmed room for the indisposed next to the infirmary. It
came by boat from the collieries across Cardigan Bay –
the whole year's supply, a very large black mountain of
the stuff, on a spring tide. The barge came in precisely
at the turn of the high tide, running into the beach and
settling at its highest point as the tide ebbed and left it
high and dry. It would sail out again on the next tide,
approximately eleven hours later, empty.

Where were the mechanical diggers, the conveyor

belts, even a few seasoned coal heavers to aid its delivery? There weren't any; just novice power, for the task of removing every last knob of coal fell to the novices, and our blistered and bleeding hands bore witness to the unequal war we waged with just a shovel to turn that boat around inside the tide.

Every year it was the same. The day before, novices were warned. 'Tomorrow the coal boat comes in at eight a.m.', Lawrence would say with a mischievous grin. Alarm and despondency on the faces of those who knew what that meant through bitter experience. Bewilderment on the faces of those who didn't. Further bewilderment as silently we attempted to convey to them the fate awaiting them, clutching necks, sucking fingertips, signs for death, sickness and madness, until Lawrence called the room to order.

'As the work is somewhat arduous' (further signs for disablement and death) 'those working on the boat may eat a couple of eggs today . . .' (signs for chickens, egg laying, etc. – all good puerile stuff) '. . . and will miss the Night Office for the next two nights and all services tomorrow after Prime . . .' (subdued rejoicing as we couldn't be seen to wish to miss the Divine Office) '. . . added to which you will be allowed to drink as much beer as you want during the off-loading, as experience tells us it's the only thing that quenches the thirst, dulls the pain and puts a little salt back into the body . . .' (signs for intoxication and a proliferation of drunk monk antics). Behaviour had by this time strayed far beyond the limits of monastic, even noviciate, decorum and Lawrence's lips tightened for panic was beginning to set in among the newcomers.

The reality was that all this horseplay simply revealed the panic that had without a doubt set in with the rest of us as the proximity of this appointment with fear dawned on us. Tomorrow!

Well, the morrow dawned blue and bright and eight o'clock saw us assembled, fortified by eggs and totally disorganised. Missing the Night Office may have seemed a let-off but the cruel truth was that, after a few months, variations in the daily routine invariably caused

An emptied coal boat in Priory Bay.

sleeplessness and indigestion. The beach was a-bustle when we arrived. There stood the boat high on the shingle; a giant tub blackened as if in perpetual silhouette, while a grime-streaked crew looked on with amusement at this curious collection of amateur coal heavers bearing stout shovels and slender reserves. Above the line of the barge rose the mountain of coal. Our worst fears were confirmed.

The shingle was firm enough to support the community's tipper truck which was standing alongside with man-mountain Father Columba behind the wheel. He beamed at us all, his round bespectacled face alight in the morning sun, and waved his fingers as if they had just been scalded.

We climbed on board to examine our task at close quarters, and flinched at the sheer amount of coal we saw all glinting and shiny like a slate mountain after rain. Several enormous metal buckets, about five feet deep and three feet across, were balanced on the coal, and a hoist hovered above ready to lift and swing them over the side to the waiting lorry when they were full.

'Right,' said Lawrence, also dressed in denims, presumably equipped for work. 'Now, this is the hardest part, digging the coal out until you reach the deck and can shovel off a flat surface. Let's get to it.' He paired us off, two to a bucket, attacking the mountain at both ends. I was paired with Leo, a novice with whom I had had little contact, possibly because he had some disconcerting mannerisms including an amazing ability to converse in sign language and a slightly superior smile, the sort that told you he generally knew best. Very irritating for a novice like me who certainly didn't know best but hadn't yet acquired the humility to thank the Lord for this infirmity.

'Lord,' I murmured as I gripped my shovel and clambered to a distant bucket, 'be with me today.' Which was a rather pointless plea, really, as the situation demanded something altogether stronger than a truism like that. He was with me, closer to me than was actually comfortable. And the ordeal proved far worse than I feared. At first it would have been quicker to claw out the lumps by hand than to be jarring arms and shoulders constantly as my shovel struck the unyielding pile. Within the first five minutes my left hand was bleeding from contact with a sharp edge on the shovel. Then the knuckles collided with the great bucket handle and further blood flowed. Then a splinter from the helve dug deep into a fingertip. 'Lord,' I croaked, 'Do you really have to be this close?'

Brother Leo, a small wiry workhorse of a novice, was obviously having some trouble in the humility zone as he became aware that he was shovelling three to my two. His eyes, strange now without glasses and already shadowed with black dust, cast quick reproachful glances at my meagre efforts, tormented by my lack of zeal. The first half-hour was hell. Unused muscles groaned, hearts pounded, legs, unsteadily seeking a purchase on the mountainside, trembled, and we breathed, coughed and swallowed the thick fog of rising gritty dust. As I looked across the boat I could dimly make out the other figures shovelling and pitching.

The strong sunlight played on the swirling dust making sinuous patterns like unfolding rolls of cloth. The heat of it added to our own exertions and, as the sweat poured in rivulets down blackened faces, it crossed my mind that these could be the conditions of an unrepentant sinner stoking the eternal inferno, consumed by a toil without end or purpose – an eternal chipping away at the bottomless pile without ever touching a firm base. A good meditation, I pondered dully, and it seemed to distract me a little from the nightmare of the present and the accusing glances of my frantic neighbour.

Mercifully an hour slipped by and two clean cherubic novices appeared to take our places. Leo and I tottered off exhausted, chipped and bleeding, to lie on the shingle. A can was thrust into my hand and the measure of cool tangy beer hardly touched the sides of my throat. Gradually my numbed senses came painfully to life and the banging and clanging focused my gaze on the boat. A bucket lurched over the side and disgorged its contents into the tipper truck. I noticed that Lawrence was behind the wheel. 'Cunning swine,' I murmured indignantly to myself; 'he made out he would be shovelling like us, but he soon found himself a cushy number.' Still, I mused, when you've been here as long as he has it must be tempting to avoid the dirty jobs! My soliloquy was cut short by being summoned back into the boat and consigned to a bucket again with Leo who, any smile, superior or otherwise, long since abandoned, clasped his hands together pleadingly to suggest that we should work together in harmony. My flying shovel had previously just missed his head and he almost exploded. In my irritation I banged my fists together to indicate that his frenetic activity was the real cause of the problem. 'Slow down,' I signed. He made a despairing gesture towards the mountain and then signed back, 'You've got a screw loose,' with unseemly animosity. 'You're round the bend', I retorted likewise. We glared at each other, entirely missing the irony of two black-faced, sweat-streaked, thunder-browed perfection-seekers quarrelling so shamelessly, and then drove our shovels back into the coal with twice the ferocity.

My meditation on the pain and futility of hell had gone now as I seethed, caring little what knuckles I scraped. Nothing like a rage to make you work with abandon. Bits of coal flew around our heads, not aimed deliberately but shovelled without caution. 'Big head', I fumed, and all Leo's annoying ways went through my mind. How could such an intolerant jerk think he had a monastic vocation? I could see that similar thoughts were going through his head too, by the dark glances he threw me. If the Lord was indeed with us he must have been hard put to it to restrain from banging our heads together.

Suddenly there was a different sound and I saw the glint of metal beneath the coal. Eureka! I had struck the deck and could now shovel along the level. The mountain of coal still looked as high but it didn't matter. I looked over to Leo and we grinned with relief at each other, all petulance instantly dissolved. The desperate clawing was over and, in a trice, so was our row. We could now measure our progress as the deck gradually grew beneath our feet. It was easy to work together as our strokes became more fluent. Good fortune makes buddies of us all.

It was still extremely tiring work but that shift went quickly. Shame swept over me as I realised how easily I had allowed the challenge of the task to undermine charity, the cement of monastic life. How false it was to assume you were making progress in disinterested love when you were merely not being put to the test. How sheltered we novices were with our varied and protected life, and none of the awesome isolation encountered by the senior monks with their daily 'coal boats' to endure and only prayer, vigilance and self-denial to keep them toeing the line like battle-hardened pugilists.

The shifts came and went and the bells for Sext and None rang distantly in our ears. Many cans of beer were consumed only to be released, it seemed minutes later, in the sweat which poured from me. The sun went in and it began to rain which was cooling and laid the dust. But it made us look like a herd of two-legged zebras with thin white lines from sweat and rain traced down unevenly from the crowns of our shorn heads. Our appearance was so grotesque that, what with the effects of tiredness and the beer, I began to giggle. As usual Leo did not approve and ferociously dug in with his shovel, catching his elbow on the bucket handle. With a cry of pain he dropped the tool and jumped up and down clutching his arm. I just pointed at him and roared, falling back helpless on the coal heap where I lay like a wobbling jelly. Other novices, similarly exhausted and fuddled, joined in, leaning on their shovels. Leo, to his credit, looked more hurt than angry and went very white.

A clap of hands swung our attention to a tight-lipped Lawrence peering over the side and pointing at his watch. This had an instantly sobering effect on us and suddenly I felt very tired indeed and stumbled back to work beating my breast to Leo to say how sorry I was. I went over to Lawrence and pointed out that Leo had injured himself. Mercifully for both of us he was replaced by Brother Simon, a muscular African with an ear-splitting smile who didn't seem to mind how slowly I worked. The piles were smaller now but my eagerness to finish was matched by increasing tiredness. I returned to my meditation and the idea of expiation now took hold of me. Every weary shovelful could lock me into the sufferings of the distressed and the abused all over the world, and at the same time atone for the pain inflicted through my own selfishness. This somehow lubricated my body into a slow steady rhythm and I didn't even look up when the first bell for Vespers rang. We were nearly finished and the last of the coal was gobbled up in a final spurt.

We should then have cast off our clothes and leapt into the sea like Kingsley's water babies but our abandonment was to divine providence not carnal pleasure, and we hauled our bodies up the monastery road, hoods up in single file. At least Lawrence took our shovels on his truck and, with a cheery wave, rattled on up the hill before us. 'I've been atoning for you, too', I muttered wearily to myself and then, with an effort, banished that less than perfect sentiment.

Novices returning from a work shift.

Baths and a clean change of underwear (what, two lots in one week!) awaited us, and the five-minute soak was what all this mortification had been leading up to. The discarding of the filthy clothes, the testing of the water, the sinking slowly into the depths and the almost painful pleasure as my body relaxed muscle by muscle into its warm embrace. No wonder St Benedict disapproved of his monks bathing – even three minutes of it could endanger a man's soul! I gave myself up to it wantonly and thought of the coal which had fired the boiler to heat the water to give me such intense pleasure in return for what – a few hours work, a few cuts and blisters?

Next morning at six I rewrote that equation as I stumbled down to Prime on legs that did not want to bear me and with arms that ached even to pick up a book, fingers that screamed even to turn a page.

Lawrence was in a moralising mood. 'Who hasn't learnt from yesterday's experience?' he asked. 'We could do with a few more coal boat experiences during the year. A little controlled suffering can be very edifying.' Controlled! I thought. The only control was that we ran out of coal before we ran into verbal or even physical abuse. 'How did you take the coal boat experience?' he asked me later privately. 'I offered it up,' I said simply, feeling that the litter of my day, the fury, the self-pity, the murmuring, was best left strewn about back there on the beach. It was matter for confession with Father Prior, not conversation with Father Lawrence. 'How about you?' I asked. He looked at me quizzically and then over my head at the other novices bent over their desks. 'We all have our crosses,' he said.

Chapter Fifteen

Discipline or What?

The term 'regular order' conveys a sense of neatness, predictability, everything in its place. This is the Church's definition of life lived under a rule, as opposed to the word secular or 'worldly', describing the looser lifestyle enjoyed by everybody else. We see the Italians as a life-embracing, laid-back people, short on discipline, long on mealtimes. Yet for their ancestors, the Romans, as for the Church bearing the name, order was everything. The word means a row and one instinctively thinks of their version of our number four – four little soldiers standing in line. St Benedict may have been an Italian in his love of moderation but, as far as rules were concerned, he was Roman to the core.

You just have to look at his Rule to see how prescribed and orderly our life was. One of the first chapters lists no fewer than seventy–two instruments of good works ranging from helping those in tribulation to making peace with adversaries before sunset. There was scarcely enough time in the day to remember them let alone try putting them into practice. Twelve chapters order the singing of the chant. Many chapters start with the word 'how': how monks are to sleep; how those who have been excommunicated are to make satisfaction; how boys are to be corrected (but that's another story). Others measure the food and drink or regulate the monks' clothes and shoes. Nothing was left to chance so that the long day purred its course through like a Rolls Royce.

Apart from one feature, one anomaly, which stood out from the rest of our life like a sore thumb, or rather a sore back. This was the use of the discipline, a flail made of strands of knotted cord, upon our bare backs, on Friday mornings after Prime except during Eastertide or if a major feast occurred on that day. As we came from the Office the whole community apart from the old and infirm would file to the dormitories, strip off the upper garments so that they hung down from our belts, and take down the discipline from where it hung on the wall. The Abbot would then ring his bell and we would whip our backs with the flail while he recited the long penitential fifty-first psalm, 'Have mercy on me, O God, according to your steadfast love; according to your abundant mercy blot out my transgression.' Etc. Having finished, he would ring the bell, we would don our habits, and life would resume its normal pattern as if we had just brushed our teeth.

Ours was a penitential Order following a penitential rule. We did what it told us to do. We kept silent; we abstained from meat, fish and eggs; our day allowed us no leisure time as such, filling the seventeen waking hours with work, study and prayer; we took vows not to leave the monastery, to obey our abbot in all things, and to become more wedded to the life every day. You would have thought that was enough to keep us on track for perfection. So why did we beat ourselves every Friday morning outside Eastertide? There was no instruction in the Rule, noted for covering every monastic procedure, on flogging, except perhaps a little for the most obdurate of rule-breakers. Remember this was the sixth century.

Father Lawrence showed me the knotted cord that first morning when introducing me to my cubicle.

'Don't worry about this,' he waved airily in its direction. 'It's just a little monastic thing we do every Friday. I'll tell you about it later.'

Well, I was inclined to worry about it but he forgot to tell me about it later and it all slipped from my mind. The next Friday morning as we filed out of Prime at 6.30, instead of branching off towards the noviciate, the line rounded the cloister corner and made for the stairway. Just as I mounted the first step Lawrence appeared beside me, grabbing me by the arm.

'Don't do anything,' he whispered harshly. 'Just sit on
your bed and wait for me to come.'

This completely mystified me as I didn't connect it
with all the discipline stuff. I sat on the bed and a bell
rang. There followed what I could only describe as an
industry of rope landing heavily on flesh – no screams,
grunts or even heavy breathing – just the multiple
action of thwack. Of course I immediately connected it
with the discipline hanging on my partition, but where
and why and how? Having never flogged myself nor ever
even heard of the practice, I naturally thought that the
monks were being flogged either by each other or by an
appointed flogger, rather like the canings at my Jesuit
school. Maybe there was a flogatorium down the
passage I hadn't noticed, perhaps locked to hide the
bloodstains from general view.

The bell rang again and the noise ceased as abruptly
as it had begun. Almost immediately feet shuffled past
the cubicle and suddenly Lawrence's head appeared
round the curtain and whispered, 'See you in my office.'
I joined the shufflers with a wildly beating heart.

'I'm sorry I forgot to prepare you for this,' Lawrence
said, 'but to tell you the truth I find it hard to explain
and even harder to justify why we beat ourselves at all.'

'What!' I exclaimed, 'D'you mean to say that noise was
the monks all beating themselves – on their bare flesh?'

'I'm afraid so, Daniel, and it's what you'll be doing to
yourself once you're clothed, every Friday after Prime,
for the time it takes Father Abbot to recite Psalm fifty-
one, the Miserere. I just don't want you to worry too
much about it; it's not an important part of our life – in
fact, it's a bit of an anomaly.'

'Then why do you have to do it?'

'Because the General Chapter, that's all the abbots of
the Order meeting together every couple of years, don't
want to stop doing it. Father Abbot tells me that it's
brought up every time as about half of them, the
younger half, object to it as a relic from the days of a
rather harsh reformer of the Order, Abbot de Rance.
Apparently, he found the Cistercians in a very lax state
of practice and discipline, and in his zeal to recover the

purity of life according to St Benedict, he threw in a couple of extras for good measure, including the use of the discipline. This was at his monastery at La Grande Trappe in France, hence the alternative name, Trappist, given to the order following its restoration.'

'Why do the older abbots want to keep it on, then?'

'Oh, because they think the Order's in danger of getting soft, that's all. For some of them it's the last bastion of overtly ascetic practice. For the rest it's a medieval anachronism and an irregularity. But to change it they'd need near unanimity, so I'm afraid we'll just have to wait till the old'uns die off.'

I was immensely relieved by this conversation and thought no more about it. In fact, during the remainder of my time as a postulant, that is, before clothing, I rather enjoyed sitting on my bed imagining how much the discipline was hurting individuals I was getting to know in the noviciate: Luke, ouch; Leo, ouch; Kevin, ouch. I felt sorry for poor Sam with his thin, frail-looking body and his huge, trusting blue eyes. I could see them misting over with pain as he put all his strength into each blow.

However, clothing came and went, and the following Friday found me very nervous indeed. Prime was over in a trice and the line deposited me in my cubicle in a state of complete unreadiness. The discipline slipped from my sweaty fingers and I picked it up only to put it down in order to undress. The scapula came over my head and hung down from my belt. I was fumbling with the buttons of my robe when I heard the bell ring. In a panic I tore through the buttons and heaved the shirt over my head. It was going to be over before I had started.

I lashed out over my shoulder with the flail and nearly screamed with the sudden pain as the ends of it clipped the fleshy part around my waist. Lawrence hadn't said it was going to be as painful as this, damn him. The next stroke missed my body altogether; the third fell straight down my backbone and scarcely hurt at all. The fourth stroke landed, like the first, across the waist and hurt just as much. In an automatic gesture of defence I raised my shoulders, thereby tautening the skin over my frame as the fifth came down. As with the second stroke the pain was immediately lessened. The sixth was on its way when the Abbot's bell rang and I let the discipline fall to the floor. The ordeal was over – only two minutes old and I was already searching out ways and means of ameliorating its effect, already compromising its true, if misguided, spirit.

I joined the shufflers going downstairs already my mind racing. My companions in the stairwell, what were they thinking? OK, they may, like good monks, have donned the habit of obedience, no longer questioning the rights or wrongs of the practice, all consumed in the quest to put their will at someone else's disposal. But did they use the discipline to hurt sufficiently to perform its purpose, subdue the passions and put them in their place. Or were they injudicious enough to go for glory and draw blood every time. Or did they obey the letter of the ruling but just go through the motions. How would I or anybody be able to tell (apart from finding bloodstained shirts in the laundry basket)? But then why should I want to know?

All I knew was that I was none of the three. Even more now, I thought the practice was pointless and quite out of character with the rest of our life. Therefore the only issue was one of obedience, and the only procedure, discretion. Already, so early in my monastic journey, the wisdoms demanded to sustain this way of life were becoming apparent. Words like subordination or subjugation, placing yourself under the yoke, acquired a new nobility. Ploughing a straight furrow – nothing heroic about that, and yet I could see merely from observing how unprepared I was, that everything about it was heroic. These quiet, reined-in companions of mine, by now sitting down alongside me in the refectory enjoying a long-awaited bowl of coffee, were the stuff of martyrs.

Over the following months I worked out what pain I could reasonably stand with the occasional googly that sneaked through and made me yelp, but the obedience thing, that was hard, that was a craft that would take time in the learning. But one little ray of sunshine broke through the grey clouds of my unknowing.

Brother Simon, a monk in simple vows from a sister house in Cameroon, suddenly appeared in the noviciate one day. He was on his way to Rome to study theology as part of his training for the priesthood but wanted some experience of life in a European house of the Order. He learnt quickly that it was not our custom to break out with a 'Praise the Lord!' during the community Mass (a shame, I thought), or to pump your arm or clap you on the back whenever you met outside the noviciate. But he never stopped smiling or sighing with deep contentment and that was a tonic we could all do with.

I don't know how the subject came up but suddenly the morning class focused on the use of the discipline: how we should hold it, direct it, and what force we should use when applying it.

'Until it hurts,' said Lawrence, 'otherwise there wouldn't be any point; but for God's sake don't over-indulge. I once noticed that one of the novices had a cut lip on a Friday morning and took no notice; that is until the next Friday morning when the cuts reappeared. Turned out he had really been leathering himself and had to bite his lips to stop crying out with the pain. He didn't last long, poor chap.'

Amidst the laughter I saw that Simon had a bemused expression on his face. Lawrence noticed it as well.

'Simon here had no knowledge of the discipline when he came as, very sensibly, they seem to have abandoned the practice in their house. But he was most insistent that he should conform to everything we do here, isn't that so, Simon?'

'Oh yes, Father Lawrence,' he said, the broad grin reappearing, 'but I was confused when you said that it hurt. How can that piece of rope hurt me?'

Our eyes widened with respect and awe. He was a well-built man with broad shoulders, obviously used to heavy manual work as we'd found out in the fields and on the coalboat. But surely, even a big man like him ...

'Come now, Simon, d'you mean to say that after you take your shirt off, and your back is soft and warm, it doesn't nip you a bit.'

'Take my shirt off, Father? You didn't say anything about taking my shirt off, or my robe or my scapular.'

As the situation sank in we all subsided in our chairs overcome by hysteria. Simon grinned ever more broadly now that he had caused such hilarity among his new friends. Father Lawrence, however, turned various shades of red at his oversight and was obviously undecided how to react. Then, as our laughter turned into an edgy giggling, he walked over and took Simon by the hand, raising him to his feet. He enfolded him in an embrace and clapped him hard on the back.

'Well, I'm saying it now, Brother Simon, so let's all praise the Lord!'

Chapter Sixteen

Blessed Art Thou a Monk Swimming

Monks who live on small islands develop an ambivalent attitude to water. Its advantage for us lay exclusively in the barrier it presented against untimely and unscheduled visitors. So when, in the height of summer, every last local boatman seemed to be ferrying boatloads of trippers at enormous profit back and forth across the mile-wide channel which separated us from the mainland, we could but hide away on the monastery lands and feel betrayed somehow by the water which made our island the resort's 'mystery trip' for the masses.

True, we raised vital funds from Brother Thomas's Monastery Shop and the trippers' Tea Parlour to help finance our splendid isolation, but it seemed during these months that we were selling our birthright very cheaply indeed.

More critically, the outrageous consumption of water by the visiting hordes strained the resources of our single spring of natural water to the extent that over a dry spell every sunbather's cup of tea or glass of squash had its effect on our scant reserves and, on one occasion, even cost us our weekly bath. In the best sporting tradition we never descended to praying for bad weather (how could we lose?) but we were mightily relieved when squalls and storms kept the boats on the other side and the trippers at bay.

In such a wintry climate of prejudice against visitors, saving perhaps the steady stream of aspirant young wanabes, most of whom departed whence they came sadder but wiser within days or weeks, even the Abbot

General of the Cistercian Order was not wholly welcome when his imminent arrival was announced.

Although the Order has probably had an Abbot General with his secretariat resident in Rome for a few centuries it is not in the nature of monks to be subject to a bureaucracy. The stability of independent monasteries, however, is such a delicate affair that it is certain the Order would never have lasted for 900 years without a moderating and regulating body blowing warm on the cold feet and cool on the hot heads of the maverick band of abbots who presided over the very different and unique houses in the Order. That body was the Abbot General and his visit, we assumed, was to make sure we were still living by the Rule and were not selling our parched summer visitors water at £5 a bottle.

But welcome or not he was a BIG PERSON in our lives and monks are not immune to the desire to impress. This was revealed by the noviciate being given the corporate task of scrubbing the 100 yards or so of cloister – an event unknown since the place was built. But as we all tackled our allotted sections of floor the elderly terracotta tiles, which had long since lost their glazing, eagerly drank the warm sudsy water we poured on to them while yielding little of their accumulated filth. Father Lawrence had given us the task with a grin on his face which left me in two minds as to whether this was one of those planting-cabbages-upside-down obedience tests for novices or a genuine attempt to smarten up the place.

When half an hour had produced only two tiles very slightly lighter than their neighbours we decided it was the obedience trials, which had the effect of reducing the pace and easing the tension. This was a Tay Bridge job and would see out several Abbots General in its accomplishment. Lawrence, however, had other ideas. Our lack of progress, on his arrival, brought on a sort of apoplexy, and had we been in a less public and hallowed place he would, I'm sure, have jumped up and down and howled in fury, but the cloister enjoined strict silence – even on the boss. Impetuously he seized my bucket and emptied the contents over a large area of tiling. In a frenzy he started to scrub wildly in all directions but all his frantic activity achieved was to spread the mud he lifted evenly around so that my two pinkish tiles became again indistinguishable from the rest.

We stood in a wide circle, nervously amused, and anxious that Lawrence, whose natural inclination was not to suffer failure lightly, might blow a fuse or something. He stood up and looked hard at the tiles which dried visibly as we watched, then turned to us and, in answer to somebody's fervent prayer, grinned and shrugged his shoulders. 'Follow me,' he signalled, and picking up our utensils with ill-concealed delight we followed him out of the cloister and into the fresh air.

A fierce wind had sprung up since dawn, and any piece of paper or plastic that wasn't fastened to something (this was tripper time) was whirling around like snow in a storm. Lawrence's first frustrated attempt to smarten up the place instantly exploded into a second. 'This island looks like a town tip,' he snapped, 'Look, you lot, take some sacks and fan out towards the jetty picking up any rubbish you find that the trippers have left behind.' 'That'll be a wild goose chase in this wind,' Luke muttered. 'Maybe you'd rather fetch a duster and polish all the gorse bushes on the way,' said Lawrence menacingly and we buried our murmurings. There was a lot of gorse around.

'But won't the trippers just scatter another lot in its place?' insisted Aidan. 'What trippers?' snapped Lawrence, 'There won't be any trippers today; it's far too windy.' 'But what about the Abbot General?' we all chorused spontaneously. 'Sshh,' Lawrence looked around almost nervously lest any scandalised brother should complain about the ceaseless chatter. 'Oh, the monastery launch should make it all right. I only hope he won't have eaten before crossing, that's all. Look, are you going to get on with this job or do I have to go and get some dusters.' We fled with our bags and chased litter over the gorse and down the dunes, mostly unavailingly, but it was fun.

After None, when I normally would have changed for afternoon work and joined a party, Lawrence called me over. 'Look, Father Abbot and I have got to go down to the slip and meet Father General off the boat. I'd like you to come as a spare bag carrier. He's been known to arrive with boxes of books and other heavy material so you'd better bring the hand trolley. He once came with a couple of cases of wine because his previous stop had been at the mother-house in France, and they'd asked him to bring our Christmas ration of wine over to avoid the freight charges.'

'I bet he had fun getting them through customs,' I remarked, but was immediately motioned to silence as the Abbot walked across to where we were standing. He nodded to us breezily and immediately turned to lead the way to the jetty. He hooded up as did Lawrence behind him and me behind Lawrence. Nothing defined our monastic state more starkly than this tiny file of alonenesses wending its way down the island road.

I contrasted the two monks before me as I followed behind: Father Abbot, so private, so taciturn, no point offered for you to gain a purchase on him; so preoccupied with some other vision that you wondered if he was aware of your presence; so exemplary a solitary, so distancing a pastor. And then Father Lawrence, so full of bubble and dash yet so constrained by all the rules that you felt the restless energy always probing for a weakness to let it out, whether in the form of biting humour or fretful petulance or just a ferocious onslaught on some manual work. There isn't a monk here, I reflected, whose unique character isn't on show for all to see – forty separate people all at different stages of submission to a Rule which promises ultimate freedom and felicity to those who can learn to die to themselves. No wonder we needed an Abbot General who was . . . who was probably feeling very ill right now.

I looked ahead as we neared the jetty. Though it was tucked away in a natural harbour the water looked quite choppy here and the tyres which flanked the concrete slipway were jumping in the ropes which held them in place. Out there, however, in the channel the seas looked enormous and a tiny boat making its way towards us kept disappearing from view as it dipped deep into a trough only to emerge a little larger on the crest of the next wave. As we waited in silence I was able to make out Brother Thomas at the helm, but I didn't notice anyone other than the boatman until the boat had nearly come alongside. There seated in the tiny wheelhouse, tonsured head in hands, was the ashen shadow of an Abbot General, mercifully with not a trace of a large package on board.

Suddenly he looked up in surprise as if survival had not previously occurred to him. He rose unsteadily to his feet, a large man, his close-cropped head looking incongruous on top of a black clerical suit and collar. He smiled weakly at the three of us and was ushered gently to the side of the boat by the seaman who had just made fast. He stepped nervously towards the edge and Lawrence, with a broad smile of welcome, advanced and took his extended hand. But as he did so a mischievous wave lifted the boat and the aft end swung away from the wall. The hapless General, with feet on board but hands on shore, was instantly stretched into a more or less horizontal position and, with Thomas now clinging on to one end and the rest of us grabbing whatever we could of the other, our revered visitor made a passing imitation of a gang plank, and was able to observe the heaving waters from the closest proximity. While it was not the most dignified of arrivals, there was a striking similarity to the condition of the Apostle, Peter, Christianity's first Abbot General, when his newly found aquatic prowess deserted him on the Sea of Galilee. But that was for lack of faith, not sea legs.

With no other hands to spare we were forced to use the person of the prostrate General to haul Thomas and the boat gently back to the quayside, whereupon he was unceremoniously dumped more or less upright on dry land. He flopped down on the nearest bollard and heaved several deep breaths into his lungs, no doubt using the time to settle his scattered wits and get used once again to the idea of life before death. Lawrence and I could hardly refrain from giggling, while the Abbot looked on grim-faced as if envisaging how this debacle would look on the General's report. Thomas, who seemed to be taking the event worse than the General himself, sat in his cabin mopping his brow with a large handkerchief.

It's amazing what a few moments on Mother Earth can do for a seasick land-lubber, and when the Abbot General next raised his head there was colour in his cheeks and as near a twinkle in his eye as you could expect from a man just seized from the jaws of death.

'I thought I was a goner,' he said in a thick accent, which I learned later was French Canadian, accounting, no doubt, for his lapses into these quaint Americanisms. He got up and immediately embraced the Abbot and Lawrence whom he obviously knew of old, exchanging familiarities with them, surprisingly in his native French. He turned to me too and embraced me and I felt a great natural affection flow from him.

'Daniel,' he said as he stood back to look me over. 'Thank the Lord for novices. So what do you think of this new home of yours on an island. I hope you are a good swimmer.'

'No,' I replied. What point was there in fabricating to reassure him. 'I never learned. That's how they keep me here.'

I felt the Abbot twitch at my merry quip but it was lost on the General. 'But that's terrible for someone living on the sea like this. I know we have to die to ourselves but we don't have to accelerate God's disposition.' I didn't tell him that I hadn't been anywhere near the sea since the day I arrived, and that the only water I was ever in danger from was the stuff coming out of Father Maurice's kitchen.

He turned to the Abbot who looked embarrassed, shrugged his shoulders and grinned, and reached for the General's suitcase.

'Come on, Larry,' said the General and, linking arms with the novice-master and the Abbot, they walked off towards the monastery, while I received some small items from Brother Thomas to carry and brought up the rear.

Larry indeed, I exploded inside; just wait till I tell that to the boys.

The Abbot particularly surprised me with his affability, laughing and gesticulating, easily matching Lawrence's natural effusion. Was it the arrival of a superior that had lightened the burden he habitually wore, I wondered? Or was there some dispensation from being monastic when the Abbot General came? Where did the Rule's insistence on perpetual sobriety stand? There were a few questions there that needed answering, I thought.

It was desperately hard to restrain myself from going into voluminous detail as to the manner of the General's arrival when I rejoined the novices before Vespers, but the sign language just wasn't adequate and I gave up when I saw they weren't getting the drift. All eyes sought him as we gathered for the evening Office, and I was surprised at this tall upstanding figure, every inch a monk in his clean white cowl, standing beside the Abbot. A great improvement on the wreck we had rescued from a ducking not two hours ago.

The next morning after Prime we assembled for Chapter in the cloister, eagerly awaiting his greeting and news. It so happened than the chapter read from the Rule that morning contained the instruction that monks should refrain from taking baths unless they were sick, very young or very old. Vital as baths were after days of concrete making, earth shifting or muckraking, they also carried with them that sense of luxury and privacy which stood out in sharp contrast with everything else we did. Not quite an occasion of sin, the temptation to linger (or malinger as the Rule would see it) was hard to resist were not the queue of sweaty novices outside the bathroom a timely reminder of the treachery of carnal dalliance.

Judging by the smile which passed between the Abbot and the General, the reference was not lost on the latter. Then Father Abbot introduced the General who, though he was about to speak, nevertheless raised his arms to us in a silent embrace.

'Benedicite, brother Cistercians. It is so good to be with you again and I look forward to renewing some old friendships and making some new ones during the next few days.

'St Benedict's apparent nervousness about water, exemplified in today's chapter, matches my own following yesterday's rough crossing ...' (an unaccustomed titter passed round the community like air released from an ancient balloon) ' ... and I shall certainly not be leaving until the sea looks like a monastery fish pond' (more titters). 'It put me in mind of the saying attributed to St Antoine of the Desert, 'A monk out of his cell is like a fish out of water', although yesterday I was more like a monk in the water than a fish out of it.' (Here the protracted joke received the acclamation of open laughter and old Father Herman actually clapped!) He went on, 'But seriously, I have more cause than most to stand by the wisdom of this saying. Brothers, never aspire to be an Abbot General, for by the time I leave Rome for my visitations, I am really gasping for the wholesome air of community life. You are fortunate fishes indeed to live in a cell suspended in the sea, as it must deter all but essential travelling.

'St Paul says that our baptism is more than a simple washing away of our sins, like the weekly bath on all that dirt. It is rather a co-burial with Jesus Christ, a sort of drowning, so that, being raised with him, we actually move into a new kind of existence. You could say that just as his three days in the tomb was an expression of eternity caught in time, so our stay here in the monastery is a sort of burial, a sort of death. This is our baptism, brothers. We are changed people but we are also still in the process of changing. This is why our vow of stability is so important, because it prevents us from escaping this process, in our bodies, in our minds and in our spirits. It altogether pins us down.

'However, the process of baptism does not involve actual drowning, so you can imagine my surprise when I learnt yesterday, having escaped a watery grave by the skin of an onion, that you are not all swimmers. Imagine, if young Daniel had fallen into the water in coming to my assistance yesterday, who would have come to his?' (Some strangulated sign-making among the novices indicated a whole flotilla of rescuers diving to my aid.) 'So I have consulted with Father Abbot and he has agreed that all those who wish to learn and those who wish to teach or just to practise, should be encouraged to spend a little time during the summer months in the sea, though, obviously, with no relaxation of the Rule. Then perhaps I will depart with one less worry to worry about. Now let me pass on some news about the other houses some of you may be familiar with.'

I couldn't believe my ears and the glances darting around our corner conveyed the corporate amazement. Swimming! In the sea! Without clothes on! Anyone, even the Abbot! Could life ever be the same again? I was both excited and dismayed. One moment he was advocating serenity, and the next he was prescribing an orgy!

Back in the noviciate the mood was less restrained. The rule of silence may not have been broken but you could have driven a coach and horses through its spirit. Images, honed to hysterical clarity by a few deft signs, had the Abbot drowning, Lawrence saving him, then fat Father Herman engulfing them both, holy Bede meditating on the move, Father Maurice barbequeing on the beach. When it got to dear old dotty Father Finbar the possibilities proved so overwhelming that, had Lawrence not walked through the door, something would surely have given, so threatened was our hold on self-containment.

He took in our manic intensity at a glance.

'About the swimming,' he started, only to be interrupted by a gale of released tension in the form of snorts, sniggers, gurgling, and an open exhibition of varied strokes, drowning and life-saving postures. He reddened and the Abbot's man emerged.

'About the swimming,' he repeated in a tone that placed the practice of this gentle sport alongside rape and pillage. 'I may tell you that Father Abbot agreed to this lunatic suggestion only under great duress and the force of the Abbot General's obvious fear of water. Everything about it offends against our tradition. Really . . .!'

He was now quite worked up and we all realised it would be a brave man who reasoned with him. Anyway, he was right, up to a point, and my mind switched, as it often did, to dwell on the reasons for my being there. Bathing was not one of them.

'I mean, does St Benedict mention bathing in the Rule?' he went on. 'All right, so he didn't live on an island, but he did live on a mountain at Monte Cassino. Did he instruct his novices in the art of rock climbing? Do we see a chapter on belaying and tying clove hitches? An article on the best routes up the Dolomites?'

At this Brother Leo sniggered and the rest of us seized the opportunity to break the tension by laughing inordinately. Lawrence grinned at his own humour and the tirade, his brief act of rebellion against obedience to the General's authority, was over.

'Anyway, the instructions are that bathing is to be permitted, initially for all novices, with swimmers to teach non-swimmers, on Sunday afternoons between None and Vespers and . . .' he turned suddenly to me, '. . . since you got us, however inadvertently, into this mess, Daniel, you had better be the star pupil and learn in one afternoon, or I'll have you permanently wearing water wings as a penance.' It was my turn to laugh, along with the rest, at the bizarre notion that the first thing I had ever been given to do under obedience and pain of censure in my monastic life, was to learn to swim. My spirits lifted considerably as there was no longer any dilemma, no crisis of conscience. I wouldn't be frolicking in the water – just immersing myself in the dictates of the Rule.

'Now for the practicalities,' continued Lawrence,' You can keep the under-breeches and towels you would normally discard after your Saturday bath, and return them to the laundry after the swimming. You will not break the rule of silence under any circumstances, so if you see someone in difficulties you had better learn to swim real quick or else say the *De profundis* for their departing soul. Seriously, you must carry on any instruction by signs, and . . .' he concluded with the benign smile of a shark contemplating a wriggling pair of legs under the water line, '. . . woe betide anyone I find enjoying themselves.'

He strode out of the room leaving us unsure as to whether his parting remark was a joke or not. A lasting hysteria immediately broke out, and when we burst out of the noviciate for the Office I felt exhausted and my sides ached with the laughter and levity, and even in choir the contagion of sporadic giggling expressed our manic reaction to this epoch-making decision.

The Abbot General left a few days later on a millpond sea. The trippers' plastic bags still adhered to the gorse bushes. The cloister tiles remained unfathomably dark, but, according to Lawrence, though we may have not received the Best Kept Monastery award, we had nevertheless been adjudged regular and orthodox and therefore likely to escape scrutiny for several years to come. Sunday came around and a curious nervousness descended on the noviciate. The General had gone but a thwarted abbot and novice-master remained. We all felt caught up in the midst of warring forces with the overwhelming conviction that, somehow, no-one was going to win.

It was not warm. The same frisky wind blew as on the day of the General's coming. After None we gathered in the boot room as we would for daily work. The option to go or not which applied to professed monks was not ours, yet there was a sprinkling of them in the assembly. Surprisingly, or perhaps not so, the more noticeably ascetic monks were not there – rather the more laid-back, free-wheeling members of the community; big, bluff Father John, sleuth-eyed Norman, smiley Brendan, man-mountain Columba and, of course, the rotund Father Maurice, always game for a laugh. Father Francis, the infirmarian, stood aloof, presumably attending under orders to administer first-aid, perhaps even the kiss of life. The Abbot rather unsportingly did not appear (were these not, after all, his sheep who, if not lost, tended to wander about a bit?) but Lawrence, complete with towel and clean underwear like the rest of us, took on the leadership of the party.

'We'll go to Sandy Bay,' he announced with a savage grin. 'It's a steep beach, so swim you'll have to from the moment you enter the water, or else ...' he thrust his thumb up under his chin – the sign for extinction, which cheered me up no end. 'Just a sec, though,' he exclaimed, and bounded across to the vehicle shed to reappear immediately rolling two large inflated tractor inner tubes with a length of rope slung around his shoulder. 'I don't want any drownings on my hands,' he said tersely, passing the tyres over to two novices. 'Like Father General said, safer to die a confessor to the faith than a martyr to the elements.'

He raised his hood, tucked the rope under his scapular and led the intrepid band of tradition-breakers into the teeth of the gale, past the vegetable gardens, on to the only made-up island road and out towards Sandy Bay. Although it was within the monastic enclosure (that part of the island denied to the public) Sandy Bay did not attract the leisure-bound monk as much as the more interesting limestone caves and coves on the northern side of the island. Here the fields gave way to dunes which then shelved steeply down to the sea across a boring landscape of deep loose yellow sand. The crocodile of twenty or so hooded men, professed monks in their black scapulas, novices in their white, travelled briskly at first, two abreast across the fields like a zebra crossing on the move. But the line slowed to a crawl as the deep dry sand, blown up by the inrushing wind, stung our faces and got into our boots. At a stroke the prospect of a gentle, warm afternoon dip changed to that of an ordeal by wind and water. The Abbot General already seemed less than generous in his concern for our welfare.

Deciding that we were close enough to the water's edge, Lawrence stopped abruptly and without delay started to strip; first his black scapular, then his ankle-length white robe. He kicked off his shoes, removed his leggings and stood there, exposed to the elements in his faded blue denim knee breeches and striped, collarless undershirt, reminiscent of an old-time bare-knuckled boxer coming up to scratch.

There was no shelter to be seen so there was nothing for it but to strip where we stood, the wind singing in our ears and covering our clothes with sand even as we

put them down. Having undressed we clustered uncer-
tainly together, a right weedy looking bunch, almost
indecently deprived of the dignity conferred on us by our
flowing clothes. We waited for the party to begin with
the enthusiasm of a class of ne'er-do-wells waiting
outside the headmaster's office.

Lawrence made some tentative signs to indicate the
parties of swimmers and non-swimmers. I trudged over
to the smaller group and awaited, like the reluctant
debutante, my choice of partner for the dance. There
was a brief pause as we all eyed each other shyly, no
one wanting to make the first move. Then suddenly big
Father Columba over with the swimmers tore off his
shirt revealing a massive snow-white torso, charged the
few yards down to the water and, with a great shout
that seemed to have been waiting twenty years to come
forth, flung himself into the waves and disappeared in a
plume of spray. This jerked the hardier of the swimmers
out of their lethargy and they followed Columba like the
Gaderene swine, preferring instant paralysis to the slow
torture of getting wet by degrees. The rest of us peeled
off our shirts reluctantly and stood ankle-deep in sand
and water, longing for the less challenging things in life
like scrubbing the cloister or divesting the island of
plastic bags, even dusting all the gorse bushes on the
island, one by one.

And then, oh horror, amidst a cloud of spray that froze
me to the marrow, Columba surfaced like a sea monster
two yards in front of me. 'Come on, Daniel,' he sang out
and, diving forward, plucked me up like a baby and
tossed me over his shoulder into the waves right out of
my depth. As I clawed in panic at the water I contemplated in quite a detached way that this would not have
been quite the baptism that St Paul had in mind. I rose
choking to the surface to see Lawrence, beside himself
with fury, pitching an inner tube in my direction, at the
same time shouting without restraint, 'For God's sake,
Columba, put a sock in it.' I grabbed the tube with relief
and, since the Rule of Silence seemed to have gone out
of the window, heard myself shouting back, 'Thanks, I
thought I was a goner!' Madness indeed! Columba

turned and disappeared seawards whooping with the manic joy of a liberated killer whale.

As I regained my composure an astonishing spectacle materialised. Monks whom, for over a year, I had engaged only with a sober inclination of the head and shoulders, were all laughing, shouting and yes, pushing each other around. The action of cold water on warm bodies had obviously unlocked a floodgate of emotional energy that even Father Basil's death and the joys of Easter and Christmas had kept contained. It was as if we had discovered a postscript to St Benedict's Rule which ran, 'When two or more of the brethren shall enter the sea together, the rule book shall be discarded and mayhem will reign.' In truth, where flailing arms meant survival in the swirling seas, our sign language became as irrelevant as table manners in a famine.

We were all out of our depth but none more so than Lawrence, painfully presiding over a riot of non-conformity, a maelstrom of monastic madness. All he could do was to stand, the waves lapping round his knee-breeches, holding the cords of the tubes, and look very cold and very miserable. Will he ever forgive us for this, I wondered? As I looked at him I thought of the mortifications of St Aelred, an English monk of an earlier age, who used to stand neck-deep in a Yorkshire water hole on a winter's morning to subdue his passions. The only passion that seemed to be tormenting Lawrence was his overwhelming desire to be somewhere else and abandon this crowd of renegades to their lawlessness.

The warmth that such frenetic activity brought to our unaccustomed nakedness soon wore off, and our sun-starved bodies turned gradually to blue. Long before the stipulated hour we had all returned to the shore, dried and dressed ourselves in our itchy sand-clogged clothes. We had long used up our *joie de vivre*, and a dense silence descended on us novices with the putting on of our clothes. We stood untidily and reflective in the deep sand, locked back into our corporate silence, looking out to sea, not a sign in circulation. Like small boys after a large tea our appetite had been more than satisfied to the point of discomfort.

Columba, last to return, huffed and puffed cheerfully and noisily as he rubbed himself dry but, the monastic mantle donned once more, he too stood as quietly as the rest of us. I reflected on the genie who had briefly bewitched us all, and had now left us each alone, uncertain whether the bathing party had demonstrated or betrayed the community of faith to which we had long since committed everything we possessed.

We turned and trudged towards Vespers behind a bowed Lawrence. Stranded at the water's edge and in that wind for that hour with no exercise other than a vast interior rage, he didn't survive the experiment and was in bed before Compline with a temperature. For the rest of us it provided an exotic piece in the mosaic of our monastic life.

Next Sunday it was not mentioned (and we didn't dare) and the party was never repeated, at least within the noviciate. Perhaps Columba and Maurice still trudge out to Sandy Bay on Sundays after None, and whoop like porpoises for an hour, but for the rest of us it was definitely safer to struggle to stay awake reading a commentary on the Psalms in a warm noviciate. The episode seemed to prove nothing more than the old adage, ascribed to nobody in particular, that a monk swimming is not a blessed art.

Chapter Seventeen

What are Friends for?

I suppose Hubert had a head start on the other novices in the order of my affections; well, let's say we had a different sort of relationship altogether, simply because we had known each other before our entry into the religious life. We had met at college and became close friends, sharing a resolve to do something with our faith rather than adapt it to the world's ways and blunt the edge of the gospel call.

Nevertheless I was surprised when he wrote to me at the Abbey announcing his intention of joining the Order. Ours was known to be one of the toughest disciplines with its silence, its personal proximity and the accent on heavy manual work – I had told him as much in a letter I had written him shortly after my clothing. I remembered Bertie as a sensitive soul, an incurable romantic who loved his independence and creature comforts.

Anyway, he arrived in late August, and after the initial fairly painful adjustments seemed to take the life in his stride. He had retained his whimsical sense of the ridiculous which seemed to be essential to survival; he was soon at ease with the chant; and though not particularly robust seemed to cope with the physical work, neither holding back nor seeking to outdo others in grasping the nettle. I tended to assume an avuncular role and was guilty of abusing the sign language (which was never meant as a vehicle for conversation) by overly trying to protect him from the hazards I had encountered during my early months.

On his part he always seemed to turn to me when he was in difficulties. When the hay bales proved heavy he would come over and give me a helpless look and we would fork them up together. Whether in class or field I would find him beside me wanting to share his insufficiency. This could be irksome and I would sometimes make the sign for novice-master quite vehemently. 'It's him you should be asking, Bertie, not me!' A hurt look would then steal over his face as if I were rejecting him, and the thought that I probably was usually made me seek to reassure him on the next approach. I regretted my early protectiveness and worried that this dependency might jeopardise his powers of endurance.

My self-regulated programme of ascetic training drove me to do as much as I could without assistance and limited my chats with Father Lawrence to no more than two a week. Bertie's simplicity caught the backwash of insecurity behind my zeal. A part of me felt envious of his 'softness' in seeking help, and I somehow admired the sheer frequency of his recourse to Father Lawrence. It spoke of a moderation I noticed in the behaviour of older monks, a sort of cruising speed down the monastic motorway that came from wisdom and maturity. At the same time, however, it strengthened my resolve to go for gold and, if anything, it made me try harder.

One evening Bertie placed before me on my desk a photograph of his family he had just received in a letter. I found letters from home quite a problem because they interrupted the flow of my new life. It was like a hand from the past grabbing me by the shoulder, forcing me to look backwards. Although I only received one letter a month by arrangement, it had the power to disrupt my life for a day or so if I felt particularly raw or vulnerable at the time. I had known Bertie's family from college days, and particularly his sister with whom I had developed a mildly flirtatious relationship whenever she visited him. Her strikingly pretty face, smiling out at me from the photo, tweaked me savagely for a moment and all sorts of appetites I had long thought discarded flooded back.

I looked up to see him grinning and rubbing his chest to signify 'Nice, eh!' I smiled bleakly but snarled underneath, 'Look, you keep one foot in your family if you

like, but I don't want time bombs like that tossed casu-
ally into my life.' I had to cope with that haunting face
and figure popping up in my thoughts for several days
and nights.

During that winter the main work of the community
was to lay a concrete road from the jetty past the
monastery to the farm. A grant from the Ministry of
Agriculture had enabled us to buy cement powder and
the necessary dumpers, thumpers and assorted iron-
mongery for the job, while everything else – sand,
stones and sweated labour – came free. And sweated it
was. On the meagre diet we novices allowed ourselves,
the grind of a four-hour afternoon shift left our bodies
trembling with fatigue.

Bertie and I always seemed to end up with a pair of
enormous builder's shovels, and the task of repeatedly
filling the hopper of the cement mixer, first with shovel-
fuls of ballast, then a measure of cement, then some
more of the shingle and finally a couple of bucketfuls of
water, would have been arduous at the rate we had to
perform even for well-fed toughies.

The scene was hardly contemplative. The combined
noise and bustle of mixer and dumper trucks, plus a
vibrator board to shake down the concrete into one long
sinuous grey snake, was bad enough, but when the haze
from the fine powder and exhaust fumes grew so thick
as to blot out both sun and sky, the experience became
as purgatorial as the labour that fed it. Our silence
seemed irrelevant in all this tumult, and I cocooned
myself against the pain and the bedlam by doggedly
repeating a mantra or trying to meditate on the Gospel
of the day, or by wandering sadly through dreams of my
childhood.

If it was purgatory for me it was pure hell for Bertie. I
did what I could to lighten his load, carrying the bags of
cement from the stack, shovelling sometimes two to his
one, but his slight frame never looked at ease with that
shovel which he seldom managed to fill. And after we
had jelly-walked our way back to the monastery I would
catch him falling asleep during Vespers or just too tired
to eat his supper.

The tipper-truck driver off to gather shingle for the road.

The worst torture of all, however, was to our hands. Even wearing industrial rubber gloves (and who could shovel effectively in those loose-fitting things) the continual wetting caused by carrying slopping buckets of water allied to the cold damp weather which allowed nothing to dry, caused a chapping of the hands which transformed them in days from fine instruments of precision to swollen lumps of meat. Added to which the odd grain of sand would work itself through the top layer of skin and cause a tiny puncture of rawness electrifyingly sore to the touch.

It was the ideal torment for a novice seeking perfection for it never went away. Though we would wryly smile as we went through the agonising process of washing them clean after work, my hands seemed to me like a pair of trophies preserved as a testimony to the ascetic life and accepted as providentially as the water and wind which had made them so.

You can imagine my amazement, therefore, when one day while we were preparing for the afternoon's work, I saw Bertie applying a barrier cream of some sort to his hands and wrists and working it in to them. 'Who gave', I signed. 'The infirmarian,' he signed back with sticky hands, 'the infirmarian and Lawrence.' I was initially aghast that this milksop of a monk should seek to circumvent the forces of natural mortification in this way. But as the afternoon wore on and I flinched every time I jarred my hands, while Bertie worked as hard and as happily as I had ever seen him, I begrudgingly accorded him a certain measure of discretion, although still maintaining that I had chosen the better part. You can imagine how, in those deafeningly noisy yet totally silent hours, my mind had a field day of endless, anguished debate. This alone should have told me that there was a basic flaw in my judgement, but who could accept that doing God's will was as simple as protecting my hands from the elements. Had I come all this way, and given up this much in the pursuit of simplicity, for it to be accomplished in such a simple way?

After work we stood exhausted in the washroom at adjacent bowls washing heads and arms that were caked with the fine cement dust. Bertie's hands certainly seemed in better shape now and after drying them he rubbed in yet another lotion. He looked over to me and observing my curious gaze, grinned, reddening slightly, and passed over the jar. How should I refuse it, I wondered; with a disdainful toss of the head indicating contempt, or a meaningful get-thee-behind-me-Satan stare? I smiled; 'Do I knock it straight back or spread it on bread?', I signed and passed it back. The moment was saved but I knew that an opportunity was lost.

That night Bertie and I stood next to each other during that part of the Night Office called Vigils. At this hour, about 3 a.m., the small lights illuminating the large psalters left much of the church in deep shadow, and followed every movement of cloak and cowl with muted flashes of white darting back and forth in the choir. I was thankful as usual that our practice was to sing the night-time chant on a monotone which was about all my sleep-relaxed throat was capable of at that hour.

At the end of the psalm we all bowed low to sing the *Gloria Patri* verse, in honour of the Blessed Trinity, which concludes every psalm. As we raised ourselves I noticed that Bertie was still bowing. What was he doing – picking up something that had fallen to the floor, perhaps? Then as we sat down I looked up into his lowered face and froze with horror. Even in the scant light I could make out the deep bluish purple which suffused his contorted features. I lowered his seat immediately and leaning across rocked him gently back into a sitting position. As I did so his head fell back revealing a ghastly expression of bulging eyes and open mouth and the beginning of a violent jerking of the head and shoulders.

I had never encountered epilepsy before and sat back appalled by the grotesque condition of my friend. Although the next psalm was already under way the sense that something was wrong was making others around us react. Sam, next to me, leapt across as Bertie pitched forward. A flash of white from the other side of the choir brought Father Francis, the infirmarian, leaping to our place. He knelt down beside Bertie and, holding him round the shoulders, eased him into a curled position on the floor with his head and shoulders resting on his lap.

As if this were not enough Bertie now began to scream with unearthly shrillness. The chant faltered and then stopped altogether as others rushed across, and together they raised up the now threshing figure with Francis continuing to hold the head close to his own. Gradually they threaded their way through the choir stalls and carried the jerking, shrieking Bertie towards the door and out into the cloister, but even when the door was closed his cries forced their way back into the church and assailed my ears. The rest of the community resumed the Office but I sat on in my stall numbed by the shock of it all.

What could have happened to my Bertie? I could only think of demonic possession, but in one so normal, why? I couldn't bear the thought of him in so much torment and kept glancing next to me trying to tell myself it had all been a dream, but the seat remained vacant for the rest of the offices.

Later that morning Lawrence explained to us in the noviciate the nature of the fit and its sudden re-occurrence in Bertie, unknown to me, after a lapse of many years. And then, just before Mass, Bertie appeared, looking normal, thank God, but drawn and tired. Instinctively I hugged him, and as we drew apart he kept his hands on my shoulders and gazed at me for several seconds with that old soppy smile I was so fond of. Then he sighed and his eyes seemed to fill with tears and he turned away. And life, crushingly oblivious of all its minor cuts and bruises, rolled on.

Sunday afternoons between None at 2 p.m. and Vespers at 5.30 was an empty space in the week which we could fill as we pleased, reading a good book – if we could find one, or writing the occasional letter home or going for a walk. One mild Sunday in February I walked out towards an isolated cove within that part of the island reserved for monastic use only. Away from corrective eyes (although the life was designed to etch outward decorum into personal habit), I began to rock-hop my way down the limestone cliffs towards the incoming tide, exulting in the sudden power of move-ment which carried me precipitously from one boulder to the next. Totally absorbed I was thunderstruck to hear my name called out loudly, and not my religious name but my nickname from college days. Looking up I saw Bertie sitting crouched against the cliff base, merging in with the sea-bleached stone behind him.

'Dizzy' he called, 'over here.' My heart sank; what did he think he was doing breaking the silence like that? I waved and approached, my heart sinking even further as his face, blotched and tear-stained, came into view. 'Dizzy, Dizzy' he croaked as I came up to him, 'what am I going to do?' As I looked down at him I asked myself that question. What was I going to do – now? Never did brotherly detachment seem so unavailing, so meaning-less, as I stood now awkward and silent beside my friend. My heart went out to him in his obvious misery and I stretched my hand nervously towards his shoulder. With a sudden movement he grabbed my hand and pulled me down to him causing me to topple partly on top of him. He clutched at me desperately and I also held him, and with heads close together I could feel his chest and shoulders heaving with convulsive sobs and his gasping breath playing on to my ear. Was he having a fit, I wondered, as I waited for him to calm down, but he gradually came to rest, and we remained silent there in the gentle beat of the tide for what seemed an age.

'What am I going to do?' he repeated eventually, as we drew apart and half knelt on the rock holding hands. 'Bertie,' I said, abandoning the rule of silence for the first time, 'Whatever the problem is you're not alone, not even here, especially not here.' 'I can't go on,' he whispered, 'I can't. I feel I'm being torn apart. I try so hard to meet the challenge, not only of the rules and the detachment, but of the work and the cold and the food. I go to Lawrence and he tells me to take it easy, that I've got a whole life ahead of me. He gives me cream for my hands, encourages me to write home, tells me to eat well – and it all makes sense. Then I come out and have to live with you and the others working like navvies, fasting, putting up with chapped hands and God knows what, silent, detached, contemplative, and I'm back in turmoil again. I didn't come here to take it easy. And all the things I read on the life back up what you're doing and label me a slacker and a murmurer.'

I sat down beside him and stared out to sea, across the line of white crested waves stretching out to the empty horizon. I couldn't speak for the ache in my heart. Had my pride done this to him? Competing in an unequal match when all the time I should have been supporting him and praying for his faltering progress. I looked at his tear-tracked face, his hurt disillusioned eyes. 'But what about obedience; what about humility?' I ventured weakly, 'The Rule's quite clear about them being the most important things. You've always stood out in my eyes precisely because you don't seem to rely on your own strength but seek advice and then try to follow it. I don't expect the Bertie I know of old to be a heavyweight hero, just the gentle person St Benedict wants you to be.'

As we sat there I remembered the old college times when whole nights were squandered in easy conversation and nothing threatened the long future of our youth. We glanced at each other, smiling, and as if by a telepathic link he said, 'D'you remember that night we both got drunk and walked home arm in arm swearing eternal brotherhood. I've wanted so often to remind you of that over these last months. The times I've longed to be with you like this to pour out all my doubts and fears in a way I could never do to Lawrence. The times I couldn't cope with the loneliness and the pain; I really needed ours to be a special relationship, like it was, just when things got too bad.'

My spine tingled with the finality of what he was saying and he sensed the sudden distancing. The tears leapt to his eyes again and he said quickly before his sadness overcame him again, 'But it can never be like that now, can it, Dizz?' I shook my head and felt tears on my own cheek. 'You know it can't, Bertie,' I whispered, 'It has to become something else.' 'But I can't become something else,' he cried out. 'And I want you to be the way you were; everything the way it was. I feel everything has just slipped out of my reach.'

He buried his head in his hands and rocked to and fro in a tearing grief. What could I do? I feared the desperate warmth of his embrace if I reached out to him again. There was no future in this closeness, not in this life here. I felt I had to leave him, rightly or wrongly, before I went down with him. 'Bertie,' I said quietly, 'I've got to go, but we are brothers, you know; we'll always be brothers. Remember St Paul – "Our conversation is in heaven."'

An arm emerged from the huddled figure and reached towards me. 'Goodbye Daniel . . . brother,' he said, 'I do love you.' I touched his fingers but they made no attempt to grasp mine. Down there, the pain, briefly shared, had turned in on itself and I was free to take my leave. I walked away on trembling legs, looking back one more time on his gently rocking figure as I crested the ridge which hid him and revealed the monastery, my chosen home. I walked homewards confused and crushed. In this exhibition of his weakness and attach-ments, all I could see, strangely, was his strength and independence. His unarmed vulnerability had shown up my paper-thin asceticism for the conceit it was. But I was to stay here and work it out over the bitter-sweet years ahead, whereas he was going to leave, seemingly a failure, much like his master.

Hubert left the monastery that week, slipping off quietly one morning. We exchanged no more words but our occasional glances conveyed the closeness of our Sunday encounter. On the morning of his departure he caught my attention just before Mass and kissed his fingertips, which I reciprocated. At the Kiss of Peace we held each other so firmly but could say nothing in the fullness of our hearts. A week or so later he wrote briefly asking for my prayers for the next part of his odyssey, 'I don't care where,' he wrote, 'as long as God allows me longer chats – and lighter shovels.'

Yes, and eternal youth, I added, with a sudden insight I probably mistook for wisdom.

Chapter Eighteen

As Mad as a Trappist

It might seem appropriate to apply the tag, 'You don't have to be mad to work here, but it helps' to those who work out their salvation within the four walls of a monastery. You could also say that St Paul's assertion that a guy ' . . . must learn to be a fool before he can really learn to be wise' might have been true applied to first-century Corinthians, but to the latter-day enlightened Christian . . . well, really, I mean to say . . .

Being distanced from the outside world by our seclusion, our manifestly different way of living, plus a mile of water, may have lent enchantment to our humble community. But, medieval clothes and funny haircuts aside, this distancing plus the silence and removal of all distractions, tended to bring on a concentration of the mind that put enchantment and all things ephemeral well beyond the pale.

As Father Lawrence said on my arrival, 'You'll find the first month pretty awful, a bit like withdrawal from an addiction. Surrounded by shelf upon shelf of devotional books, learned exegesis, twenty different translations of the Bible, and even a section on comparative religion, you won't want to pick up one of them. Everything will be as dry as dust; you'll feel drained, wrung out, longing for that elusive whisky or cigarette, the merest familiarity with what used to be, but there no longer.'

In the event I thought I was going out of my mind – and into an arid plateau of desolation; though some would recognise it as a form of brainwashing or even the normal, if extended, rigours of induction. But after that evacuation I began to build, as it were, on a clear

base, and the excitement of matching learning to experience gave my spirit wings. The honeymoon period had
begun.

Others were not so fortunate. A heavily-built older
man, introduced to us as Grant, joined the noviciate,
and exuded a breezy cheerfulness which was a welcome
distraction from the morgue-like sobriety of the atmosphere at the time. After a week or so, however, the
cheerfulness evaporated and we guessed he was beginning to go through it as the rest of us had done. Then
the breeze changed to a sort of ill wind, and to the
rumblings below were added mutterings above. Again I
put it down to his adjustment to our stodgy diet and
Father Maurice's daily affirmation that, with the heavenly banquet in our sights, who cared what the food tasted
like down here.

Poor Grant continued to suffer. His sighs, whether at
the desk or in the field, grew louder and began to be
accompanied by murmurs of discontent, anathema in
The Rule to the spirit of the community. Bent over my
study I would hear an explosive grunt behind me,
followed by a half-whispered 'I can't be having that' or
'That doesn't make sense' and, half-turning, I would
catch sight of his full-jowled florid face, creased with
anguish, as he pencilled notes with great vehemence
down the margins of the book before him. Writing on the
book! This was beginning to look serious.

OK. In school, college or even the local library, this
behaviour would not be seen as the first indications of
madness. Eccentric yes, even reprobate, but not certifi-
able. But learning to live by The Rule was a long, intense
lesson in containment, in the hope that, by living like a
monk on the outside we would, God willing, gradually
mature on the inside until we met up with the Holy Spirit
at the very core of our being. That, to St Benedict, was the
ultimate sanity. There were monks, there are usually one
or two in every community, who get the outside bit right
but then more or less give up the struggle, settle for the
status quo. Now that, even I could see, was madness; to
give up so much and then do nothing with it!

It was evident that Grant was not winning on that first

Harvesting the vegetable crop.

lap of containment. He was beginning to fray at the edges, and the glances we shared with each other betrayed our common concern. Should we share it with Father Lawrence? Did he know already? It even crossed my mind that Grant might have been planted among us, a tare among the wheat, to test our own resolution; but this was quickly put aside as being, in itself, a road towards the quicksands of instability.

Time dragged on and Grant's unease deepened. One afternoon we were sent by Brother Denis to turn over a vegetable bed before he planted it with asparagus. It was a grey day as we trudged there with our forks through the cloddy soil, and the mood didn't lighten as we discovered, under the soil, a rich tapestry of roots and couch grass amidst the gelatinous mud. Still, monks will be monks, and we tackled the impossible task without demur even though we knew we lacked the faith to render the ground clean by the intensity of our prayer. We were more comfortable with the pain.

Not so Grant. He was huffing and puffing right from the start, but after about half an hour he suddenly exploded with wrath and threw his fork down on the ground. 'Why did he give us forks for this job?' he growled loudly for all to hear. 'You can't clean twitch grass with a bloody fork! We need spades – any fool should know that.'

In the prevailing silence his words came like a thunderclap, and we all stopped digging and looked over at him, standing back from the line, red-faced, arms folded. What were we to do? Short of going over and giving him a little hug, which might possibly antagonise him even more or, even worse, cause him to break down in tears, nothing. So we stood for a few moments, looking awkward, and then, one by one, resumed our labours.

This set Grant going again. 'What's the point . . . brothers,' he railed, sounding for all the world like a shop steward rallying the workers. 'We need spades, not forks,' he glared around at us. 'Give us the tools and we'll finish the job.' Now that was pure Winston Churchill addressing the nation during the Second World War. This time we didn't stop and it was beginning to produce the odd suppressed giggle along the line.

Rembert, the senior one of the group, just coming up for his solemn profession, detached himself to try and prevent the outbursts turning into farce. He took Grant by the arm and led him aside, talking to him softly. In a while I noticed Grant sitting down, head bowed and his shoulders gently heaving. It looked as if the dam had burst and all the grief and frustration that had been mounting over the recent weeks was in full flow down the wreckage of his short-lived monastic venture. Later he walked off with Rembert. We carried on, our hearts pounding with the upset of it all and, as if to prove him so right, had to abandon our forks and tear at the undergrowth with our bare hands to make any progress. We would demand spades the next time, that was for sure.

We didn't see Grant again as he had moved into the guesthouse by the time we returned, nor did Father Lawrence make any reference to his departure. It seemed somewhat cruel but The Rule, that spiritual straight-edge, had winnowed the chaff from the wheat and we were all a little wiser, especially, we hoped, Grant, from the experience.

Six months and several novices later – even Rembert had left, having decided not to continue with his solemn vows (and that was a real shock) – we were deep into winter and proceeding apace with the road being built from the jetty to the farm. Every able-bodied monk was engaged in one way or another, from working the mechanical shovel which gathered the shingle from the beach for the concrete, to the setting of the kerb-stones in place when the roadway had set. Father Abbot and Father Prior manned the vibrating machine – another straight-edge making order and containment of the chaos of the concrete mix. Father Lawrence, typically, bounced around on his mechanical moke, carrying supplies hither and thither, and, of course, the noviciate were assigned to the hand-hardening, back-breaking work wherever required.

The focal point of the whole operation, by which the speed of completion could be measured, was the concrete mixer; and crucial to that was the rapid filling of the machine hopper with the correct amounts of ballast (from the beach), cement powder and water. Two at a time, the novices exhausted themselves filling the hopper, waiting briefly while it was hoisted into the mixer, and then filling it again once it was lowered. All under the watchful if roving eye of Lawrence who saw to it that we were never short of the wherewithal. After half an hour another pair were yoked to the task and construction rolled remorselessly on.

It was my turn on shift and I turned, tiredly, to open up another bag of cement. But this time, as I leant down to slice the bag with the blade of my shovel, a puff of the caustic cement powder flew upwards and straight into my eyes. I shut them instinctively with the burning pain and, in spasm, the lids refused to open. I reeled away from the work, screaming with the agony, and was aware of a commotion as everybody downed tools and ran to my side. 'Open your eyes,' I heard. 'I can't, I can't,' I moaned. 'I'll get Francis,' I heard Lawrence roar and off he went. I could feel hands on my shoulder as I knelt on the floor with my hands clutching my head. The pain seemed to be driving inwards as if the centre of my head was being riven.

A calm voice said with authority, 'Now lie on your back, Daniel, and don't mind what I do. It will make the pain better.' It was Father Francis, our doctor infirm-arian, and the next moment he had seized my eyes in turn, forcing them open with both hands. 'Direct the hose into them,' he said, and a jet of immense force hit the raw eyeballs. I screamed again and tried to close my lids but he held them firm. After what seemed an age, satisfied that none of the burning powder remained, the hands were relaxed and my eyes closed once more, although the burning ache made me want to retch as I lay shaking on my side.

But I was in the way and production had to go on. Whether or not the Abbot had come to see why the concrete no longer flowed, I couldn't see, even with my eyelids open. Father Francis led me into the cloister and round to the infirmary with its vacant bed under the window. 'Now just you sit there a moment. I'm going to put some drops of anaesthetic into your eyes which will dilate them and, more important, take the pain away. Then you can take your work clothes off and slip into bed to try and get some sleep, the best cure ' There followed a moment of rare magic as he squeezed the drops in. I felt my pupils widening, widening, until just a red blur blocked my vision. At the same time I could feel the pain recede and my body, racked with tension, relax. I slipped into bed and unconsciousness almost immediately.

It appeared that only one of my eyes was badly affect-ed but the treatment of cleaning them of the discharge was so painful that the bucket was always by my side. Eventually I was able to leave the infirmary and return to the noviciate, a patch over the bad eye and with strict instructions not to attempt to read with the other. I wasn't to study; I couldn't work; I was exempted the night office; what was a novice to do?

'Go for walks as long as you stay in the enclosure. Father Edmund has a gramophone and some records which you can listen to in the guesthouse chapel. Eat in the sick refectory with Father Finbar where you can have meat, fish and eggs, and may God and Father Maurice have mercy on your soul.' This was Father Lawrence who added grimly, 'And don't get too used to it. As mountaineers say of the ascent, 'Try not to lose the height you've gained.' Believe me, you'll only regret it.'

He stopped short of telling me not to enjoy myself, so I did. No part of the enclosure, roughly half the island, was left unexplored. Idyllic bays of rock and sand; little caverns exposed between the tides in the limestone rock; long paths around the sleeping fields; patches of original woodland. On one icy walk I saw ahead of me a large black bird dart down a path trying to hide. When I pursued it the curlew made abortive attempts to fly away but couldn't. Its wings seemed to be frozen, and as I cornered it the eyes stretched wide in terror and the great curved beak opened and shut revealing tiny scraps of dirt and ice.

I suddenly felt at one with God's world of living creatures. I picked it up and covered it in the folds of the black cloak I was wearing and turned my steps towards the noviciate where I could warm its frozen body. But as I uncovered my hand to open the door the bird, its wings already loosened, swooped out of my hold and was away, up, and heading for the sea in an instant. I wanted to run inside and tell them all my incredible story but suddenly held back, aware that our lives were lived apart now and would be until I could take up the flow once again. A warning moment.

Again, I was sitting in the chapel listening to the majestic rendering of a Bach Partita on the harpsichord. I turned the volume up to its highest and sat there with tears streaming down my face. It was as if, like Grant, all the tension of this unequal fight was released, though, unlike Grant, all I felt was a delirious happiness. It was ecstasy but also a warning that I was really enjoying myself much too much for comfort.

Eventually the day approached to return to normal noviciate life. The eyes were better and the patch had already been removed. I felt on the top of my form, renewed in body and spirit, able to take on, if not demons, at least Father Lawrence, the novice-tamer, cracking his whip in a thousand subtle ways. Of course it was hard getting up so early; I fell asleep during mental prayer; I couldn't wait for coffee and a crust after Lauds; I was bored stiff during the long private study period before and after Prime.

By the time we were into the community Mass, some six hours after getting up I was exhausted. Well, my legs were trembling which was how they felt after concrete making, so it must be tiredness. But as I sat down during the class period they were still shaking; in fact, the slight buzz was not only in my legs but throughout my whole body. I realised I was anxious about it, uneasy, and that this distracted me from – no, got in the way of applying myself to study, to work and to prayer. Well, where prayer was concerned it took over completely, my anxious mind running round and round in circles of restless anxiety about running round and round in circles of restless anxiety.

'Don't worry about it,' said Lawrence when I took it to him that evening. 'It's bound to be difficult to pick up the life again just like that. I told you it would be. It'll come soon enough – just don't worry about it.'

He didn't tell me, however, how to stop worrying about something I was worrying about without knowing what I was worrying about. Indeed, his tone had an edge to it that sounded as if, underneath, he was worrying about what I didn't know I was worrying about.

After a restless night I found that my condition had not altered except, perhaps that it had got somehow deeper. I was desperately miserable and had no appetite for food nor anything else. But I didn't want Lawrence interrogating me so I kept out of his way, not even looking at him in class or the allocation of work. As we were going out to the Compline, the final Office of the day, he came out of his room as I was passing and he drew me back inside.

'Feeling better, Daniel?' He asked, 'Wobbly legs OK?'

'Not really,' I replied, 'In fact they're a bit wobblier.'

'Look, maybe you're a bit more tired than you think.

Don't come down to Night Office and Lauds. And try to eat well – I noticed you hardly ate anything today. Now that's not good enough. We've got to give it our best shot, you know. Don't let the enemy get to us, OK.'

He didn't expand so I didn't know which enemy was getting to him or if he thought it was the same enemy that was getting to me.

I was awake – I had hardly slept – when the bell rang for Night Office, and I listened to my fellow novices creak out of their beds and plod along the corridor and down the steps. Then there was silence followed by the distant intonation of the monotone chant. That was when the anxiety turned into dread. I was in a nameless world of waiting in suspense, waiting for the chant to stop, then waiting for it to start again, then waiting for the first footstep up the stairs, empty when nothing happened, fearful when it did. Where was I, who was I in all this?

Eventually Lawrence's head poked round the doorway. 'You missed Prime.'

'I can't,' I whispered.

'Now look, you've got to get a grip on yourself.' Suddenly the humour had gone leaving only the bite. What could I say? I turned to the wall, desperate to shut him out, shut everything out. I sensed he had gone and lay there curled up, in limbo.

I became aware that someone had come quietly in and was sitting on the side of the bed.

'Hello, young fellow.' It was Father Francis, the infirmarian. 'Father Lawrence tells me you're not feeling too well. Says you've a touch of the jitters, the heebie-jeebies. Now, if you could sit yourself up I'll have a little look at you.'

Well, at least he wasn't telling me to get a grip on myself so, with what seemed a supreme effort, I turned to face him. He had a reassuring smile on his face.

'Now let's have a look at those eyes of yours.' He fished a pencil torch out of his pocket and looked closely. I could smell the coffee on his breath.

'Well, nothing there to worry about. Now, for the rest

I think you need a little rub of the magic wand.' What was he talking about?

'We'll need to get you down to the infirmary, I think; that's where we keep the magic wand, you know. Just slip your shoes on and see if you can make it down the stairs with me. That's it,' as I shakily got to my feet, 'Hold on to my arm if you need to.'

I had no idea of the time and was only dimly aware of the morning bustle in the cloister. I clung to him as we slowly made our way to his room. There seemed no sense nor reason in anything, and I was conscious only of his presence as he hummed cheerfully getting this and that on the edge of my existence. I focused on him bending down over me, a glass and two tablets in his hands.

'Right, now for the rub of the magic wand, Daniel. Just take these and wait for the magic. We'll have you playing for Celtic before you know it.'

What was he talking about, I asked myself as I mechanically took the tablets? Celtic? Magic wand? Strange man, but somehow a comfort.

'Now just sit there; I have to go out for a minute, and if you feel tired you may lie on the bed. Just remember, you've had the rub of the wand and you have to wait patiently for the effect.' He was gone.

What was he talking about? I sat, head in hands, conscious only of the tangle of thoughts and feelings swirling about, none of them good.

Francis didn't return and I began to feel light-headed, so I got up with a great effort and laid down on the bed I had vacated not so long ago after my accident. Some of the memories of that agony came back to me. Had it all started then? What was wrong with me? Was this the onset of madness?

Suddenly I was aware that the creases in my brow were being smoothed out as if by the gentlest of hands, and that this released warm waves of easement, creeping through the top of my head, down the back of my neck and over the shoulders. Then the waves reversed and swept up and over my head. I was drifting into unconsciousness but with what seemed a smile on my face, saying 'Thank you, Lord, for the rub of the wand.'

It was, of course, a tranquilliser I had taken, and to which I had responded so readily. Wary of Lawrence's draconian bedside manner, Francis took over my second convalescence, decreasing the dosage gradually but returning me to the noviciate and the full noviciate life within the week. Lawrence seemed cool towards me for several days and didn't call me in for a chat. Maybe he'd been warned by Father Francis that, in the words of St Charles Borromeo, a spoonful of sugar was better than a barrelful of vinegar, and he just didn't feel up to that sort of molly-coddling.

One evening, having worked all afternoon with Father Oswald and his battery hens, I met Lawrence on my way to Compline and he pulled me into his office.

'How were your little mates, then?' I was mystified. 'Who do you mean?'

'Why, the chickens of course. Who else, apart from you, is prone to sudden acute attacks of anxiety.'

Ouch! If this was Lawrence's way of making the peace . . .

'Was that the official diagnosis, then?' I asked.

'Well, what do you think? Who's the novice who likes to live the life at 100 miles an hour?'

I was thunderstruck. Did I have that reputation? I knew that I tried very hard to live the vows to the letter, even though I hadn't yet taken any. I also knew that I had repeated attacks of acid and jippy tummy and seldom really felt relaxed.

'Is that wrong, then' I asked.

'Well, shall we say that if you go on like this, you won't make old bones, as my granny used to say.'

This was a very different Lawrence from the acerbic novice-master of my breakdown.

'Well, why were you so heavy on me when I was feeling low, telling me to snap out of it, etc. etc?'

He sat back, colouring up.

'Was I that bad?' he said.

'Yes, that bad, I'm afraid. I think you even put the wind up Father Francis.'

'Oh dear!' He was still for a moment and then smiled

at me, blushing. I'd never seen him blush before – hadn't thought him capable of it.

'We're very alike, you and I, birds of a feather – yes, a bit like Ossie's brood, in fact. I tend to go at things like a bull at a gate, you may have noticed. Indeed, I had an episode like yours when I was a novice, under Father Finbar. And if you think I'm hard, thank God you weren't exposed to his bedside manner, bless him. He well and truly gave me the works when I went all wobbly-legged. And tranquillisers weren't on the menu; neither was Father Francis. So I just hung in there and sweated it through – the most miserable three months of my life. When I saw you going down that road I'm afraid I panicked and did a Finbar. Sorry! And thank God old Fran came to the rescue, eh.'

He was still blushing; I could have hugged him.

'I really thought I was going mad at one stage, as mad as a hatter.'

'As mad as a Trappist, you mean,' he chortled. 'You know, when the Holy Trinity are giving out laurels at the great prize giving in the sky, I'm sure we'll get the triangular hats instead – the ones with the big D on them – D for Dope.'

'Or D for Difficult, like the rock-climbing grade,' I added. 'I do tend to make things hard for myself.'

He rose, a sign that our reconciliation was complete. 'I hope that, one day, the Lord will say to you, "You can stop climbing, Daniel; you reached the top a long time ago.'

Chapter Nineteen

Forgive us our Trespasses

It would have been unusual for anybody living on an island less than a mile wide not to chart their lives by the sea. But such was the insistence on protecting the novice's life from any contact with the outside world that we were never encouraged to go near it. We didn't need to sail on it or swim in it, and we didn't fish in it because we didn't eat fish, although one or other of the older monks could, on occasion, be seen fishing for bass off a low rock to provide a guesthouse supper.

However, it provided the backcloth, pleasant or dismal, depending on the weather, to everything we did. More, it seasoned the air we breathed, it purified our light, it gave us the sea birds in great profusion (a hoopoe had previously been just a great Scrabble word for using up 'o's); driftwood washed up on the beach gave us enough kindling for our big boiler and the island hearths; most of all it gave us that sense of isolation from the rest of mankind – a boundary which defined our community in a way that no fences or gates could have done.

Having said that, there were occasions when even the most diligent novice would seek a change of scenery, a walk just for the sake of a walk, without risk of being labelled restless or incurring censure. Sunday afternoon was such an opportunity when the slot between None and Vespers, filled on weekdays by manual work, lay fallow. The coastline to the west and north was within the monastic enclosure and prohibited to the general public, and the bays and limestone coves provided an idyllic adventure playground to the energetic novice who could play Robinson Crusoe on virgin beaches till it was time to grow up again.

One such cove, Paul Jones Bay, reputed to be used in times past by a pirate and smuggler of that name because of its seclusion from mainland vigilantes, became my favourite recreational outlet. It lay immediately beyond a dense pine wood which had defied all Brother Denis' attempts to gain land for cultivation. A narrow path threading its way through generations of needles suddenly gave way to a shallow clearing and a sharp drop of some sixty feet on to rocks and sand. A precipitous route to one side gave access to the agile or else it was a lengthy walk round the sea line at low tide. It was not often frequented for this reason and the fanciful notion that it was my bay added to its Sunday afternoon appeal.

Such excursions sometimes yielded a reward other than the exercise, usually washed up by the sea. I remember finding a huge dead fish on the beach one day whose mouth, when I picked it up, dropped open to reveal a gaping chasm I could have climbed into without any trouble. On another occasion so many starfish were washed in that the gulls glutted themselves on their soft underparts, lifting them up to smash them down on the rocks high above the tide. The stench of their decomposition kept me away for a fortnight.

On one occasion, I walked to the bay at dead of night. There was a period between the night office and the dawn Office of Lauds which varied slightly according to season and was assigned to private prayer. It had been customary for us to spend it in church warding off sleep with some difficulty in the stuffy atmosphere. We had complained about this and it was decided to allow us to stretch our legs and pray where and how we wished – a miracle of democracy in an absolute if benign dictatorship.

At the first opportunity, therefore, about four o'clock the next morning, I turned my steps towards Paul Jones Bay in a spirit I must allow a little removed from prayer. A clear moonlit sky saw me through the gardens without any trouble, but the moment I entered the pine wood I felt less certain; in fact I felt lost and scared. Soon I had strayed from the narrow path (there was a moral in that) and was being clawed at by every low branch or thorn bush encountered, stumbling over shrubs, stubbing my feet on the occasional rock. Something scampered away from under my feet and a bloodcurdling shriek seconds later announced its demise, probably due to me blowing its cover. My heart pounded in my chest and the blind panic I felt rising needed all my common sense to quell – and I was supposed to be in prayer!

Suddenly I was out of the wood and very nearly over the cliff. I stood stock still shaking and panting. There below me lay the sea lapping gently, the colour of pewter. The silence was absolute and I knelt down sitting on my heels, unsure whether to praise God for his silent world, thank him for my deliverance or apologise for my folly. As I knelt there a slight movement to one side attracted my attention and I picked out a gull perched just below the top of the cliff, fast asleep, with its head tucked underneath its wing. I ran my eyes along the ledge and noticed more sleeping birds: then, along every terraced moulding in the cliff face to see row upon row of hundreds of birds, all white-robed like their human brothers and at rest, secure in their cliffside stalls. I was dumbstruck and could only thank God in a silent prayer that I was there, receiving peace from their peace. The minutes passed in quiet until I remembered with a sudden shock that I was going to be late for Lauds if I didn't make an immediate move. I rose gently and reluctantly, submitting myself to another rough ride across the wood, though this time too uplifted to be fearful.

Of course, I was late; I picked up the drone of the chant as I got to the side door and crept in unobtrusively. I sat down inconspicuously enough until a loud crackle told me, and my neighbours, that I had sat on a small branch and, looking down, was appalled to see my whole tunic bedecked with needles, leaves and burrs like some vagabond Worzel Gummidge. It's a fair cop, I said to myself and, after choir, awaited Father

Lawrence's lashing sarcasm almost with detachment. I scanned the Rule for excommunicable offences but, apart from being late for Office, there was no punishment for impersonating a tree. When, later, I owned up to Lawrence and enthusiastically described the wonder of the sleeping birds he just snorted and asked where I thought they slept – in a sea-front bed and breakfast, perhaps?

One Sunday afternoon in May I took my habitual stroll through the pine wood, cruising over the needles, noticing how the bluebells forced their way up no matter what, when I heard the sound of voices, something alien to my perception of this part of the island. I made my way cautiously forward to the cliff edge and, without being observed, spotted a large white launch in Paul Jones Bay. A rowing boat was drawn up on the sand and several men and a woman were clambering around among the rocks conversing in echoing tones. I couldn't believe it – people, in my bay. They couldn't be smugglers, not so openly on a Sunday afternoon. Nor were they just affluent trippers since one of them carried a millboard and paper and another a measuring tape. Prospectors, perhaps, but for what? Should I approach them, ask them for a piece of cheese like Ben Gunn; or clear them off our property, though they could claim the common right to stay below the high water level. Instinct told me not to get involved. As Lawrence would have said, it was no job for a novice to interview visitors, however suspicious.

I ran back to the novitiate and, barging into his room, told him of the invasion breathlessly. 'OK, calm down,' he said, 'they're probably here quite innocently. I've known boats anchor there before, just looking for a quiet spot to do some sunbathing or snorkelling.' Nevertheless, when I sat down at my desk I saw him pass the window heading for Paul Jones Bay at a pace.

I popped into Lawrence after supper, unable to restrain my curiosity. 'Oh that,' he said airily,' actually they were from a film company. When I confronted them with the fact that they were trespassing they assumed an innocent air and said they had no idea, but had been attracted by the dimensions and desolate nature of the cove which would be perfect for a scene in a film they were making. They said they would pay handsomely for the use of the site, so I referred them to the Abbot whom they could contact in the normal way, on a weekday. They said they would and left. I saw them off and watched them head for the mainland. Probably the last we'll see of them.' I knew somehow that it wouldn't be.

About a fortnight later the Abbot announced in Chapter that a company was doing some filming in Paul Jones Bay, so the bay and the cliff top area would be off limits until they had finished about a fortnight later. We quizzed Father Lawrence that morning, but he didn't know a lot more, just that they would be erecting a set, gaining access throughout by the sea so as to minimise the disturbance, and that they had made the Abbot an offer he couldn't refuse. 'Armchairs for the novitiate?' I asked. 'Books for the library, I hope,' retorted Lawrence who was also the house librarian. 'Do they want any extras?' joked Luke, but Lawrence was instantly serious. 'Look, this has nothing to do with us so I don't want any sly walks to Paul Jones Bay. You became monks to keep in touch with reality. Their business is to feed fantasies. Our worlds are a million miles apart.' We heard nothing more about it except later, through the grapevine, that filming had started.

Two days later, I was on kitchen duty and Father Maurice decided to make a guesthouse cake. His excursions into patisserie were few and far between and usually followed a compliment on his cooking (equally rare) by a guest which was brought back with great enthusiasm by Father Aelred. If the praise came from a child it merited a cake, and the whole performance of putting the simple ingredients together would be carried out with an air of festival, an impish smile and intoned lullabies remembered from childhood. The iced monster would later be carried by Maurice with great panache round to the guesthouse at tea time, and the luckless young creep who had praised him subjected to a bewildering billing and cooing from the lovable cook.

Such an indiscretion had obviously just been committed by a young guest, and Maurice, in full culinary flight,
was suddenly checked by the discovery that he was
clean out of eggs. His cap of rage went flying into the air
but he was only stumped for a minute. Remembering
that it was, by sheer coincidence, the time of the year
when seagulls were laying eggs on their cliff top nests
he summoned me explaining, with a mixture of sign
language and Franglais running commentary, my
mission.

'Les seagulls ...' flap, flap, with his arms, 'le nid ...
nest ... des oeufs, ... Va-t-en ... take ... l'un seule-
ment, s'il vous plait ... Attention, eh!'

I knew exactly what he meant since I had been on a
similar expedition before. Seagulls always lay their eggs
in clutches of three for comfort, and to take one egg
from a nest merely unbalances the hen who promptly
goes about laying another to restore herself to an even
keel. The eggs were larger, stronger and fishier than the
normal domestic egg but were quite adequate for
cooking, well, for Father Maurice's cooking.

I needed no encouragement to leave the kitchen for
the windy heights of the cliff top with its clumps of
sweet-smelling thrift. I was up there in a few minutes
and quickly located a lonely spot where nests had been
prepared in little hollows every few yards. The mission
was not without its danger as vigilant fathers on the
look out for just such predators as myself would buzz
me, swooping in within inches of my head with a menac-
ing screech. However, by running and ducking at the
moment of attack I managed to raid four nests, pocket-
ed one large warm egg from each and turned for home.

As I did so, I was attracted by a commotion of birds in
the sky to my left. Of course, Paul Jones Bay was the
next cove along and there would be plenty going on
there to attract these bright-eyed gulls. Suddenly, I
found my feet turning towards the activity. I could not
resist the opportunity to see what they were doing to
my bay. No one would know, unless Lawrence himself
were there, acting as local consultant on island features
– maybe even playing a bit part as a wandering holy

man. I approached quietly towards a good vantage point
from which I could take in the whole scene without
being observed.

I could not believe what I saw. Was this my bay?
There was a large white-walled cottage up there on the
top just where I had seen the host of sleeping birds.
How had I never noticed it before? The high masts with
spotlights on the tops; the confusion of power lines
criss-crossing the beach, the fifty or so people all
working purposefully though independently, moving
over the sand and rocks like ants; the launch and small
boats involved offshore or pulled into the beach; and
was that really a U-boat just outside the bay floating
peacefully on the gentle swell. So this was a film set. It
was fascinating – I was drawn to stay and observe the
activity, but I had to get back or Maurice would wonder
if I had gone to the mainland to get his eggs.

I decided to walk back through the pine wood and
made my way round to it carefully. I had to pass behind
the white cottage so I turned to inspect it to make sure
it was as temporary as it must be. As I crept close to it
I could see that it was just a shell with no interior or
back to it at all. The walls were made of a light material
though very cunningly dressed to look quite rustic even
from close quarters. How else could they have brought
it over on the launch. It was so funny I wanted to share
it with the others, but realised I was condemned to
silence and ... Oh God, I was going to be late ... I
stepped back quickly and almost into the arms of a
young woman who had appeared from nowhere.

'Watch what you're doing!' she barked in her fright,
'and who the hell are you anyway, snooping on the set
... oh my God, you must be one of ... from the
monastery over ...' She was in her twenties, slim and
dressed in a purple shirt and blue jeans. Her face was
deeply tanned and her eyes in her alarm were enormous. I felt I had seen her somewhere before – perhaps
she was an actress of repute.

What was I to do? Barge past her and fly away like a
hoopoe caught on the hop. Every norm of monasticism
was bidding me to make such a retreat, yet a stronger

instinct made me tarry and normalise the encounter. 'I'm sorry,' I stammered, 'I shouldn't have been snooping – I was just passing.' I turned to go, 'Please don't go,' she said quickly. 'After all, it is your island and we're the intruders.' She smiled and immediately relaxed in spite of being in such close company with an alien species. 'Tell me, what do you do here as a monk? I guess I'm really fascinated by all this monastic stuff – I was thrilled when David said he was bringing the set here. Say, what's that egg you're holding, for Chris . . .?' She put her hand over her mouth in embarrassment.

I looked at the egg I had taken out in my nervousness. 'Oh, I couldn't possibly explain our life to you; I hardly understand it myself yet – I'm only a novice.' God, were all women as confident and pushy these days or had she learnt it from the trade she was in? 'The egg is easier, borrowed from a seagull for a guesthouse cake. But look, I shouldn't really be talking to you; our Rule forbids talking altogether, except in emergencies to strangers like yourself, except that this isn't an emergency. I'm afraid it's a curiosity.'

She laughed. 'Well, that puts me in my place. But look here, I'm a seeker after the truth, like yourself, and I've always wanted to ask one of you guys the question why . . . what right do you think you have to cut yourself off from the rest of us, the way you do.'

I was a little nettled by her aggression but I couldn't resist the challenge. 'Well then, what is it that fascinates you about us if we're just a lot of selfish loners. Isn't it rather that our search for the truth leads us away from the world because God has gone before us commanding us to find him. Also because we admit we are unequal to the task of finding God out there in the world. I mean, how do you hope to find the truth in a world of fantasy like yours?' Oh dear, I had already said too much, and now I had challenged her.

'Fantasy,' she snorted, colouring up. 'Fiddlesticks! Mine is a job just like yours. The truth lies in the people I work with and play with. The films are just stories about other people's truths and they can serve just as worthy a purpose in their way as you think you can in yours.'

We both paused and then she smiled. I was surprised how normal I felt. Where was my confusion and guilt?

'Look,' she said, 'I can imagine how complex your life is, and I really do admire your commitment even if I don't understand it. But tell me, does this life really fulfil you – does it make you happy?'

I reflected a moment. My thoughts were in a constant state of turmoil these days, but that was not through unfulfilment – just not having hours enough in the day to read, to meditate and to pray. After nearly a year I was head over heels in love. 'I've never been happier,' I said. 'For the first time in my life, in the words of the song, I know where I'm going and I know who's going with me. To be making a journey with the one you love has to be heaven on earth, doesn't it?'

She looked, almost stared at me for what seemed an age. 'Oh, I don't know about any journey. I take life as it comes. I have someone I love very much. I want to campaign against the injustice I see all around me. Life will never be dull,' she blushed a little. 'Actually, one of my adolescent ambitions was to make a film about a nun. I'd do it in black and white and in total silence. I'd show her conquest of sin by a thousand daily crucifixions hidden in a life of self-denial. Your idea seems positively romantic by comparison.'

'Sounds like a pretty boring film to me,' I commented, 'I think U-boats off the British coast will get bigger audiences any day. The inner beauty of our life would be hard to capture. Though working with our cook, Father Maurice, in his grotty kitchen, would get the comedy award any day.'

I remembered the eggs with a start. 'Gosh, he'll kill me if I don't get these eggs to him. Look, come to Compline in the church, any evening at seven fifteen. It's very beautiful – still gives me goose pimples. Goodbye.'

She held out her hand as if to stop me. 'What's your name? Could I meet you again perhaps; there's so many questions I want to ask. Please!'

I turned and ran into the pine wood scarcely caring whether I broke the eggs or not. I was mad to have stayed. What did I think I was doing. I could feel the excitement of her last invitation already beginning to challenge the hard-won silences within me. How would I cope with her memory at night in the warmth and tiredness of my bed. Or those long afternoons in the fields – would she haunt my tedious exercises of detachment from day dreaming? What an indulgence I had granted the Tempter! What a fool I had been!

Father Maurice got his eggs. The guesthouse child presumably got his cake. I got a bad attack of conscience. I had certainly done nothing wrong. I hadn't sinned had I? I had merely responded to another's need. I had been courteous and fairly brief. But could I share my trespasses at Paul Jones Bay with Father Lawrence. No, that was a step I feared to take. I dared not expose myself to his scorn. He might also view it more seriously than I did. I couldn't risk upsetting . . . everything.

Compline that night came and went without a sound from the gallery, though I was aware for several Complines to come of her invisible presence. I said nothing, and suffered abundantly. The nightmares and the daydreams punished me hard and caused many a heartache.

One day Lawrence reported to the assembled novices that a young lady had enquired at the guesthouse about a young monk she had met . . . carrying an egg. 'I told Aelred it couldn't have been one of us as I would have heard about it, surely,' he looked around as we all giggled at the very idea . . . carrying an egg! I hesitated and the opportunity for heroism (or martyrdom) was gone. In time I got over the confusion and the guilt, and the memory faded, carrying with it a little of my carefree love of the life. I was more guarded, less the liberated soul St Benedict had in mind for me.

Months later, with Paul Jones Bay now back in bounds, I went there as a pilgrim one Sunday afternoon. It felt fine. It was great to tread through those pine needles again and scramble down to that deserted beach. It was so easy to praise God in the economy of this landscape, in the spaciousness of my life. As I re-entered the wood at the top of the cliff a flash of white caught my attention. It looked like a page from a small notebook pinned to a tree. My blood suddenly froze and my heart thumped in my chest. Had it . . .? Could she . . .? Should I . . .? In a torment of conflicting feelings I tore it from the tree, hardly daring to fasten my gaze on the sheet. I needn't have bothered. It may have contained a message once, but the weather had totally erased it.

Empty and defeated I slowly walked back to the noviciate, tearing the paper pieces into smaller pieces. Suddenly the devil was back on my shoulder, the burden of folly and weakness weighing me down. Then a further thought stopped me, sweating, in my tracks. I could share the load, seek its absolution in confession, perhaps, though I doubted there was actual sin involved. But if I were to honour the truth . . . the truth that she, a mere dealer in fantasies, claimed to value so much in her work . . . then I would have to reveal all, first, to Lawrence?

But how could I, now, after all this time?

But, for any peace of mind in the immediate future, how could I not?

Chapter Twenty

Family

For the zealous monk family can be a problem. Monastic tradition, i.e., the Rule, the Sayings of the Desert Fathers, etc., assume that the break between the monk and his former life is complete and final. The solemn promise of Stability directs him to stay rooted in the monastery, while the promise of Conversion would have the monk count the past as historic and the present as imperfect, but sufficient. The family ceases to exist and the community takes its place. Simple.

And simple enough it was for me, some nine months into the life. I had survived the trauma of separation and now, like the Easter bunny, bounding joyfully among the foothills, sniffing and nibbling at God's new creation, flexing my puny muscles, unmindful of the precipitous ascent and the distant hawk – wasn't I monasticism's mountain lion. Family! Who needed family?

Well, my family needed family. Or, to be precise, my mother needed me. When she had dried her tears on my departure, and subsequently heard from me that I was now a bona fide novice, the hope burgeoned in her that while she may have lost a son she might well have gained a community.

Her letters arrived without fail on the first Saturday of every month and Father Lawrence decreed that while I was subject to him the law of charity overrode my desire for sanctuary and I should reply as frequently. So a filial letter sped to the capital by boat and train every first Monday describing the island, the monastery, the weather, the meals, even the daily programme, while the other ninety-nine per cent of my life remained hidden from her as I had no words to convey to those I loved how in love with this life I had become.

Her letters, sweet though they were and charged with sighs, proved a constant irritant to the tender tissue of my new persona. An innocent remark would go like, 'West Ham are doing very well at the moment, especially Groom who's scoring lots of goals, so your Dad's happy. Do you remember the one he scored in the cup final last year?' Of course I remembered, and come Vespers or the afternoon work period, my attention to duty would fight a losing battle with a succession of Match of the Day action replays and Groom's volley into the top corner.

This might be followed by the, surely, less innocent comment: 'I saw Marian last Sunday at Mass. She's looking lovelier than ever and I heard she's getting engaged to ... guess who ... none other than Mark Prior who you always thought was a bit of a drip.' Of course, in my new-found strength I could cope with the vision of an ever lovelier Marian, but somehow she would find her way on to my pillow as I tried to drift into sleep, and I was thankful for my rarely used rosary beads, a loving parent's parting gift, to control my thoughts and my fingers.

'You should treat it, I certainly shall, as a valuable indicator of your ability to live at ease with yourself,' Father Lawrence commented crisply when I shared my discomfort. 'If you're constantly being upset by simple items of news from home, it means you're probably living the life here under tension, and that's dangerous if it's sustained for too long. One of the purposes of the two-year novitiate is that it gives you time to relax under the Rule and learn the art of separating the essential from the peripheral – the great spiritual gift of discernment. Another purpose is to show if you have what it takes.'

'Yes,' I replied, feeling the sting of his diagnosis, 'but raking up old memories just muddies the water that this life is supposed to be clearing. It's like a punch that gets through your defence because you're not expecting it to come from such a loving source.'

'Which just goes to show that you're a bit too intense about everything at the moment, Daniel,' he observed tartly. 'Anyway, with summer a'coming you can be sure that, even as we speak, plans will be taking shape back on the ranch for a family holiday on this romantic island. The idea of seeing their son and brother, visiting his mysterious island home and having a lovely holiday at no great expense, will have occurred to your family even if it hadn't to you. And it would be churlish to deny them a little taste of the fruits that you enjoy all the time.' He was surely winding me up. 'So if you think getting letters is distracting just you wait until the guesthouse is full of your nearests and dearests and you know that they're there or up in the gallery, and see how well you concentrate on the deeper meaning of life then.'

He was right. As a seasoned novice I was now making up for my hesitant start and living life in the fast lane. No study was too profound to challenge my desire to penetrate and absorb the monastic spirituality. No task too arduous or menial to quench my zeal for bringing my body, Brother Ass, into subjection. Yet, for this knight in arms who sought only greater dragons to slay, the prospect of a family visit had me running scared.

I couldn't help thinking of my first day here and the happy, bouncing O'Connell family visiting their Kevin. Had it been mere coincidence that he had left the monastery a few months after their visit or had its disruption of his fledgling life been too much to take. And yet there was Father Aelred, the guest-master, daily consorting with the whole world without turning a hair – not that he had a hair on his smooth dome worth turning!

So anxious was I that I summoned the courage to knock at the Abbot's door. Father Lawrence might not approve of novices seeking second opinions but I felt a crisis coming on. He looked up from his desk as I walked over the bare floorboards to sit beside my austere master. I was staggered to see that he was reading what looked like *The Times*. Families! Newspapers! Was this flight from the world really only for the brochures?

'It seems to be the custom around here for novices to

have their folks down, though I can never see why,' he said breezily when I had stumbled through my enquiry. 'My mother would move in permanently if I gave her half a chance. I mean, the pluses are all on their side while we have only the Gospel to cling to. When Jesus says, 'Who is my mother; who is my brother?' he is clearly stating that the Kingdom supersedes the family. Goodness, what more can we do than run away to a small island in the Atlantic Ocean, but even then they don't seem to get the message. I certainly wouldn't encourage them to come, but you'd better see what your novice-master has to say. His family visits regularly enough without bothering him.'

Well, if you want a hard line go to a hard man. Yet, strangely, his dismissal of the family as an evil you grow out of, like spots, was too harsh a judgement for my tender condition and I quickly bounced back to Lawrence. Predictably, this family lover struck a different note.

'We're not in the fantasy business here, you know, so don't imagine you're so heavenly yet that you can cut the cord of your earthly origins. Don't get too precious about this separation from the world. Keep your old girlfriends at bay if you can but hearing about West Ham's fortunes is hardly tempting providence (so he did read my letters!). Most parents go away after their visit reassured that their baby boy is in good hands – some even give a donation,' he added gaily. 'It all helps to pay for your privileged seclusion.'

As if they had been colluding, the very next letter from my mother brought the announcement of her intentions. 'You haven't said anything further about our visit since you mentioned it in your first letter, but Daddy and I can't wait to see the monastery and the island you describe so beautifully in your letters.' I ground my teeth at this indiscretion. Why couldn't I have said it was like the Falklands! 'Anyway, we'd like to come in August sometime, if that's all right, so that Mick and Jenny and the kids can make it, and perhaps Maureen and Eric and family as well if they can get down from Scotland.'

My heart missed a beat – the whole bloomin' family was coming. A quick calculation told me that this made twelve adults and children in all. I knew I would find it hard to cope with but, at this rate, could the community survive! I rushed in to Lawrence, who raised his eyebrows at this very unquiet novice, and blurted out the terrible news. His reaction was amazing. 'Twelve, eh. Now let's see; if we sleep the larger of the families in the cottage by the jetty, and move in some beds to the large bedroom in the guesthouse . . .' I was flabbergasted. It was all a game to him, a strategy of sleeping and eating. To me it was a tragedy in the making.

'But what about the sheer numbers,' I pleaded. 'How will Maurice cope with the extra cooking?' 'How will they cope with Maurice's cooking, more like it,' he laughed. 'Don't worry, you seem to forget we live by faith here.' 'Yes,' I replied, worn down by the indifference of his worldliness. 'But it's my faith I'm worried about. How am I going to manage? 'Ah,' said Lawrence, immediately serious. 'That's the problem, is it – ordeal by family? Numbers don't come into it, do they, as much as chemistry. Now we're going to see what you're made of.' Too right! I felt I was playing in a match with the referee blatantly in favour of the other side. Win I knew I couldn't, but twelve to one!

As August approached my mother broke the rules and letters appeared every Saturday, shorter, perhaps, but loaded with menace. 'We're all getting so excited. Micky's picking us up in London so we'll arrive together while your sister and Eric make their own way down.' 'I really hope the weather turns out nice 'cos I've bought a lovely off-white summery dress. Dad says it'll match your habit perfectly. Maybe I can slip into the monastery when nobody's looking.' It was all a game; everybody was playing games, but I was the one who stood to get hurt.

I even raised it one evening with Father Prior, the Abbot's deputy, to whom I went weekly for confession. Neither ascetic like the Abbot nor free-thinker like Lawrence, he might provide me with an escape clause, but no. 'We are monks, yes, but not the *monachus* of the third century living alone in the desert. We haven't run away from the Church as they did because the laxity of its life was a scandal to them. We are still in and of the Church and everything we do is prompted by love, is it not. We must ask ourselves, Daniel, which is the greater denial; to keep them away or to allow them to come. Or again, where is the growth; you must always ask yourself where is the growth.' I gave up resisting but still couldn't feel the growth.

The great day dawned and the Abbot's rising bell at 3.00 a.m. had an ominous ring to it. All the different parts of the day: the application to the Divine Office, feeding the prayer by recurrent acts of consciousness of what was passing before my eyes and through my mind – well, that went for a burton. Silent prayer before Lauds passed prayerlessly. Instead I just knelt watching the deep blue of the early morning sky through the window become ever lighter and brighter. Study time tasted like a piece of stale bread, while even the real bread and coffee after Prime seemed to have lost some of its delight. I threw myself into the morning work like a maniac and never had the toilets shone for so little gritting of the teeth.

By the time Vespers arrived I was living in a different world. I scarcely knew when to turn the page, and was distractedly moving on to the second psalm when a child's voice from the gallery exploded in my head and left shock waves dancing up and down my spine. They had arrived. The enquiring voice continued. 'Is this a church, daddy?' 'Sshh!' 'I can hear the men singing, daddy, but I can't see them.' 'Sssshhh!' 'Is Uncle Paddy down there, daddy?' 'Sssssssshhhhhh!' I looked up red of face and prepared to smile it out but not an eye strayed from the psalters, not a snigger from a fellow novice. Then there was a crash from the gallery and a wail of such ferocity as to cause a slight ripple in the chant. A scuffle ensued and a door banged shut and one small child's introduction to music a thousand years old was prematurely aborted. Silence reigned but a rage surged irrationally within me caught as I was in the crossfire of the Opus Dei and this Opera Comique. Vespers drew to a close and as we filed into supper the odd nudge from a shrouded friend told me that I had not imagined the interruption.

After supper Father Lawrence caught me up on the way back to the novitiate. 'Normally you would have to wait until tomorrow afternoon to greet your folks but I must be getting soft in my old age. Why not pop into the guesthouse now and put yourself out of your misery. Somebody obviously wants his Uncle Paddy. Mind you're back for Compline though – the show must go on.'

In the guesthouse all the noise was coming from the dining room. I hesitated, pondering that if we were called a religious Order then what was going on in there was a demonic disorder. If that was free speech then thank God for elected silence. But for all that the voices thrilled me for they belonged to the people I loved, and I sprang into the room with a shout of welcome.

It stopped the show. In a moment of stunned silence I looked at the twelve faces gazing up at me in a frozen frame and it occurred to me that seated round this table was a gathering a third of the size of the community which took up a large vaulted refectory to eat its meals. Then pandemonium broke loose. My mother shrieked 'Paddy! and moved like greased lightening to be first in my arms sobbing, 'Lovely, lovely!' Dad, clutching Mum and slapping me on the back was quite inarticulate. Then everybody leapt up and an ill-formed rugby scrum in which I was both participant and ball battled it out in the doorway. Through the mill I could see Father Aelred standing apart like a anxious referee, one eye on the scrum, no doubt to see that I was being heeled cleanly, and the other on the steaming meal lying neglected on the table.

It was as I feared. In that instant it seemed that nine months of commitment and pain had been erased and all the controls so arduously superimposed on my instinct for freewheeling through life were effortlessly set aside. I was back in my original element and as happy as a pig in a puddle. I was also the centre of attention, a novelty I found hard to cope with as I got a cuddle here, answered a searching question there, and had difficulty stopping a small niece from seeing what I wore under my habit.

The bell rang for Compline. 'I have to go; that's my bedtime,' I said, extricating myself from the heaving humanity. 'Bedtime!' the kids screeched, 'Nobody goes to bed this early.' 'They do round here,' I joked, 'who do you think has to wake the birds in the morning.' My mother pouted; 'It's not fair ...' 'Mother!' Mick cautioned, 'no complaints – you promised.' 'Oh well, when can we see you again, my love – tomorrow morning?' I looked at them all, oh so wanting to stay, tears of happiness, tears of anger at the hurt, tears of a million filtered memories, here in this room. 'Tomorrow afternoon, perhaps, that's the rule. But you mustn't let all this lovely food get cold, must they Father. See you after None.' I touched my lips – our sign of thanksgiving.

Joining the other novices as they assembled for Compline I was glad of my raised hood to hide the hopeless confusion I felt. The choir was full of shades as the evening sun drew in, and I drifted through a childhood long ago, long ago.

The following day passed as the previous one, full of distraction and drifting as if I were anaesthetized. It was all going on down there but nothing reached me, whereas normally I was so in touch. Now my senses were all targeted on the afternoon and whatever response I must have given to anything or body monastic until that time were glazed and token. When I eventually let myself into the guesthouse, however, the greeting was gentler. Only the immediate family were there; Mum, Dad, Mick and Maureen. The others had already taken advantage of the fine weather and gone down to one of the beaches where we were to join them.

'Well, dear, how are you? After you telling us you had put on so much weight when you first came, I was expecting to see a Friar Tuck.' This was my mother pinching my arms as if I were a prize turkey. 'No,' I replied, wriggling out of her clutches, 'I put on a lot because of all the stodge in our diet but I'm back to my fighting weight now and getting slimmer by the day.'

'Well, I think you've sorted yourself out a nice little number here,' said Mick, ever one to see commercial possibilities in any proposition however sublime. 'Lovely surroundings, friendly community, no responsibilities, low income, I grant you, but no overheads.' I knew he was joking but how could he guess the burden this privilege laid upon me, upon all of us. I reddened, not wanting one of our point-scoring matches so soon. 'It has its price,' I said, gently punching him on the chin. 'What d'you mean, no birds, of the unfeathered variety, eh, Pad?' He winked at Maureen who giggled. 'Stop it, you two,' protested my mother. 'Show some respect. 'Come on,' I said, moving for the door. 'Let's join the others on the shore and I'll show you a few birds that'll really make you whistle.'

'So do you think you'll be happy here?' my father asked as we went outside. Of all the family Dad seemed the least at ease, somehow unequal to the monastic dimension. His was your Cockney/Irish Catholic faith, justified in works of mercy, displayed in gaudy processions, priest-centred and macho, still full of granddad's displaced Irish patriotism. Further, he had always organised the holidays, where beaches had convenient conveniences and ice creams and jellied eels were never too far away. Here he was a confused camp follower and still a long way from being convinced that I was in the right place. There were volumes of unanswered questions behind his innocent enquiry. 'I'm working at it, Dad,' I replied, 'but the same things are hard wherever you are. It's not the silence nor the funny food we eat. It's the people you live with that make life difficult – the guy next to you in choir who sings flat or your fellow novice who doesn't pull his weight in the garden.'

We walked out into the heat and, as if prompted by the warmth, my mother and sister instinctively linked arms with me with Dad and Mick following behind. So many years since the five of us had walked anywhere together. 'I had to come to a monastery to get my family together,' I commented blithely. 'No, you came to a place of peace to be at peace,' purred mother, 'and peace is where my family is.' 'Ah, but one person's peace is another person's ...' I squeezed Maureen's arm before she completed the sentence; she looked up and we smiled at each other. She would know what I was really going through – she always did, but I so wanted today to pass without even a raised eyebrow. If they were luxuriating in the novelty of my island home, I was back in a familiar heaven and I now wanted my fill of it whatever the later heartache.

We sauntered through yellow fields and golden memories until we came to a grassy bank in the field which sloped steeply down to peter out in dunes and then stretch smoothly out to the shoreline. There the children darted and dived at the water's edge while all else shimmered as a calm sea rolled out to merge into a cloudless sky. 'This is heaven,' breathed Maureen. 'It'd make a smashing marina,' Mick added. I closed my eyes. The thought crossed my mind that this was as good a moment as any to die. I had fought the good fight; I meant well but life had caught up with me. At this blissful crossroads where things could only get tougher, whatever the direction, what a wonderful solution it would be. But no murderous assassin, no fatal heart attack came to deliver me, not even a fiery chariot to bear me up, so with a sigh I opened my eyes and took the purgatory road.

It was downhill all the way. The noise and needs of the smaller children, the insatiable curiosity of the teenagers; playing French cricket here, exploring a deep rock pool there; and every momentary pause plugged with a distracted question about the monastic life. 'Will you stop kicking sand over me like that!' ... 'But what did it feel like to kneel in front of the community with a broken plate in your hand?' 'Oh, Mick, look where Greg is. He shouldn't be going out as far as that on his own.' 'I mean, do they laugh at you or snub you to really humiliate you?' 'Mick, are you going to swim out to him or do I have to?' 'Do you have to take a vow not to break anything?'

Before I knew it the bell for Vespers was ringing and I stood up amidst loud protests from the whole party which, it has to be admitted, were muted when I explained that only I had to go. I hugged my mother and her eyes filled with tears. 'This is so lovely, Pad. Thank you for everything. I couldn't bear to have lost you altogether.'

As I strode up the field I smarted. Looking back I saw them all playing a ball game, and could imagine the kids saying, 'Right, let's enjoy ourselves now he's gone.' Did they need me now that they had placed me in the frame? All the essentials details had been covered. The rest was the holiday, the sun and the sea and re-creation. Oh, to be truly noble; to accord them all that graciously; happy to be counted as a quaint but loved accessory to a memorable vacation. At least it would disguise the pain of wanting so much to be wanted so much.

Amidst my many wanderings at Vespers, one of the shorter psalms did manage to rescue my attention. It ran:

> How good and pleasant it is when brothers live in unity.
> It is like precious oil over the head,
> upon the beard of Aaron,
> running down the collar of his robes;
> like the dew of Hermon which falls upon the mountains
> of Zion.
> For there the Lord has commanded his blessing
> life for evermore.

The imagery was striking but obscure. In those days when there was nowhere else to go, brothers like the sons of Jacob must have endlessly fought out their petty rivalries with each other, making this image a thing of rare beauty. Today we could run away to many monasteries – singletons to a city bedsit, newly-weds to some newtown semi, leaving happy families to the TV ads. It was certainly no hardship to all meet up once in a blue moon in a place like this. Yet that heavy sweet oil dripping over the head of Aaron suited our world of affectionate nostalgia this afternoon.

Oil on the head ... the picture sprang to mind of myself at the age of three or so sitting on Dad's shoulders just coming off the beach on a seaside holiday. I had complained of feeling unwell and suddenly up it all came; breakfast, ice cream, sea water and sand, over his head, running down the collar of his clothes. I recalled the instant relief in my tummy, then the horror as I surveyed the yellow matted hair beneath me, then some reassurance from the shrieks of laughter of the rest of the family, gazing spellbound at the face I couldn't see – brothers united indeed at father's disarray.

I remembered Dad, surely quicker to forgive than any Old Testament patriarch, running straight out, fully clothed, into the sea, with me now the one to shriek still astride his shoulders, and the terrifying enormity of the splash as we plunged locked together into the waves. How proud I was to march back to the house, now enthroned on bare shoulders broad and brown; and he the king, both serving and forgiving. My soft remembered childhood long ago.

And so the week passed. All the images passing distractedly before my eyes as we sang the psalter seemed to apply to me. It was me who was being winnowed on the threshing room floor. It was my metal being refined in the fire. I was being put to the test to see, in Lawrence's words, if I had what it took. On one afternoon I had to forego the family as all hands were needed to harvest the long field, and a helpless rage rose within me at the injustice. How could they treat my family like this, a sword to pierce their loving hearts. I apologised humbly to them for this shameful treatment the following afternoon – much to their amazement.

The last afternoon came and went like the others – in being family; after all, that was what we were best at, perhaps the only thing we were good at. It was life by extrusion; the genius lay in the formula which could be effortlessly pumped out while the ingredients were present and active. The cut-off was brief and tearful.

As I promised to write regularly I was conscious of signing my hard-won birthright away for a drip-feed of football results, parish titbits, births, deaths and marriages, continually tugging me back to a life that could only sow tares among my wheat. Perhaps I could set all their letters aside to read and respond to collectively at Christmas, say, but I knew even as I thought it that I couldn't cope with the burning tears inside each unopened, unanswered letter. It had become blazingly clear to me that all I wanted was them, not anything they could tell me; a sort of heaven of belonging effortlessly and eternally. What hurt so much was that at this moment my heaven was with them and not with the community, and that I had had to leave them to realise how much I wanted them.

Later, when I poured out all this grief on the sanguine shoulders of Father Prior, he shrugged them as if to shed a superfluous load. 'But you still have them, my dear boy. They've gone away but the bond, the love you can take for granted, still remains. I love members of my family to come and yes, parting is such sweet sorrow, but they have their separate lives to lead – they have always done – and so do I. What I think you have to decide is whether or not this newly awakened feeling you have is a genuine disinterested love that can allow them to be – with you but apart from you – or a homesickness which is more to do with how you feel about being here with us than being there with them.'

I looked back at them that afternoon, standing there in tableau, Mum and Dad holding each other amidst a ticktack of waving white hands. Then one of the children, it was Mary, detached herself and ran to catch me up. I groaned – not now, Mary, not now. She came puffing alongside and linked her arm through mine. 'Do you mind if I walk back to the monastery with you,' she asked a little nervously. 'Not at all, my love,' I lied, 'but they won't let you in, I'm afraid. You're under age and, in case you hadn't noticed it, you're a girl and you've got trousers on, and only men in long skirts are allowed.' 'Oh, stop it, silly! I don't want to join your Order, but that's what I've been wanting to talk to you about ever since we came. Being here where God seems to be around every corner has made me realise more than ever that I want to offer my life to him, like you have, but perhaps in a different sort of way.'

I stopped abruptly in shock and looked down at her

smiling, blushing face. How like Maureen she was with those same hazel eyes animated and humorous, the thinning face, the rounding arms and shoulders fashioning in her a womanhood I hadn't noticed. How crass of me to assume that my life was the only one God had an interest in changing around here. Oh, the beauty of that first flush of assent, when the heart in full flow makes no conditions in response to the call, 'Come, follow me!' 'Welcome aboard,' I said rather weakly. 'It's not always heaven like this, I have to warn you.' She smiled, nodding, waiting for further words of wisdom to fall.

But I had none – me! – how could I respond to this white-hot purity at a moment of such paralysing doubt and confusion. And yet I had to. Her trust was so vulnerable that I could imagine God, our Creator, who holds all things in being through his love and concern, hanging breathlessly on my response. A sacred moment.

'Before I came here, Mary,' I ventured hesitantly, 'all the decisions I had previously made in my life – what I should study, how I should make a living, who I should choose to live with – these were the stuff and substance of existence. But when the call to serve God awoke, or rather exploded, inside me, all these other realities just faded into insignificance. I suddenly became aware of this other journey I was on, had always been on, and the importance from now on of keeping God in my sights. It seems right for me to be in this monastery but that may change. In the old days monks used to journey into the desert in response to the insistent summoning in their hearts, 'Follow me!' Wherever it leads you it's being true to that call that matters.'

Had I said enough? Had I said too much? I paused and looked into her innocent eyes. 'Have you thought which way you want to go?'

'Well, every time I hear or read the Gospel, Jesus always seems to be with poor, sick or afflicted people. He seems to choose to be with them, he tells us to be like them, and the things he has to say he says to them. But our life at home isn't like that. We're not poor and I don't know any poor people, and I suppose I'm really discouraged from getting to know any. There aren't any at our church, that's for sure.'

At that moment the bell rang for Vespers. Unless I went straightaway I would be late and certainly incur Lawrence's displeasure. Oh for the wisdom to know what to do, what to say. Mary's vocation – the biggest thing in her young life. But then again, what could I say in the next ten minutes that would make any difference. Wisdom suddenly told me that the bell had answered my question.

I gave her a hug. 'Mary, I have to fly or I'm in deep trouble. I promise I'll write (another millstone!). And yes, you must love and serve the poor. Never let God out of your sight. He loves you so pass it on. You're very special.' I left her by the little island church and sprinted for the Enclosure door and arrived in choir, my robe everywhere but in the right place, just as the Abbot knocked for the Office to proceed.

It was over. My heart was pumping. My mind was racing. I could feel the calmness and detachment around me but in my state of stress it was a wall to separate, not arms to enfold. Was I glad to be here? Who were these people anyway – were we the poor in our privileged seclusion, our customised clothing, counselling and support ever to hand, forgiveness and reconciliation for the asking? Were we the great unwashed and unloved to whom Jesus had brought the Good News?

And what was this I had said about my life here not necessarily being permanent. Before, I had been so in tune with it all, so excited with each new discovery, so fulfilled by its profundity. I had been part of a tight ship – if ever there was a journey I should be on, this was it. Now I was all at sea. A week ago when the first wave hit me my prayer had been, 'Father, forgive them, for they know not what they do.' Now, in the tidal wave of their departure, it had become, 'My God, my God, why have you forsaken me?'

Chapter Twenty-One

Where were you on 22 November 1963?

Monks, like chickens, are creatures of habit. Give them the right diet of bodily toil, mental exercise and prayerful aspiration, plus one and a half square meals a day, a measure of sleep, and the occasional opportunity to bathe and to shrive, and the golden egg will roll out into the tray with monotonous regularity. Of such is the kingdom of heaven – well, for monks at least.

The rest of us crave distraction, anything to fill the void – those endless moments of emptiness that surround the basic functions of our lives. Today we have instant access to the sum of human knowledge at the flick of a switch. News and opinion floods in from home and abroad, restrained from swamping our minds only by a conscious choice on our part. Somebody is always hovering out there in the ether, waiting to entertain us wherever we are, and so insistent is their summons that we often have to shift somewhere else in order to decline their invitation leaking out of an adjacent headphone, window or passing car. People converse across the world as they walk the streets or drive around town, and technology is increasingly translating the office to the home so that even retreating to the innermost parts of one's ultimate sanctuary can seem a selfish option in our communication-crazed age.

Media was not a word known to our monks. To them medium meant the mid-point between two extremes and it didn't require a plural. To use it to describe the pandemonium waiting just on the other side of the monastery wall would have seemed a very extreme point in any direction.

The only method of communication from outer life was Chapter, the meeting after Prime for the recitation of one chapter of the Rule and any notices or comments that the Abbot might wish to convey to the community. A media-addicted abbot might have told us many things: the current exchange rate of the dollar; who was at number one in the pop charts, or at number ten in the government; the latest news on the origin of the universe or the destruction of the planet. But ours told us nothing more than oiled the wheels of our enclosed life: the need for a new boiler in the laundry; the arrival of a visiting scholar or, to add a frisson of excitement to our mundane lives, the imminence of a gale in the Bristol Channel.

I had the further blessing of the monthly letter from home which gave me an added polarity of knowledge all parties lacked. I could have informed the folks at home of the place of angels in the heavenly hierarchy; I could have informed my fellow novices of the place of West Ham in the Football League, but I couldn't have told either party very much more about anything in between.

The plan was obvious. We had all come a long way, often at great personal cost, to achieve single-mindedness. The system had been drained of trivia for the express purpose of re-packing it with the knowledge and presence of God. The initial evacuation for me had taken some months and had been unpleasant, often painful, like the withdrawal of any addiction. The re-packing had its own dangers too, like the chap in the Gospel who, rid of one diabolical possession, put up a Vacancy sign and was promptly repossessed by seven devils all worse than the first. False notions creeping in to fill a spiritual void have marked the paths of most of the great religious loonies in history.

The Bible and the Rule was the staple diet of the novice's mind, with the Sayings of the Desert Fathers thrown in to add the leaven of example to the dough of ordinance. On such a sound and inspirational base could be added a judicious range of studies: the lives of the saints and a large and challenging tome on

Abandonment to Divine Providence. With the occasional article taken from a contemporary learned journal, your monk, by the time he took his solemn profession, was a walking meditation and prayer machine with every moment of every seventeen-hour day filled with humble ponderings on his own unworthiness and the ineffable joy to come for those who persevered in this vale of tears. The enjoyment of a glorious sunset only served to emphasise the transience of earthly pleasures.

Well, that was the theory. In the event the quirks of humanity, unforeseen by the Rule though evident enough in the Scriptures, constantly interfered, like trip-wires, on the paths of the righteous. Whether dropped in places sacred or profane, the banana skins of life brought out the same reactions in the monk, however modulated, as they did in lesser mortals. If the incidents were rarer they were the more enjoyed, the more memorable for that.

But the Abbot did his best and little disturbed our daily attempts to focus hearts and minds in the vertical rather than the horizontal plane. And, as if to emphasise our other-worldliness, in one corner of the cloister between the washroom and the stairs was a small notice board which suffered the fate of most notice boards by being unnoticed, not because of the usual bewildering profusion of items defying the observer's attention span, but because from the day of my joining there had never been a notice put on it. As popes and councils came and went with never a notice appearing, one could conjecture that the only announcement deemed worthy enough by the Abbot to grace this space would read: 'The world is terminating sometime after Compline tonight. Please carry on as normal.'

22 November came and went and, as on the 10,000 days that had preceded it, the abbey was closed for business by 8 p.m. By this time all novices had cleaned their teeth, laid their golden eggs, and were stretched out, shoeless but fully clothed on their beds, awaiting the last trump or the rising bell, whichever came the earlier. 'I don't want any heroes,' was Father Lawrence's stern admonition. 'When you've made your profession

you can pray the night away for all I care, but while I'm in charge all my novices get in seven hours sleep or I want to know the reason why.'

As ever my arousal from sleep came with the creaking on the dormitory stairs of the anonymous bell-ringer prior to his summons to the new day. The bell preceded Vigils, the night Office, by some ten minutes, but a late sleeper could leap from bed into his shoes, grab his choir robe and be bodily present in church inside sixty seconds. Those who preferred to wake up gradually and aid consciousness with a quick douche under the tap were grateful for the other nine.

But on this twenty-third day of November something was different. Even getting down the dormitory stairs became progressively difficult as the white-robed figures ahead of me slowed down and, as in a motorway tailback, finally came to a jostling uncomprehending halt. Had we been hens we would all, by now, have reached a high state of panic. But we were monks, and years of training in detachment stood us in good stead for a crisis like this. It crossed my mind that what I thought was the bell might have indeed been the last trumpet of judgement, and that the congestion was being caused by the presence of the Ineffable Other in the cloister below. But a slight movement in the crowd enabled me to round the stairwell and take in a spectacle compared with which the end of life on earth might well have seemed anti-climactic.

There was a notice on the notice board.

It was clearly the worst time to have put it up, for every monk had honed the interval between rising and the start of Vigils to his own ability or inclination. A human blockage like this was putting everyone's personal timetable at risk. The Abbot had probably thought that no one in their befuddlement would notice a small square of paper on the board, and that all would take the opportunity to read it at their leisure after Lauds or Prime. But some bright waker had obviously seen it, paused to read it, and so brought about the massing of cowls and robes into one great heaving snowball of consternation. An Occasion of Fault on the grand scale.

Worse was to come. Those in the front of the crowd happened to be the older members of the community, mostly of Belgian extraction and least aware of the world we novices had only recently left. As we pressed forward from the back to learn what earth-shattering news the notice contained, we were frustrated by their slowness to just read the message and move on. We could see them shrugging their Gallic shoulders with varying degrees of incomprehension. And imperceptibly the practice of a lifetime, the commandment which more than anything else captures the essence of monasticism: namely, that silence be observed in the cloisters at all times, began to fray at the edges.

Querulous murmurings like: 'Qui est ce Kennedy la?' 'President de quoi?' 'Ou est Dallas?' 'Je ne comprens riens!' came floating across the air, magnified by their very inadmissibility in the hallowed precinct.

I saw Maurice say something clownish to Father Columba and the whispers turned to rumbles as the big man noised his appreciation to all and sundry. And as each of them had to jerk their heads by ninety degrees one way or the other to make visual contact because of their all-enveloping hoods, the clockwork movements of arms, shoulders and heads, all going nineteen to the dozen, looked for all the world like some mechanical puppet show, and totally obscured the notice and its import from the rest of us, though the facts, garbled in their truncated questionings, were beginning to filter through.

To the pantomime taking place in the front were now added the explosions of impatience and law and order from the rear, with its *Sshhs* from one quarter, *Pssts* from another and *Ttchhs* from somewhere else. Amazed by the whole debacle I now had a glimmering of how the message ran and wondered at its significance in our lives unless, perhaps, it foreshadowed some imminent nuclear apocalypse. But, surely, it hardly concerned me. Had I not fled the world! What concerned me was the halt it had imposed on the inexorable passage of the day. The ten minutes was well up by now and I needed now more than ever that splash of cold water to bring me to my senses; a short, sharp shock to convince me that all this was not a particularly nasty nightmare.

It was not long in coming. I was just edging round the back of the throng towards the washroom when a clap like a rifle shot called the proceedings to immediate attention. In the frozen silence the barrel of each hood gradually swung around in the direction of the noise to reveal a purple-faced Abbot standing on the dormitory stairs, no doubt deeply regretting his misjudged sense of timing. With exaggerated gestures he slapped a finger to his pursed lips several times and then pointed it fiercely at the watch on his left wrist. In so doing he caught the cross hanging at his chest, causing it to fly over his left shoulder, nearly doing damage to the monk standing behind, and land with a thump on his right one. And there he stood caught in this dramatic pose daring the slightest contradiction. He could have been Moses coming down from the heights of Sinai and catching the Israelites in flagrante delicto.

The message was clear – Vigils or else; and the company to a man put down his golden calf, picked up his golden egg, and sheepishly shuffled off unwashed to the church where each could meditate if not repent at leisure.

Later that day the notice board was removed which, we surmised, was not so much a reprisal or even a reproof, but a tactical aid to good order and monastic discipline. Henceforward important news would be relayed by an emergency Chapter, the traditional summons to which came via the great bell echoing sonorously over field and forest. This we all agreed was more effective, more pleasing on the ear, more commensurate to the gravity of the occasion, more appropriate to the ebb and flow of our life, than any ill-conceived attempt at breaking the news.

Chapter Twenty-Two

Teething Troubles

I became aware during the Community Mass that I had a toothache; first, a slight unease, then the knowledge: ouch! That hurts. I really loved the Community Mass, relaxing into it like a tired body into a soothing bath. It restored my strength; it informed my day; it embraced my soul. I emerged as a man with a mission. But today I emerged as a man with a problem. Where do you get a dentist on a small island?

This was no minor issue. I was getting on for a year into my noviciate and fully convinced that this was the life for me. The family had long since made their visit, a cruel experience, tearing at my heartstrings, but I was well over it now. I understood the promise of Stability I would be making in a year's time. I was a member of this community, under this Abbot, on this island, physically, mentally, emotionally. Life might be a journey but this train wasn't going to leave the track for anyone.

Pain was my meditation all that morning. And that was another thing. The monastic life was about asceticism, the exercise of self-denial, patience, bearing things. I had found it easy, exhilarating even, and going the extra mile or two was no trouble at all. But to bear a pain that was in top gear seconds after take-off seemed to be more like masochism than asceticism, except this was a pain I could scarcely endure never mind enjoy.

I heroically put off taking my complaint to the novice-master until after lunch, a meal always eagerly awaited, as a bowl of coffee would be all I had consumed in the nine hours since rising. Maybe he had observed my stoic refusal as the trolley came round, for he ushered me into his room before I could knock on his door.

'Novices don't miss meals, Daniel. Are you unwell or something?'

'Yes,' I replied, not wanting to open my mouth too much to let the cold air in. 'Something ... something of a toothache.'

'Oh, well that's no good; you'd better take yourself off to the Infirmary and see the doc. He'll be there or thereabouts until None. Go on, off you go.'

Thanks for the sympathy, I thought, but I kissed my fingertips and betook myself to the cloister where the infirmary stood next to the calefactory. I knocked on the door and received an affirmative knock in reply. Father Francis, a raw-faced white-haired monk sat at his desk surrounded by shelves sporting a bewildering variety of bottles and packets. A hard-looking bed lay underneath the window and the prevailing smell was pharmaceutical with a memory of today's lunch. The kitchen was next door.

'Sit down, Daniel, and how are you today?'

'May I speak,' I muttered, still keeping my mouth semi-closed.

'Well, finding out what's wrong with you might prove a little difficult if you don't.' He smiled, 'Just a few words might help. Your soul is safe with me.'

I explained briefly my trouble.

'Let's have a look,' he said gently, slipping on a pair of latex gloves and picking up a pencil torch, 'Where does it hurt?'

'Ngaagh,' I uttered fearfully, opening my mouth and indicating a rear molar on the left.

'This one?' he asked, and tapped it slightly with the tip of the torch. The pain shot up to the top of my head as if he'd hit it with a hammer.

'Ngaagh!!' this time an octave higher.

'Hmm,' he said after a little look around the rest of my mouth. He sat down.

'When was the last time you went to the dentist, Daniel? A few years, I reckon.'

I stayed silent, trying to remember. Had I been since leaving school?

'Look, I'll make an emergency appointment with the dentist we use on the mainland. But I guess it'll take a few visits to get your teeth sorted out.'

I was thunderstruck. Leave the island! Over the months I had been lulled into the notion that life was complete here and that, if I chose to stay, I would never have to cross that mile of water again. I had imagined that, if a dentist couldn't be found within the community (they had managed to find a doctor!) they would ship one in, complete, of course, with dental surgery and assistant.

Armed with some painkillers I rushed back to Father Lawrence.

'I've got to go to the mainland to a dentist.'

'That'll probably be tomorrow morning on the first boat,' he said, looking at the tide chart on his wall, 'which will leave the jetty at about 8.30. I'll let you know after work – that is, if you can manage some work this afternoon; better than kicking your heels here in the noviciate, feeling sorry for yourself. Anyway, take a good strong dose of those tablets and see what you can manage.'

I wanted to ask him everything about my trip but my priority was getting rid of this pain, thanking the Lord that I lived in the age of aspirin. My work effort was, to say the least, distracted, and I found that the simple repetition of a mantra, any devotional line from a psalm, induced a kind of trance-like feeling, not good for the work but it kept the gremlins at bay.

After supper I knocked on Lawrence's door. He didn't look pleased.

'Father Francis tells me you'll need several visits. You may regret them more than the toothache – can disturb a fragile novice.' I wasn't in a mood to argue. The sharp pain had settled into a dull ache and I felt very fragile indeed.

'Anyway, you've got an appointment at 9.30 with a Mr Morgan at 36 Harbour Lane,' he passed me a local street map with the address picked out in biro. 'You'll wear exactly what you've got on now, and when it's over straight back to the quayside. Take a book to read and avoid conversations. The habit seems to excite a certain type of person who believes it their duty to challenge us to explain our way of life and then justify it and other things like free will and transubstantiation. Just smile and keep glued to the book. It's called custody of the eyes. This isn't a catch-up outing after a year's separation. It's a visit to the dentist, nothing more. Have you got that?'

He seemed to be more on edge than I was so I mumbled my thanks and left, smouldering. After all, I didn't invent the wretched toothache and I couldn't believe he was so concerned for my welfare. After Compline I took some more tablets and, surprisingly, gradually drifted into a sound sleep.

I would have really enjoyed the strange experience of walking, on my own, down to the jetty away from the monastery, had it not been for the insistent throb of the tooth and a jangled nervousness. I'm a natural coward; I don't have to work at it. Brave enough when my blood is up, say, in a rugby maul or outraged by some injustice, but faced by unknown forces, the unexplained or unexpected, I quail, the fight draining from me. The cheery bonhomie of the boatmen distanced me from the human race, and I stood, a man apart, in the prow of the ferry careless of the swell splashing and the heaving waves. Rubbery legs added to the debility as we disembarked, and the utter strangeness of standing in a hubbub of idle chatter together with the proximity of these alien creatures with their long, coiffured hair, high voices and all the perfumes of Arabia, literally made my head spin. I closed my eyes and clutched at the first mantra that came to mind, *Domine ad adjuvandum me festina*, 'Lord, help me, and be quick about it!', the intoned verse at the beginning of all the Hours.

'You all right, young man?' I opened my eyes to see an elderly woman peering at me, speaking for a small crowd of assorted townsfolk behind her.

'Who, me?' I replied, now mortified with embarrassment, 'Just getting my bearings.' She looked as if she wanted to go on, to reassure herself of my well–being, but she kept silent, continuing to gaze at me. I got out the map.

'Harbour Lane?' I scanned the group but they averted their eyes and edged away; then I noticed the woman pointing to a street sign, Harbour Lane, behind my head.

Marvellous, I thought, now I'm a congenital idiot as well as a clown, and, to add offence to idiocy, I kissed my fingertips instinctively, meaning to thank her. I saw her lips purse as if in disapproval, so to avoid any ensuing recrimination I walked past her and on to the lane. I'd been off the boat for two minutes and already I'd nearly started an uprising.

As I walked I recalled Father Prior telling me, during one of my confession slots, how when the original Belgian monks first took possession of the island, the mainlanders were enraged by the sale of their island to foreigners, and would hurl abuse at the hapless brethren whenever they came ashore. I was picturing them dodging handfuls of rotting fish when I came upon No. 36 with its brass plate, Alan and Beth Morgan, Dental Surgeons. As I knocked the legs started to tremble again and the mantra flowed as if I had turned on a tap.

A pretty woman in her thirties dressed in a white smock opened the door.

'Do come in; you'll be Brother Daniel.'

I followed her down a corridor and into the surgery where she ushered me into the chair. I sat down, a little calmer, and waited for the dentist to come. The woman put some instruments down on a surface and came and sat next to me.

'Right, Daniel, could you tell me what the trouble is?'

I sat bolt upright, appalled. How could this happen? In the whole of my life I had never been treated by a female dentist; I had not even contemplated their existence. And here I was trapped with no escape route open to me.

'Lawrence said Mr Morgan,' I said in a strangled voice.

'Yes, my husband does usually see the monks, but I'm afraid he's away on a course this week. I'm his wife,

Beth, and knowing that you were an emergency . . .' she
tailed off, smiling and blushing a little.

It crossed my mind to get up, apologise and leave. But
I dreaded Lawrence's response and I couldn't go on
bearing this pain indefinitely. I lay back defeated and
deeply ashamed that this attractive woman would be
discovering neglect on such an enormous scale in my
mouth.

She picked up probe and mirror and gradually made
her way round my teeth without saying a word or
expressing her horror in any way. Her touch was so delicate that I felt nothing, and just lay rigid in the chair
with my eyes closed. This didn't prevent me from catching the scent of her cosmetics which, in my unprepared
state, I found mildly intoxicating. She turned away and
made some notes several times during the examination.
I opened my eyes to find her looking down at me.

'Well, Daniel, there's quite a lot of work to be done,
I'm afraid, and one or two of your teeth are beyond
repair. Are you quite fit: no medication, no conditions
like heart, diabetes, asthma? No?' when I shook my
head, 'Then which one is giving you the trouble?'

I indicated the back molar and she pouted sympathet-
ically.

'I'm afraid that one has got to come out. Half of it has
broken away already. Are you happy about me extracting it today?'

Desperate I was; happy I was not, but what alternative did I have. As far as Lawrence was concerned my
monastic detachment was on the line. More to the point,
what would the lovely Mrs Morgan think if I backed
down. Again I was trapped.

I looked at her petite build and those slender arms
and she smiled knowingly in response.

'You men,' she said, grinning, 'You think it's all about
muscles. Trust me; it's all in the wrists. Hang on while I
get my assistant.'

Well, I wasn't going anywhere so I hung on, trying to
cope with the confusion fate had visited upon me in the
little time I had strayed from the fold. No women in my
life for a year and suddenly I was surrounded by them,

beautiful sirens with power and authority. And I was their victim. 'Led like a lamb to the slaughter' – I could empathise with Isaiah's suffering servant, even if I was likely to survive, this time.

The two women came in, Beth's assistant more my age and grinning. What had Beth been saying? I withered at the thought. Come on and get it over.

'Have you had an injection before? Don't worry,' she purred as I shook my head. All I could remember were those dreadful visits of my childhood; sitting fearfully in line, then up the dark, steep staircase, into the brightly lit surgery, the grinning tiger face poster on the wall, the masked face above me, the contraption placed over my nose and mouth, the strange smell of gas, and . . . oblivion. Then waking up with tears wet on my cheeks. She took the syringe from the assistant and gently eased it into my mouth, 'You'll hardly feel it.'

And she was right; I hardly did as she slid the anaesthetic into my gum two or three times.

'Just sit tight there and wait for it to go numb while I prepare. And please try to relax; come on, uncross those legs, breathe deep and, yes, just relax. It'll be out before you know it, I promise.'

As I sat there I could feel the pain receding and an immense calm began to take over. I was almost asleep when I became aware of her fingers in my mouth, flicking the tooth and rubbing my gums.

'Feel anything?' I shook my head, and she picked up her instrument, whatever it was. I heard it lock on to my tooth as she braced herself alongside me, her lips in a firm line. I saw two little dimples form in her chin as she tensed, and at the same time felt a tremendous pull on my jaw and heard a creak like a rusty door. A bead of sweat formed on her upper lip as I gazed fascinated.

Suddenly it was over and she stood away, forceps in her hand and a bloody tooth in its jaws. 'There you are,' she said a little breathlessly, 'Child's play, even though it was broken. There's a little blood so rinse out and take a couple of codeine for the pain when the feeling comes back.'

She walked over to the assistant and I lay back in the

chair in a state of total euphoria. As yet there was no pain, there was no tooth, there was no fear. The monastery seemed a million miles away. Mrs Morgan was an angel briefly entering my life. Tidings of great joy. A high tide of peace. This was not real and the child in me felt tears running down my cheeks.

'Are you all right,' said the assistant bending over me.

'Yesh,' I mumbled through my numbed mouth, 'Tearsh of relief; tearsh of joy.'

I bent over the basin and rinsed my mouth and swallowed the tablets.

'Can you make the same time next week,' Mrs Morgan, radiant in my eyes forever, had the appointment book open. 'If we make it the same time every week Alan should have you finished in a month.'

She saw the flash of disappointment on my face and misinterpreted the cause.

'I'm sorry you've got to come again. I know how you monks hate to leave your monastery. We really love having you all so close to us on the island; you're a very special bunch of guys. We're proud to be your dentists, aren't we, Ann. Like a visit from on high when one of you comes for treatment.'

She blushed again and then shook me by the hand.

I was embarrassed; I was confused; I was infatuated. I smiled a lopsided smile and kissed my fingertips, walked awkwardly from the room, down the corridor and out into the crisp air with my hood up and a handkerchief over my mouth.

It was one of those beginning-of-the-rest-of-my-life moments. There was still no pain, although my jaw felt uncomfortable, and I was walking on air. I was also walking in the wrong direction as I had turned right not left outside the door, but I didn't care. My steps took me uphill following the line of the coast and I soon reached a vantage point from which, as I paused and turned about, I could see the colourful, bustling town spread below me and, as I turned seawards, the island with its monastery silently tucked underneath the rise to Chapel Point and the lighthouse. Without knowing it the familiar mantra started within me, 'God, come to my aid; O Lord, make haste to help me!' What was the matter with me? It wasn't as if there was a choice. However intoxicating my slight brush with the world had been, and I could still see and smell the nearness of Mrs Morgan as she bent over me, I was in the wrong place. My world lay out there within that ill-assorted job lot of a community, whose gaze, however dimmed, was heavenwards. Everything else was a distraction. I had better be going home.

I turned and made my way down, past No. 36 back to the quayside. There was no sign of the monastery boat; it had probably returned to the island with its cargo. The idea of kicking my heels waiting for it to return, reading Lawrence's blessed book, didn't appeal to me in the slightest. I turned my steps up into the town and sauntered among the shoppers, looking into the shop windows as I passed. It was like being on a film set: everything was familiar but nothing was real; snatches of conversation, the moving lips on the TV screens in the rental shop, the endless sales promotions; huge implants of trivia, all seemingly designed to divert, to keep us preoccupied with the social mechanisms of life, not life itself or its true purpose.

Suddenly I passed a window that was different, and familiar. The sign read, The Monastery Shop, and it displayed a strange hotchpotch of items: cards, pictures, some pottery, bottles of sweets, phials of Island Gorse, Lavender Water; even a section devoted to Monastery Produce – our long loaves, pats of butter, fresh eggs and an assortment of vegetables. It seemed popular judging by the flow of customers. And there by the counter was Brother Thomas whom we rarely saw in choir except at weekends. A monk like the rest of us but here he was chatting and laughing as if this was the routine that energised his life. It was highly disconcerting and worrying for me. Hadn't he been a novice once, offering his life to the God of silence and contemplation. Was this a shameful opting out I was observing, or a mind-boggling act of sacrificial obedience?

As I stood there, stunned by the thought, he looked up and saw me and bustled out of the shop.

'There you are, Daniel. Father Lawrence was hoping

you'd get the boat back but it left a quarter of an hour ago. You've been to the dentist, I hear.'

'Mmm,' I murmured through the handkerchief. I didn't really want to get into conversation and, anyway, I had nothing to say.

'There'll be another boat in about an hour and a half. You could help me unload some stuff that's just arrived or would you rather go for a walk?'

I thought of an endless line of shops followed by an endless line of neat little houses all forming an endless ring of supply, creating and feeding demand. I had seen enough and opted for filling the storage shelves of The Monastery Shop accompanied by the endless chatter filtering through. By the time Thomas came to tell me that the boat had arrived I was finding it all rather irksome and longing for the company of people bent on keeping the silence, like the preservation of something precious, something too easily lost.

Again I stood, a man apart, on the return journey. My mood was debonair, despite the aching jaw and an aware-ness in the stomach of a meal missed. There would be aching jaws to come and unprepared encounters but for this suffering servant they would hopefully be healing experiences. I remembered Lawrence's jibe. Fragile novice I might be but at least I understood what he meant now. A brush with temptation. What did the proverb say, 'To know oneself is the beginning of wisdom.'

I arrived back in the noviciate as None ended, and mixed in with the other novices as they prepared for afternoon work. Lawrence ignored me as he doled out the tasks. Then he turned to me with a funny look on his face.

'Well, you decided to come back, then.'

'Mmm,' I decided to play numb; why be a butt for his sarcasm.

'Do you want to work or would you rather finish your book?'

The book! I must have left it at the shop. He spotted the look on my face and rolled his eyes. I decided now was not the time to tell him of my further appointments, nor ever to let him in on the turmoil I had faced. If there

was matter for confession Father Prior would be the one
to hear it. Otherwise ...

'Mmm,' I said through the handkerchief pointing to the
fields.

'Get out,' he said but with the hint of a smile, 'and for
your penance recite the Invitatory psalm, you know,
'God, come to my aid; O Lord, make haste to help me',
and this time mean it.'

Chapter Twenty-Three

Michaelmas Days

Michaelmas fell on 29 September and with it the anniversary of my reception as a novice. I was in a reflective mood during the community Mass. Being an angelic feast the liturgy was rich with apocalyptic references. There was the prophet Daniel's vision of the Ancient of Days with robe as white as snow (a little different from mine now several weeks unwashed), ' . . . waited on by a thousand thousand, with ten thousand times ten thousand standing before him'. This passage always left me distractedly adding up the last set of noughts to make a total: eight in all which made a hundred million . . . now was that a billion or was a billion one thousand million? And then . . . what sort of arena would house that number – the Isle of Wight? . . . Australia? . . . and what sort of amplification would they need? . . .

By this time we were into the next reading, the account from Revelations of war breaking out in heaven and Michael and the angels hurling down to earth the great dragon, the devil of Satan, and all his angels. 'If we were only to pierce the barriers which enclose our human condition,' I remembered from a sermon by St Bernard, 'and perceive the war raging between the angels for our souls, our hearts would surely shrivel in an instant'.

The imagery was confusing: one passage spoke of immense order and peace – a billion or more angels doing homage to the Ancient One; the other of continuing conflict and chaos, presumably while there were still souls to win or lose. What was it Father Anthony, our

farm manager, had said during a sermon he gave one
feast day in Chapter after Prime:

> As monks we must remember our angelic dimension. Ours
> is not to evangelise the world as missionaries, taking the
> Gospel to the ends of the earth; nor to feed the hungry,
> tend the sick, nor visit those in prison; not even to console
> the faithful. All we are asked to do to fulfil our vocation is to
> bear witness to this great struggle between good and evil
> going on around us, by our humbleness, brotherly love and
> prayer. And that's what I guess angels do all the time.

It was difficult to imagine less angelic material than
rosy, earthbound Anthony, more often to be seen
cursing a steaming, reluctant tractor or benignly slapping the rump of a pedigree large white, but his vision
did give a clue to the mystery of good and evil, order
and chaos co-existing. However, we were not angels,
and humbleness and brotherly love was a painful
process each of us were engaged in, a sort of chaos
within the order, chaos perhaps becoming order. Each
one of us was a battlefield, every creature of free will,
angel or human, a battlefield. Even in heaven? Yes, I
supposed, even in heaven – where good and evil
contended like corpuscles in the blood; nature, as ever,
a perfect, if clouded, image of the supernatural. We were
filing out before I even realised that Mass was over. I
resisted the temptation to worry over such a colossal
distraction. 'Amen, Lord,' I breathed. 'Give them back,
pass them on, offer them up, and then run!' Father Prior
had counselled on errant thoughts. 'Sod off, Satan,' I
added.

'Happy anniversary, Daniel, and many of them,'
chirped Father Lawrence as we returned to the novitiate
for class. 'And as a special treat, Father Abbot wants to
see you at ten.' The sharp intake of breath on all sides
marked the gravity of my ordeal (he must be just as po-
faced with everybody, I thought) and caused Lawrence's
eyebrows to shoot up. 'You may gasp,' he snorted, 'and
break the spirit of silence in so doing, but just remember
that we are the nursery garden of this community, and
every professed monk has a vested interest in seeing

that the shoots are springing up straight and true. You should see how the arrival of each new postulant cheers up the older monks – and how they sigh when he leaves! So it's natural for the Abbot to want to make his own appraisal of each novice and what better time than halfway through your novitiate. If you've survived a year there must be something going for you, unless I'm making your lives too comfortable, of course.'

Another communal gasp was nipped in the bud as Lawrence glared around him. 'Go on, off you go, brother; you've got about three-quarters of an hour to prepare yourself and think up some reasons why you should want to stay here – or leave if you prefer,' he added with a mean grin. 'Why not go for a walk, but don't jump off the cliff – it won't be that bad, I promise.'

I escaped through a column of covertly upturned thumbs and made for the sea.

A breath of fear caused me to shiver as I ploughed through the forest and over the spongy meadowgrass. The future I had taken for granted seemed suddenly uncertain, suddenly in someone else's hands. I was so in love with this life, so completely at home. I had survived the trauma of my family's visit; indeed it had forced me to choose so decisively that when the pain had subsided my assent to God had felt complete. I had been blind but now I saw. They would come again but as guests to visit, not as bailiffs to repossess.

But this new vision had not allowed for abbots' appraisals. If only Father Lawrence were abbot, or Father Jerome, our hard but kindly Prior, the angel of unlight whispered in my ear. Reason told me that I had given him no cause to wish to send me away; surely he must grant me at least the other year to become the sort of person he wanted in his community. But what if he could see some deep flaw in my character that no amount of monastic formation would put right? Wouldn't he think it kinder to strip the diseased branch from the vine straightaway, no messing. The dry, brusque way he responded whenever we had conversed bore all the marks of an abbot who couldn't wait to get me out of his . . . tonsure.

Novices making 'Abbot's Kitchen' apple jelly in the refectory.

And what a waste of a life that would be. From the different tasks I had been given to perform I had come to know virtually the whole community. Maurice I knew and loved, not only from the exposure to his creative cooking but from the regular duties in his darksome but strangely entertaining kitchen. Edmund, choirmaster and fruiterer, must have had a soft spot for me to keep me in his *Schola* and ask for my help in the orchard picking his cider apples. I had warmed to taciturn, meticulous Oswald with his hens living out their sad lives in barbarous wire cages. How many eggs had I harvested since I came ... how many miles of sharp-smelling droppings had I reeled in from the trays beneath.

There was expressive, swash-buckling Anthony, and silent, almost furtive Wilfrid, on the farm, both of whom I cherished as an extension of the joy and peace I felt whenever I was in the company of the warm, smelly animals, our twin contemplative community. Then there was Brother Denis, resolutely enlarging his market garden year after year, reclaiming every last yard of soil until it became rock and tumbled into the sea. He was always glad of an audience to hear his endless theories on land management – much to the discomfiture of novices who might disagree, but who feared far more the wrath of the novice-master if he found that they had broken the silence.

The monastery had become a honeycomb of rich environments to me as I toiled from day to day: in the bakery with Father Dominic, the only smell that tempted me outside the refectory; the wardrobe – where Brother Malachy laboured under the ancient title of chamberlain, and made and repaired our woollen habits and workclothes of strong denim; the pottery, a new world of clay and kiln, opened under Brother Rembert, already skilled before he entered – and sadly left; the silent order of the sacristy; the foaming chaos of the laundry. It seemed to me like a medieval village, full of the bustle of life where all the tools of office made music, and where an endless investment of afternoons begged to be shaped into offerings of prayer and reflection wherever I happened to be working.

Yes, this was the life I wanted. No brochure or prospectus could even begin to describe this interweave of richness, its beckoning depths, its draining beauty.

But I had a problem – we all had a problem as far as I could see – with the Abbot. The monastic life is a contradiction in terms: a bunch of strangers from God knows where, all single-mindedly seeking God in the emptiness of their own hearts, yet living and dying together under the gospel imperative to lay down their lives for one another. But human love (and I for one hadn't renounced my membership of the human race) shows itself in body language – words and actions that spring from feelings of tenderness, affirming us in our insecurity and barrenness. A love not demonstrated leaves us unsure, always fearing offence given or received. That would be bad enough from a fellow novice, but from an abbot!

The nervous novice of forty minutes ago was reduced to sweated dread as I knocked on the Abbot's door at ten. Such funk merited a Borgia at least, but received by contrast a mild 'Hallo there,' from Father Abbot, tall of stature, spare of frame, caught in the act of reading a newspaper – yes, a daily newspaper, spread right across his desk.

'Take a chair,' he said nonchalantly, and continued to read from the paper. I sat down, still seeking composure, taking in at a glance the bareness of the room save for a fold-up bed and cupboard in one corner and a bookcase behind him stuffed with directories, maps, a Michelin guide, a Jerusalem Bible and a pile of old newspapers and magazines. He sat at a desk which held a telephone, a typewriter and a wire tray brimming with correspondence – or were they reports on recalcitrant novices? Not much to feed the soul here, I thought. The moments passed. It surely wasn't for me to break the silence; I was hardly breaking in on his devotions – unless the daily news was part of it. The tension became unbearable.

'I never thought I'd see *The Times* again,' I ventured, feigning light-heartedness.

'Nor will you,' he retorted with a sigh, at last folding the newspaper up, 'unless you are unlucky enough to become Abbot some day. Someone has to keep abreast of the world if only to keep the rest of the community protected from it . . . and as this job carries responsibility for the island and everything on it – a sort of feudal lord without any real powers . . .' I waited for the rest of the sentence, all sorts of senses vitalised by the glimpse of the day's news, upside-down though it was, meaningless though it seemed . . . but no, he gazed hard-eyed through his steel-rimmed glasses, whistling tunelessly, and then jerked suddenly into consciousness.

'Right, so you've come for your mid-noviciate chat. You probably know I'm not much of a talker, but I do have to assess your novice-master's observations on your first year . . .' he opened a file that had been lying under the newspaper and studied the top sheet with great interest.

'Well,' he said at length, 'Father Lawrence is an optimist by nature – perhaps that's why he's so good at his job.' He smiled a bleak smile. 'For what it's worth, he thinks you've got what it takes, though he says you're a bit jumpy and impetuous. A man of action, he calls you, inclined to be a little over-zealous.'

He looked at me over the file. 'These are, of course, the hallmarks of the world rather than the cloister, and yours could be a busyness that finds obedience tiresome, stability irritating and conversion of manners – especially conversion of manners, incomprehensible.' He paused, and as if reflecting that this seemed a touch harsh, he went on, 'However, that's what noviciates are for, to help you change, radically, your perception of the world, and re-train body and soul to the yoke of service and humility.'

My heart sank. Was this what he really wanted; what the Rule demanded – a zombie like Brother Sylvester, a recent arrival, who never looked at you, rarely smiled, never 'signed' frivolously, always arranged everything neatly on his desk, went through a whole afternoon's work with never a gesture of need or an observation. Strewth, he was there already, a saint in sheep's clothing.

'He adds that you seemed to find your parents' visit quite difficult and took some while to recover your equilibrium afterwards.' He removed his glasses and looked at me, his face softer without them. 'This is a little more serious as it could be an indication that that's where you really belong, where most people belong, in the heart of those dearest to them. After all, for most novices this period under the Rule is only a temporary solution to their searching for a vocation elsewhere.'

'Oh no, Father,' I leapt in, alarmed by his implication. 'No, this is my family now. I know that as sure as I was born, but it took the agony of their visit to make me realise it. Yes, I went through a real crisis then, but I'm sure I came out of it stronger in my attachment here, and count the experience as a valuable part of my development.

'Good, good,' he said softly, 'well, time will tell, and

you have the second year to measure up to the demands of becoming a monk.'

'Oh, great!' I said, with a sudden uplift of hope after the panic – all that worry for nothing. A strange buoyancy made me add, with all the impetuousness he had just drawn to my attention, 'It's a wonderful life, a crazy but wonderful life. It's right what Paul says about being a fool for Christ's sake.'

His eyes widened as I spoke. 'What do you mean?'

'Well, it's idiocy really, isn't it.' I felt I was treading on air. 'We wrench ourselves away from our family. We travel to the back of beyond, put on silly clothes, pray in a foreign language, conform to a ridiculous sign system when a well-chosen word would suffice. We remain estranged from the people we live and die alongside and yet call them brothers, and then have to become 'normal' once a year for the sake of those we have left behind. But I guess I would rather be here in this place at this moment than anywhere else in the world.'

The Abbot sat there fingering his glasses. What was he thinking, dear God? Had I blown it with my prattle of joy? He put on his glasses again and the hard lines reappeared.

'What an extraordinary thing to say,' he said quietly. 'You mean to say that you've been here for over a year and still can't accept the way of life laid down by the Order you're electing to join?'

'Of course I accept it, Father Abbot,' I felt irritated by his lack of empathy. 'But surely I don't have to agree with all of it. Can't I accept it as my . . .' I waited for a word to come – surely he could see . . . '. . . my martyrdom, my way of witnessing to the equal absurdity of Jesus, the Son of God, dying on the Cross, if I understand St Paul correctly.'

The Abbot's eyes suddenly sparkled but I wasn't sure it was friendly. There was 'error' in the air, the smell of heresy, maybe. 'Look, you've come here to spell out your faith over an indeterminate number of years, not go down heroically in the teeth of the battle. Do you think this heady feeling you are enjoying right now about the incongruities of this life is going to wear well as time passes. You know nothing yet of the pressures this life can impose. You may well enjoy the challenge of it all now, but what about when the going gets really tough, and I mean tough. When the thought of another day like the last one turns your heart to stone, day after day, month after month. If you already think that the life is ridiculous I wonder if there is any place for you alongside simple suffering souls, not cast in such an heroic mould as yourself?'

'But I didn't say I thought the life was ridiculous. There is nothing ridiculous about the Rule. The logic of it is blazingly clear to me, and the challenge it offers is one I am driven to take up. The reactions, I would have thought, were the reactions of mid-twentieth-century man to oddities like the clothing we wear or our use of the Latin in the Office and Liturgy – things that would even take a modern-day St Benedict by surprise.'

There was a pause as I waited with heart fluttering for his judgement on this outburst I never meant to happen – me, complaining at the very moment of my appraisal. Why, he could even interpret it as murmuring – St Benedict's pet hate in a troublesome monk.

He sat back in his chair and sighed, fingertips together. 'So, what would you do if you were Abbot then, subject to the annual gathering of all Cistercian Abbots, a crowd of reactionaries if ever there was one – so conservative that year after year they won't even consider throwing out our bizarre use of the discipline for fear that the Order might be seen to be getting soft.'

I was staggered at his candour, an aspect of him I had not even dreamed existed, and for sharing his thoughts and opinions – with me! Or was he? Could he just be playing the Inquisitor, leading me on to reveal the error in which I was steeped, till, with tears coursing down my face, I begged him to dispel me from the monastery at the earliest opportunity. How could I know?

'I suppose if I were Abbot,' I ventured hesitantly into the unknown – fancy telling him how to run the Order! 'If I were Abbot I would fight for the full observance of the Rule but fight equally for allowing the ordinary rather than the extraordinary in everyday life. If we drive tractors why can't we wear jeans and jumpers. If we study in a modern language why can't we pray in one. Why do I play such a large organ for such a small community when an amplified guitar would suit us better and cost us less. If we are the highest form of life in the Church surely we should be leading it not drag-ging centuries behind.'

The Abbot sat there, turning his pectoral cross this way and that way. God, I hadn't intended to say anything like this. Indeed, could I have possibly said it had I been kneeling at his side as the Customs and Ordinances required. But if he had relaxed that rule, he was surely open to other changes.

'Of course you're right,' he said suddenly with a warm wry grin, the sort of grin I had seen him show the Abbot General. Heavens above! I exploded inside. 'But just suppose I began to make changes as basic as those you suggest. Do you know what would happen? I'd have a riot on my hands, letters to the Abbot General, to the Pope even, and probably from my own Prior at that. Like the other abbots, most of this community would see it as me getting soft – soft in the head as well. They would see it as a betrayal of all they had endured over the years – an end of life as they knew it. No, with a life as tough as this you don't rock the boat without a very good reason for doing so. And as for this estrangement you feel from your fellow novices . . .' Obviously he had drawn the curtain on oddities. 'I don't see the Rule saying much about emotional relationships other than the one we sinners all have with a merciful God. A peni-tent is too aware of his own enslavement to sin to worry how good he feels about anyone else. We're all the bottom of the barrel here, you know, and if we love one another it's out of our brokenness, our common broken-ness; but it's God we're looking at and listening to, not each other. We're monks, not social workers. A hierar-chy of loners – God, Abbot, monk – that's what the desert is all about.'

'Whether it's the sixth or the twentieth century?

'Especially this self-indulgent, self-absolving century,' he retorted, leaning forward in his chair, obviously warming to his theme. 'Sin is not a communal experience and neither is repentance, and St Benedict was making sure our solitude was not going to be disturbed by idle chatter or even deep sharing.'

'Solitude, not solicitude,' I reflected.

'Right. The ox doesn't look at his companion when he's pulling the plough, but he isn't estranged from him, not at all, because he knows his support is vital to the common effort. Neither are you estranged from your fellow novices, because you know you share the same burdens, the same failures – and the same target. Just keep your eye on the furrow and let the novice-master dispense the solicitude.'

He closed the file and sat looking into the space between us. He had no more to say.

'So, you're happy for me to stay on – in the community,' I said tentatively. I still had to hear him affirm my status as continuing novice. 'Me and my heroics,' I added.

He snorted, just as Lawrence would. 'You're welcome to your heroics but you'll suffer for them, I can assure you. But do remember that obedience needs to be massaged or else it becomes a tyrant. Learn to love the habit you wear; learn to think and pray in the Latin; learn to love the organ. That's the last step of humility, the final piece in the jigsaw of our lives; what does the Rule say: 'when the monk begins to keep, without effort as if by habit, those commands he had observed before through fear'. Yes, I'm happy enough for you to stay – if your novice-master is. I just hope you're as keen to be a fool next year when you come up for profession.'

I got up to leave. Had he changed? Had our relationship moved on? I still didn't know where I stood with him – he certainly didn't wear his solicitude on his sleeve. Maybe it was buried too deep in his daily struggle for it ever to emerge in easy affection like the Prior, or lively encouragement like Lawrence. Obviously love hadn't overcome fear in his case. But at least he didn't frighten me any more.

I walked out into the Autumn sunshine and bathed in the warm quietness which enveloped me. In this quest of mine, epic in its folly, walking on the waters of reality, I felt I had taken another step forward in faith. Sam came towards me and, as ever, smiled, turned his fingers slightly towards himself (the embryonic embrace) and lowered his eyes – the copybook monastic greeting. My dear, dear Sam; now here was someone who'd always had his eyes on the furrow, bless him.

Shove over, mate; it takes two to tango.

As I approached the noviciate, Lawrence bustled out. I went to pass him, eyes on the furrow, smiled benignly, embryonic embrace, the new man.

'Anything wrong, Daniel,' he asked quizzically. 'You spend the longest interview with the Abbot in recorded history and yet haven't darted into my office to give me the blow-by-blow account. He hasn't given you the push, has he? Come on inside and tell me all.'

I sighed and followed him in. So much for the quiet life. I thought of this morning's Mass and Anthony spelling out our angelic dimension. Yes, just as God obviously had a role for the energetic Michael as his troubleshooter, so Father Lawrence was perfectly cast for driving out the demons in our lives, especially the ones we didn't even know were there. With him it wasn't a question of love casting out fear. In a way that St Benedict had obviously never considered, Lawrence's overflowing zest for life just elbowed it out of the way.

Magnificat

Lord!
How you must love the world at three in the night
When nothing moves except in service;
Nothing sounds except in praise:
The sea-slap on the rocks;
Sea-stroke on sand; gulls
Nestling each other softly asleep;
Whilst sibilant winds whistle,
Chattering though caves, layering the dunes,
Murmuring their meeting on the waves.
Yes, every sound and stir, whether we choose or no,
Is changing our sweet earth on
Processionally, in peace.
And slap and chatter, stroke and murmur
Magnify you, Lord,
Like a long loving applause.

Lord!
How you must love the world at three in the night
When no-one stirs except in duty;
Evil largely lies asleep;
And we are your only pockets of praise,
Watching for the world,
Singing each other softly awake.
The oneness of our call and answer
Strokes the antiphonal hours away,
Murmuring their meaning through the choir.
More: every move of the heart,
Whether we know or no, recharges all, renews us all
Professes all, in peace.
And watch and oneness, song and murmur
Magnify you, Lord,
Like a long, loving embrace.

If I take the wings of the morning
and dwell in the uttermost parts of the sea,
even there thy hand shall lead me
and thy right hand shall hold me (Psalm 139:9,10).

Printed in the United Kingdom by
Lightning Source UK Ltd., Milton Keynes
141963UK00001B/56/P